Children of a New World

generally, were critical to the American social experience. How the schools responded to their challenge was a central American story.[7]

Reflecting the trajectory of my interest in youth and children as subjects of historical investigation, the first section of this book is devoted to three essays on schooling and traces my thinking on this subject from the 1980s to the 2000s. All the essays in this section evidence my lifelong engagement with the school as a fundamental component of social formation. All the essays are about the children of immigrants and all are located within the bounds of American national history. Indeed, it is the modern nation-state that has made schools a necessity almost everywhere in the world, and urgently so in the United States, with its repeated and varied immigrations.[8] As I have become more engaged by the possibilities offered to our understanding of considering schooling in a global context, my views of the relationship between immigration and schooling has developed, as is evidenced in Part III, but the nation and the school remain inexorably interconnected. The three essays in Part I therefore correctly remain exclusively about schooling as a national project. Instead of organizing these chronologically either by subject or by date of publication, I begin in Chapter 1 with the latest of these essays (written in 2002), where this national framework is most clearly laid out. This is the most comprehensive of the essays on education, and the most recent. The last (Chapter 3) concentrates on a specific time and set of students' experiences and is most emphatically tied to the methods of social history. Indeed, only this essay in the entire collection draws its data from a large quantitative sample (in this case high school yearbooks), often seen as the hallmark of early social history. I have never believed that social history is coextensive with quantitative history, but in this instance I adopted this method as a necessary means to reconstruct and evaluate ethnicity as an experience in the social relations and school life of students in New York City high schools in the 1930s and 1940s. It is fair to define this section as I have, "Children in Society," since these three essays all draw upon the opening that social history gave to studying children in history and specifically the push that social history gave to examining minority groups and fundamental institutions.

ii

Social history encouraged historians to attend to the faint imprints of social life and listen to previously ignored voices from the past. In this way, social history allowed children, older children especially, to be heard within their institutional settings, such as the school and the family. And the literature of the time by those historians who looked at family life such as Virginia Yans McLaughlin, or at small communities such as Philip Greven and John Demos, or at youth-identified issues such as Joseph Hawes, Joseph Kett, and John Modell began to lay the solid foundations for a real history of children.[9] But an exclusively social history of children could never be more than partial and limited. With its bias toward empirically definable behavior patterns that made people in the past independent actors, and its emphasis on agency, social history could never entirely liberate children. Children are, at least in part, defined by their dependency and their helplessness, and their behaviors and identities are often structured by others. Their most important behaviors as children are only infrequently noted and less frequently given real importance. Just as significantly, their visibility, even when faintly apparent through the long haze of history, is usually masked by adult interpretation and mediated through adult reflection. Young children leave very few literate traces, and even artifacts like toys or prams are most often determined by adult choice.[10] It is rarely possible (though not impossible) for historians to observe children or hear them speak directly to the present.

By the 1980s and 1990s, however, cultural history helped to make these disabilities less important. Historians of culture began to assert that this lack of direct contact with children's voices and beliefs was true for almost all subjects excavated by social historians, and that neither texts, nor paintings, nor even statistics are transparent. All of them were patterned through culture (adopting Geertz), all of them existed within a penumbra of power (learning from Foucault), or were already arranged through a conspiracy of texts (adopting Derrida). Moreover, how groups were defined, and the meanings given to identities, was at the very heart of what engaged the attention of the cultural historian. As cultural historians began to challenge the clarity of social historians' views of the hidden actors of the past on these and other grounds, they paradoxically made it more likely that historians would focus on children and on childhood. If no historical subjects ever spoke plainly in their own voices or acted entirely freely, then it was not such a great disadvantage to focus on children. If social historians had opened a much wider angled lens on the past, cultural historians had made it imperative to focus on all its details. In examining details we learned much more about the large patterns of culture. Above all, childhood itself was a pattern inscribed by culture through the ways in which dependency and age, sexuality and maturity, the body and the mind were defined and delineated.

Now in the context of both social and cultural perspectives, historians looked around the more open rooms of the past and saw more and more children. Children were everywhere, not just at school and in families, but on the streets as David Nasaw demonstrated, and in the courts as Mary Odem discovered. They were deeply part of the developing social science agenda of the twentieth century as Hamilton Cravens demonstrated. But the contribution of cultural history was even more profound, because children often stood firmly in sight as historians found them deeply embedded in political language, sermons, and policy statements. The sexuality of adolescents, as Beth Bailey found, was a matter of real consequence and the subject of cultural instruction and control. And children came prominently into view in the custody and legal issues that Michael Grossberg and Mary Ann Mason explored and in the world of social welfare studied by Linda Gordon.[11] They were part of the literary landscape and the visual imagination.[12]

A newly enlarged and liberated political history also noticed the importance of children. By the twentieth century, whole federal agencies revolved around issues of children's welfare and rights, as Kriste Lindenmeyer found, and the idea of the child lurks even in the concepts of legal responsibility that define criminal intent and political citizenship.[13] Not only did many expressions of culture contain children, but there was a whole subset of cultural products focused on child rearing that gave children pride of place. And children's literature has a rich history of its own.[14] These matters gradually came to the fore and have borne fruit in excellent studies of this literature and the concerns it enshrines.[15] Cultural historians were confirming what Ariès had noticed two decades earlier: that culture defines the meaning of age and that childhood is embedded in that definition as well as in the larger belief systems of the society.[16] And Ariès's insights, though not necessarily his conclusions, have remained a touchstone of cultural and social investigation.

The emergence of social and cultural history as central disciplinary perspectives by the 1980s, and a refashioned political history which looked at social policies and law, meant that by the early 1990s the study of children could proceed without much apology. As more and more history was written and new sources became usable, they even began to yield evidence of children's own culture and their independent "agency."[17] The previous absence of children in our history became inexcusable. How could we have missed people who often make up 50 percent or more of the population and are fundamental to how a society defines itself and structures its institutions of power and continuity? How could we have missed children and the contributions they make to the family economy and the tensions of immigrant experience? The explosion of children's studies in history and other fields has followed this recognition and, while many historians still bemoan the fact that we are often more engaged in the history of childhood (how we imagine and portray children and frame their lives) than in documenting the history of children's experience and activities, there is no gainsaying the extraordinary results. Children's history has become a visible and significant specialty, now firmly anchored within its own organization, the Society for the History of Children and Youth, a specialty which monthly produces innovative and interesting additions to our knowledge of childhood and children in all parts of the society. Today, we are even hearing children's voices in books like Steven Mintz's *Huck's Raft* and understand how deeply they are embedded in the everyday artifacts of the culture as we have learned from Anne Higonnet's work on paintings, illustrations, and photographs, Gary Cross's work on toys, and Rachel Devlin's work on popular literature.[18] And this explosion has taken place far beyond the boundaries of American studies, among European historians who had been developing and challenging Ariès for decades, and increasingly also among Latin American historians and historians of China, India, and Japan.[19] Indeed, as these studies progress, the picture of children's history and of world history has been wonderfully enlarged.

As someone who had been baptized in the historical study of children early, through social history, and who had long been committed to studying culture as an important component of social experience, I needed no special conversion to explore culture both in itself and as a means toward a richer understanding of social life. Nevertheless, its new applicability to children and its potential for enlarging the study of childhood was an important gift of the new cultural turn. Children are pivotal to how a culture defines itself and its future. With the new attention to a full range of cultural expressions, I turned to understanding how Americans defined their obligations to children, and I became alerted to how modern culture dealt with both the children it raised and the children it lost and especially to the strategic role of the modern media in defining parental obligations. The elaboration of cultural signals centered on fears about losing children is a peculiarly modern experience. While grief over the loss of children is as old as parenting and was elaborately expressed in the nineteenth century, anxiety as an anticipation of such loss was a product of altered modern parental expectations. Intrigued by the media obsession with portraying child abduction in the 1980s, I began to explore how the emotional attachment to children and the social commitment to childhood that became prominent by the late nineteenth century resulted in a potent new source of social anxiety, and the learning of new emotions.[20] In Part II of this book, "Children in Culture," I include versions of two episodes I explored in my desire to understand modern fears about child loss: the first a frightening tale of young people gone bad in the 1920s in the notorious story of Leopold and Loeb; the second an examination of the strange contemporary interest in and redefinition of parental abduction. The final essay in this section, Chapter 6, also discusses anxiety about children by examining our increasingly ambiguous sentiments regarding children in the post–World War II United States. In it, I suggest that the planning and control of children that was a fundamental expression of modern parenting has now come to haunt us.

iii

The light that cultural history shed and the stimulus it provided for the study of children and childhood historically came with a broad beam. While culture has been used to illuminate small communities or subcultures, as in Clifford Geertz's famous study of the Balinese cockfight and Lawrence Levine's *Black Culture and Black Consciousness*,[21] the concept of culture can and has been used to separate much larger social and historical units; thus we often speak about Western culture or Islamic culture, or Renaissance or Chinese culture. Once culture is understood to exercise deep powers over patterns of behavior, belief, and perception, it can easily spill beyond and between national boundaries. In American historiography, this perspective on the subcultural became important in the discussions about multiculturalism in the 1980s in which historians were active participants. If groups in American society had independent cultural sources that issued in diverse forms of expression, then the nation-state was an inadequate vehicle for an exploration of its sources and its consequences. The state certainly exercised one kind of power, but culture brought its own sources of persuasion and identity. As a result, throughout most of the decade historians and many policy makers worried about the disintegrating possibilities that this seemed to threaten. This threat passed by the 1990s, absorbed as so many other similar episodes in the deep well of American pluralism, and the growing recognition that the nation exercises its own powerful cultural influence as a form of identity.[22] But by then the image of culture as a force for disintegration in the world was being replaced by new visions of culture in terms of global power. Once discussions of culture took a global turn, as it increasingly did in the 1990s, then it became significant not apart from nations but as a political strategy in discussions of the fate of nations.

This was the position that Samuel Huntington provocatively adopted when he became one of the first to use the idea of culture in order to see through the new lens of "globalization." By viewing culture, and within it the special role of religion, as the fundamental basis for historical development and contemporary identity, Huntington posited one of the primary issues of our time—a global war of cultures. His perspective has since been sharply rebutted, not least by Amartya Sen, although the current politically fueled perceptions of a world of deep cultural divides and conflicts has certainly given Huntington's ideas new life.[23] But Huntington's is not the only use to which a "globalizing" perspective can be put, as I demonstrate in the last section of this book. Globalization can prod American historians to think about American development, not as one of the global forces in Huntington's conflict-based model, but as an alternative model. American social and cultural development can be importantly understood as having early instantiated and successfully mobilized the very factors that would eventually become crucial features of globalization. Indeed, America was in fundamental ways a new global kind of nation that anticipated the newer global world we are experiencing today. In rethinking American history in this manner, we can imagine a very different outcome than the culture wars that Huntington has posited. Indeed, once we recognize that culture in the United States has been a hybrid that resulted from contributions made by different ethnic, racial, and religious groups, American experience can be viewed as evidence contrary to Huntington's vision of culture as homogeneous, univalent, and in hostile opposition to other cultures. The very diversity of American culture becomes not a fragile force in today's world preparing to defend itself against other cultures, but a counter-model for what globalization can mean. It was the possibilities offered by this perspective on American history that first engaged my thinking about globalization in an essay, published in the *Journal of Social History* in 2003, and reprinted in this volume, as the first chapter in part III, "Children of a New Global World."

"Globalization" as a term and as an idea is today fraught with some of the political weight that Huntington gave it and lends itself to contentious debates. But while Huntington sees it as a battle of armed cultures which Americans must win, many others view it as an aggressive threat by rich nations to local ecologies and autonomous cultural values. In this view, globalization is condemned as yet another expression of Western imperialism. We are made aware of this perspective every time demonstrators protest the meetings of the G-8 nations or the programs of the International Monetary Fund. In these instances, "globalization" is not a description of growing global awareness or even the complex interactions among the cultures of the world, but another instance of American and European hegemonic drives expressed through neoliberal economic policies controlled by bankers in the largest and most powerful economies.[24] From this perspective, globalization exploits the labor of the South while raining down a nasty brew of McDonald's and Coca-Cola on their young people that obliterates traditional tastes and traditions. I suggest other ways of understanding the role of these goods for young people in the last section of this book. But those who stand opposed to globalization as simply the dominance of capital creating a world in which differences will disappear cannot imagine that globalization may actually be enacted through the actions of young people in many places. This is happening today as young people who are participants in a smaller world become more familiar with difference.[25] There are some observers, such as Thomas Friedman, who view globalization as a beneficent as well as an inevitable force in the world today, but like so many others involved in this debate, these discussions tend to be without historical dimension.[26]

If we could view globalization historically, as having begun in North America starting in the seventeenth century, and use the United States as a model of its initial expression, rather than as a contemporary political villain, it might be possible to reexamine globalization as a means of taming, not obliterating, difference and creating new cultural tolerance. In the United States, a successful nation-state learned to define itself amidst cultural differences and to embrace those differences as part of its creed. American historians are familiar with the many ways in which this has not been an easy process and the many challenges it has posed in the past and continues to pose in the present. My essays in Part III make these challenges clear. Nevertheless, during the last one-half century, the American model has remained resilient and even strengthened as an ideal at home, and grown more robust as a reality. Indeed, as Part I suggests, this model has even become very much part of the American experience of schooling, the national project par excellence. The essays in this book, especially those in Parts I and III, can suggest how American history can become a touchstone for thinking about contemporary globalization, and do so where it matters most, in relation to the young.

While American history can serve as an alternative model for understanding globalization, our contemporary awareness of the present global moment can also provide a stimulant to new kinds of historical inquiry and analysis. In the essays in the third part of this book I try to use the concept of globalization as a tool to open our historical insights in the twenty-first century, to encourage us to imagine a broader and more dynamic geographical canvas for our investigations, and specifically to encourage these things in regard to the writing of the history of children from a more global point of view. A global perspective for historians is a variant of the world history that some, like William McNeill, John Gillis, and Peter Stearns, have been pursuing for some time and that Stearns has recently applied to children's history with insight and verve.[27] And while children are often today used as symbols for the worst kind of globalization (see Chapter 8), there is no better subject for an expanded global vision than the history of childhood and children. This is not only because the history of children is still a new field and therefore open to innovative ways of organizing knowledge about the subject. It is also a consequence of the nature and potential of children themselves, since children allow us to see ourselves in global terms.

At birth, all children are members of a world community, still unmarked by most social, national, and cultural boundaries. They are then at their most available to stimuli which, until fully localized within a household, a community, and a nation, could as readily take one shape as another. Thus children are by nature "citizens" of the world. How they become attached to specific identities is precisely one of the things historians want to know. Psychologists have taught us that they do this quite rapidly through personal attachment and language acquisition.[28] Adopting a wider, global perspective allows us to study this very process by looking at how children become bounded by nations and cultures, and how they contribute to those formations through their mental and behavioral actions and interactions. Today's children are in fact stimulated by global ventures. Much more easily than at any time in the past, children today can travel physically or through their imaginations to other parts of the globe and into cultures other than those to which they were born. For children born today, the world really is a much smaller place than it was to earlier generations, and this new possibility of forming attachments across boundaries can provide historians and others with unusual guidance about how identities can be re-created and expanded.

I became very much aware, in editing the *Encyclopedia of Children and Childhood in History and Society,* that so much of what we need to know about children is more meaningful and useful when studied in a comparative or global context. This is true, for example, about mortality and birth rates, vulnerability to disease, forms of infant feeding and care, sexual patterns and practices, gender formation, and child-care arrangements. Moreover, once we look at children as children, rather than as potential grownups in a particular nation, they share many things in common that historians can only grasp by looking beyond previously defined historical boundaries. On the other hand, the distinctions matter a lot, and the differences among children may be better understood and made more meaningful when we see them in a global perspective rather than in isolated national containers. This is especially true because nation-states today reflect wealth as well as power, and the lives of children in wealthy nations are light-years away from those in impoverished countries. In this sense, a global perspective encourages us to appreciate the role, power, and influence of nationality in the lives of children. It is important to note that adding a global perspective does not require that we give up national history or the history of specific groups. Looking at the globe gives us another way of seeing and another means to explore the past, but it is not exclusive or sufficient.

In the twenty-first century, globalization is also raising anew questions about the relationship between the school, the state, and the economy. In Chapter 6 I begin to suggest how families are rethinking education and consider it much more fully in Part III. As I suggest in these essays, the pressures on contemporary schools to better educate American children has developed, in part, from global competition and comparisons which are eroding the automatic expectations that American children once experienced simply by being citizens of a rich society. Schooling as a form of competitive skills acquisition now reaches firmly across borders both because of the migration of peoples and their ambitious children and in the form of investments in people in other places. These changes may undermine the close association that began to develop in the nineteenth century between schooling and state formation. In the nineteenth century, American schools helped to create American citizenship. By the middle of the twentieth century, schools expressed the successful economic identity of America as a world power. Americans invested in schooling because it confirmed citizenship while training future workers for an effective economy. And this correspondence forced parents to give over some control over their children in exchange for the successful integration of those children into the future national economy. Today, parents, especially in the middle classes, are more than ever concerned with the specific success of their own progeny, but the success of other children as important components of a national economy has become less compelling. As the skills on which our personal prosperity depends moves outside of national boundaries, the firm understanding of schools as basic components of an integrated society recedes from our sights. What the consequences of these changes will be for schooling is not yet clear, although the increasing fragmentation of schooling across the national landscape (into public, private, charter, and home-schooling projects) may be an indication of the loosening relationship between the economic and political spheres.

Finally, there is the matter of children's futures and our actions on their behalf. Since World War II, many organizations devoted to children's issues have grown from a new global vision and committed themselves to a universal perspective, as they look toward improvement by taking all children as the object of their investigation. This is true, for example, of the United Nations, which endowed children with their own rights as persons in the Universal Charter of the Rights of the Child (1989), and organizations like the World Health Organization and the Bill and Melinda Gates Foundation. We seem increasingly willing to grant to children what we are far more reluctant to grant to their parents, a universal appeal. And we are willing to approach their welfare with fewer inhibitions regarding borders and boundaries than we are other persons. This is, in good part, related to how we have come to imagine children, as I try to discuss in Part III of this book. This approach to children grows from increasingly universal commitments that began to take shape in the eighteenth and nineteenth centuries in the Western world when the earliest globalizing trends became apparent. It is therefore somewhat surprising that so much of the literature on children and globalization (and there is now a minor industry in this literature) is at once firmly planted in this vision and then proceeds to condemn globalization and its consequences for children. This literature (and other forms of media presentations) often holds globalization responsible for the problems of children in the underdeveloped world. There are some participants in these discussions such as the educational anthropologists Marcelo Suárez-Orozco and Carola Suárez-Orozco who come with a different view, suggesting how children in many parts of the world benefit from the current moment of globalization to achieve higher skills and competitive advantages. Whichever side the writer is on, however, his or her perspective is almost always defined by a humanitarian commitment that developed historically and is the subject of the final essay in this book (Chapter 9). Indeed, it is useful to remember that this universalizing of concerns about children came in an American context that was deeply challenged by immigrant children and their needs. Thus globalization, as I define it here—the process of becoming more engaged with the world and its differences—is having striking consequences, even among those who oppose contemporary "globalization."

There has never been a better or more urgent time to direct our attention to the history of children than the present moment, at the point of a new global awareness. Today, children are frequently presented in the media as the victims of globalization. How we appraise their present and their future depends on what we know about their past. It is important that the history of children and childhood that began with Western societies become part of the agenda everywhere in the world, and I am hopeful that the current attention to the children of the streets of Latin America, the brothels of Asia, the armies of Africa, and the factories of India will stimulate a serious historical inquiry that will forcefully bring children into the agenda of the historical profession. Children and childhood have important histories that only adults can write.

Thus, we are brought back to the question first opened up by social history in the 1960s. Those questions were certainly about method and subject matter, but they were also about our openness as historians and our values and commitments. For a very short moment, social history acted as if it could be value free, but its whole development in the context of its time was devoted to providing a history to those who had been forgotten, overlooked, or without manifest power. Historians brought to their studies a dedication to creating a history that, by definition, promised to empower through the vehicle of historical visibility those who had not been seen or noticed before. Today, the new global perspective allows historians once again to commit themselves, this time to a world of children without boundaries. It allows us both to examine the history of childhood in a worldwide perspective and to urge that *children be seen and that their welfare not be ignored.* In the last essay in this volume, I explicitly address just this issue: How can values that are culturally situated and historically derived be preserved in a very different time and a very different context? The new global world is indeed a different context, and it challenges us to think not only about what it means for how we study children historically, but about what this means for who we want to become.

NOTES

1. There were a handful of exceptions in American history, almost all of them related to the growing interest in the history of the family, including John Demos, *A Little Commonwealth: Family Life in Plymouth Colony* (New York: Oxford University Press, 1970), and Philip Greven, Jr., *Four Generations: Population, Land, and Family in Andover, Massachusetts* (Ithaca: Cornell University Press, 1970); Bernard Wishy, *The Child and the Republic: The Dawn of Modern American Child Nurture* (Philadelphia: University of Pennsylvania Press, 1968). In 1970, the profession also saw the first serious attempt to organize the field in a documentary collection in Robert H. Bremner, et al., ed., *Children and Youth in America: A Documentary History* (Cambridge Mass.: Harvard University Press, 1970). But a real introduction to the field did not appear until Joseph Hawes's *American Childhood: A Research Guide and Historical Handbook* (Westport, Conn.: Greenwood Press, 1985).

Even before the 1970s, two American historians had paid close attention to the subject, but their studies had not really opened up the field: Edmund S. Morgan, *The Puritan Family* (New York: Harper and Row, 1944), and Anne L. Kuhn, *The Mother's Role in Childhood Education: New England Concepts, 1830–1860* (New Haven: Yale University Press, 1947).

2. Philippe Ariès, *Centuries of Childhood,* trans. Robert Baldick (New York: Alfred A. Knopf, 1962).

3. Many of these books followed in the psychoanalytic path opened up by Erik H. Erikson, who had written books that stimulated historians. See, for example, *Young Man Luther: A Study in Psychoanalysis and History* (New York: Norton, 1958), and *Childhood and Society,* 2nd ed. (New York: Norton, 1963). For an example of this influence, see David Hunt, *Parents and Children in History: The Psychology of Family Life in Early Modern France* (New York: Basic Books, 1970). For an extreme expression of this tendency to equate children's history with an evaluation of their psychological mistreatment, which nevertheless can often provide insightful readings about children, see Lloyd de Mause, "The

Evolution of Childhood," in *The History of Childhood,* ed. by de Mause (New York: Harper Torchbook, 1974), 3–74.

4. Two of the most important expressions of this development were in the journals *Journal of Social History* (1967) and *Journal of Interdisciplinary History* (1970). Both encouraged the new history, including family history, and published articles on children. For an early bibliography on children and youth in history, see C. John Sommerville, "Toward a History of Childhood and Youth," *The Family in History: Interdisciplinary Essays,* ed. by Theodore K. Rabb and Robert I. Rotberg (New York: HarperTorchbooks, 1971), 227–235. All the essays in this collection originally appeared in the *Journal of Interdisciplinary History.* The *Journal of Family History* joined these two in 1976.

5. My interest was first defined in my dissertation, "The Fruits of Transition: American Youth in the 1920s," Columbia University, 1974, which was revised as *The Damned and the Beautiful: American Youth in the 1920s* (New York: Oxford University Press, 1977).

Philip Greven's pathbreaking examination of how child socialization fundamentally influenced American politics and society came out at about the same time, and it too absorbed psychological perspectives while undertaking to reimagine American history with children as fundamental constituents. See *The Protestant Temperament: Patterns of Child-Rearing, Religious Experience, and the Self in Early America* (New York: Alfred A. Knopf, 1977). The same year, Joseph F. Kett's *Rites of Passage: Adolescence in America, 1790 to the Present* (New York: Basic Books, 1977), made clear that youth had a real role in history.

6. This view of schooling was especially indebted to the perspective established by Michael Katz, *The Irony of Early School Reform: Educational Innovation in Mid-Nineteenth-Century Massachusetts* (Boston: Beacon Press, 1968).

7. This is the argument I made in *Outside In: Minorities and the Transformation of American Education* (New York: Oxford University Press, 1989). The book grew from various studies I undertook on aspects of schooling, broadly defined to include public schools, private schools, universities, the United States military forces, and parochial education.

8. For a discussion of the relationship between nation building and schooling, see John Meyer, et al., "World Expansion of Mass Education, 1870–1980," *Sociology of Education,* 65 (April 1992): 128–149; John Meyer, *School Knowledge for the Masses: World Models and National Primary Curricular Categories in the Twentieth Century* (Washington, D.C.: Falmer Press, 1992).

9. See Virginia Yans McLauglin, *Family and Community: Italian Immigrants in Buffalo, 1880–1930* (Ithaca, N.Y.: Cornell University Press, 1977); Joseph M. Hawes, *Children in Urban Society: Juvenile Delinquency in Nineteenth-Century America* (New York: Oxford University Press, 1971); Demos, *Little Commonwealth:* Kett, *Rites of Passage;* John Modell, *Into One's Own: From Youth to Adulthood in the United States, 1920–1975* (Berkeley: University of California Press, 1989).

10. See Gary Cross, *Kids' Stuff: Toys and the Changing World of American Childhood* (Cambridge, Mass.: Harvard University Press, 1997), and Karin Calvert, *Children in the House: The Material Culture of Early Childhood, 1600–1900* (Boston: Northeastern University Press, 1992).

11. David Nasaw, *Children of the City: At Work and at Play* (New York: Oxford University Press, 1986); Mary E. Odem, *Delinquent Daughters: Protecting and Policing Adolescent Female Sexuality in the United States, 1885–1920* (Chapel Hill: University of North Carolina Press, 1995); Hamilton Cravens, *Before Head Start: The Iowa Station and American Children* (Chapel Hill: University of North Carolina Press, 1993); Beth Bailey, *From Front Porch to Back Seat: Courtship in Twentieth-Century America* (Baltimore: Johns Hopkins University Press, 1988); Michael Grossberg, *Governing the Hearth: Law and the Family in Nineteenth-Century America* (Chapel Hill: University of North Carolina Press, 1985); Mary Ann Mason, *From Father's Property to Children's Rights: A History of Child Custody in the United States* (New York: Columbia University Press, 1994); Linda Gordon, *Heroes of Their Own Lives: The Politics and History of Family Violence* (New York: Penguin Books, 1988).

12. See, for example James R. Kincaid, *Erotic Innocence: The Culture of Child Molesting* (Durham, N.C.: Duke University Press, 1998); Anne Higonnet, *Pictures of Innocence: The History and Crisis of Ideal Childhood* (London: Thames and Hudson, 1998).

13. Kriste Lindenmeyer, *"A Right to Childhood": The U.S. Children's Bureau and Child Welfare, 1912–46* (Urbana and Chicago: University of Illinois Press, 1997). For citizenship and responsibility, see Holly Brewer, *By Birth or Consent: Children, Law, and the Anglo-American Revolution in Authority* (Chapel Hill: University of North Carolina Press, 2005).

14. The literature here is large and growing. Two examples are Gillian Avery, *Behold the Child: American Children and Their Books, 1621–1922* (Baltimore: Johns Hopkins University Press, 1994); Julia L. Mickenberg, *Learning from the Left: Children's Literature, the Cold War, and Radical Politics in the United States* (New York: Oxford University Press, 2006).

15. Among some of the best of these, see Julia Grant, *Raising Baby by the Book: The Education of American Mothers* (New Haven: Yale University Press, 1998); Ann Hulbert, *Raising America: Experts, Parents and a Century of Advice about Children* (New York: Alfred A. Knopf, 2003); Peter N. Stearns, *Anxious Parents: A History of Modern Childrearing in America* (New York: New York University Press, 2003).

16. Howard Chudacoff, *How Old Are You? Age Consciousness in American Culture* (Princeton, N.J.: Princeton University Press, 1989).

17. Henry Jenkins, ed., *The Child Culture Reader* (New York: New York University Press, 1998).

18. Steven Mintz, *Huck's Raft: A History of American Childhood* (Cambridge, Mass.: Harvard University Press, 2004); Higonnet, *Pictures of Innocence;* Cross, *Kids' Stuff;* Rachel Devlin, *Relative Intimacy: Fathers, Adolescent Daughters, and Postwar American Culture* (Chapel Hill: University of North Carolina Press, 2005).

19. For important new work on Latin America and Asia, see Tobias Hecht, ed., *Minor Omissions: Children in Latin American History and Society* (Madison: University of Wisconsin Press, 2002); Brian Platt, "Japanese Childhood, Modern Childhood," *Journal of Social History,* 38 (Summer 2005): 965–985; Anne Behnke Kinney, *Representations of Childhood and Youth in Early China* (Stanford, Calif.: Stanford University Press, 2004); Ping-Chen Hsiung, *A Tender Voyage: Children and Childhood in Late Imperial China* (Stanford, Calif.:, Stanford University Press, 2005).

20. Paula S. Fass, *Kidnapped: Child Abduction in America* (New York: Oxford University Press, 1997; paperback, Oxford University Press, 2001). For a discussion of how this anxiety became learned, see my article, "Abduction Stories That Changed Our Lives: From Charley Ross to Modern Behavior," in *American Behavioral History: An Introduction,* ed. by Peter N. Stearns (New York: New York University Press, 2005), 42–57.

21. Clifford Geertz, "Deep Play: Notes on the Balinese Cockfight," in Geertz, *The Interpretation of Cultures* (New York: Basic Books, 1973), 412–453; Lawrence W. Levine, *Black Culture and Black Consciousness: Afro-American Folk Thought from Slavery to Freedom* (New York: Oxford University Press, 1977).

22. David Hollinger, *Postethnic America: Beyond Multiculturalism* (New York: Basic Books, 1995); Benedict Anderson, *Imagined Communities: Reflections on the Origin and Spread of Nationalism* (London: Verso, 1991).

23. Samuel P. Huntington, *The Clash of Civilizations and the Remaking of the World Order* (New York: Simon and Schuster, 1996). Amartya Sen's response to Huntington appears in "East and West: The Reach of Reason," *New York Review of Books,* 47 (July 20, 2000).

24. See for example, *Children on the Streets of the Americas: Globalization, Homelessness and Education in the United States, Brazil and Cuba,* ed. by Roslyn Arlin Mickelson (London and New York: Routledge, 2000); *The Anthology of Development and Globalization: From Classical Political Economy to Contemporary Neoliberalism,* edited by Marc Edelman and Angelique Haugerud (Oxford, England: Blackwell, 2005).

25. See Joe L. Kinechoe, "Complex Politics of McDonald's," in *Kidworld: Childhood Studies, Global Perspectives, and Education,* ed. by Gaile S. Cannella and Joe L. Kincheloe (New York: Peter Lang, 2002). An alternative perspective is presented in Virginia Murphy-Berman and Natalie Hevener Kaufman, "Globalization in Cross-Cultural Perspective," in

Natalie Hevener Kaufman and Irene Rizzini, eds., *Globalization and Children: Exploring Potentials for Enhancing Opportunities in the Lives of Children and Youth* (New York: Kluwer Academic, 2002), and Ben White, "Globalization and the Child Labor Problem," Working Paper Series No. 221, Institute of Social Studies, The Hague, The Netherlands, June 1996.

26. Thomas L. Friedman's most recent book about globalization is *The World Is Flat: A Brief History of the Twenty-First Century* (New York: Farrar, Straus and Giroux, 2005). This is the third in a series that began with *The Lexus and the Olive Tree* (1999) and *Longitudes and Attitudes* (2002). For a very different perspective, which sees globalization today as no more than a continuation of earlier trends in industrialization and labor exploitation, see Jeremy Seabrook, *Children of Other Worlds: Exploitation in the Global Market* (London: Pluto Press, 2001), and a review of Friedman, "The World Is Round," by John Gray in *New York Review of Books,* 52 (August 11, 2005): 13–15.

27. John R. Gillis, *A World of Their Own Making: Myth, Ritual, and the Quest for Family Values* (New York: Basic Books, 1996); William H. McNeill, *Plagues and Peoples* (Garden City, N.Y.: Anchor Press, 1976; revised 1989); Peter N. Stearns, *Childhood in World History* (New York: Routledge, 2006).

28. Alison Gopnik, Andrew N. Meltzoff, and Patricia K. Kuhl, *The Scientist in the Crib: Minds, Brains, and How Children Learn* (New York: William Morrow, 1999); *From Neurons to Neighborhoods: The Science of Early Childhood Development,* edited by Jack P. Shonkoff and Deborah A. Philips for the National Research Council and the Institute of Medicine (Washington, D.C.: National Academy Press, 2000).

PART I

Children in Society

Introduction to Part I

The three essays in this section address a fundamental question of American social life: How does a nation of immigrants become a cohesive but still democratic community? In the first of these essays (Chapter 1), an introduction to education and immigration written for Blackwell's *A Companion to American Immigration,* I suggest that the school has from the beginning been organized to address this task. But, unlike those historians who describe the school as simply an instrument of control and order, I believe that it has functioned as a more flexible institution that has demonstrated the capacity to respond to the populations it serves. While American education has been committed to the task of nation building, schools have also been forced to respond to the diverse aspirations of their constituents. In this way, the schools have been part of the pluralistic reality of American social life. Almost from the beginning of publicly supported, common schooling, Catholic schools have competed among the immigrant population. With available alternatives, American schooling has never been monolithic. And schools both rewarded certain kinds of conformity in behavior and were forced to accept a fair amount of continuing diversity.

What it means to build a national community has also changed over time in the United States, with economic rewards steadily gaining ground and eventually overriding civic concerns as the primary responsibility of schooling with regard to immigrants. Similarly, from the point of view of national policy, the locus of political debate has shifted. In the nineteenth century, it was primary education that was most urgent, in the first half of the twentieth century, secondary schooling, and then after that higher education at colleges and universities. While the rewards of schooling have always been more individual centered rather than community oriented, this tendency became steadily more apparent throughout the twentieth century.

The essay on IQ (Chapter 2), published in 1980 in the *American Journal of Education,* is the oldest in the book. It represents my first effort to examine the relationship between schools and their minority populations, and to appraise the matter of school rewards. In it, I suggest that the very commitment to educational democracy expressed in individualistic terms pushed the schools to find efficient means toward the ends of serving a large and diverse population. The IQ as a particular kind of sorting device allowed schools to remain democratic and technically to become attuned to modern demands for scientific means that gave priority to individual achievement. At the same time, the IQ also encoded a set of limiting cultural preconceptions about the talents and abilities of the immigrant communities who began to send their children in such large numbers to the schools starting in the second and third decades of the twentieth century. The IQ was thus an ambiguous cultural instrument, framed to respond to democratic goals but deeply tainted by contemporary cultural values and anxieties.

The third essay (Chapter 3) attempts to look directly at student experience in the schools, and specifically at how ethnicity remained alive in the schools for the second generation of European immigrants. Using New York as the primary site for second-generation experience, I created a large sample of student yearbooks from eight high schools across the city's three major immigrant boroughs during the 1930s and 1940s. By charting each individual's participation in voluntary extracurricular activities, I found strong evidence for the continuing existence and importance of ethnic identification among members of the second generation even in this most assimilative arena. This, I suggest, is what "Americanization" really entailed, a melding of the incorporative drives of school framers with the complex generational, individual, and group-oriented needs of the students served by the schools. The patterns of ethnic association varied by school environment and were flexible and dynamic. American diversity was thus contained within the boundaries of the schools, but never squeezed out. Rather, ethnicity was reframed in new terms that could vary from one setting to another. This article first appeared in a longer version as Chapter 3 of *Outside In: Minorities and the Transformation of American Education* (1989). It was condensed and reprinted as "Creating New Identities: Youth and Ethnicity in New York City High Schools in the 1930s and 1940s," for the collection *Generations of Youth* (New York University Press), which is the version that is published here.

1

Immigration and Education in the United States

Education has been central to immigrant experience in the United States and fundamental to the creation of the American nation. Education broadly understood is the whole manner in which the young are inducted into the society and enculturated to its norms, habits, and values. For the children of immigrants, this could be a very complex and conflicted experience which involved a variety of sometimes competing formal and informal institutions and organizations—family and other relatives, church, work, peers, sports, clubs, and, in the modern period, expressions of popular entertainment, such as music, movies, television, the Internet, and mall culture. For the purposes of this article, however, our attention will be limited to the education of immigrants at and through school and I will address these other matters only as they intersect with schooling.

Similarly, it can be argued that all European and African migrants to those parts of North America during the seventeenth and eighteenth centuries that became the United States were immigrants. This would include the colonizers of Spanish and French America, and African slaves, as well as the British settlers of the East Coast. I will not be using this expansive definition in this essay, but will instead restrict myself to those peoples who freely came to the United States after the establishment of the union articulated by the Constitution in 1789. This is not intended to deny the immigrant nature of those early settlers. It is rather to clarify the ways in which schooling, which did not exist as a nation-building enterprise until after the formation of the permanent union, was an expression of national goals and purposes, and to distinguish immigrants who came freely from slaves who did not. Indeed, in the American context, schooling and immigration are two profoundly interconnected elements in the process of creating a nation in a society that, unlike other societies, could not draw upon common history and memory, rituals, or language toward this end.

The absence of homogeneity in population, experience, and social habits was from the beginning an American characteristic, related to the unsystematic manner in which the British North American colonies were settled. Benjamin Rush had this in mind in 1786, on the eve of the formation of the permanent American union, when he proposed that schools, "by producing one general, and uniform system of education" would make Americans "more homogeneous," and "fit them for uniform and peaceable government."[1] Rush's insight, based on already existing experience, would subsequently govern school development as immigration became a serious and important component of the rapid national expansion in the nineteenth century. Indeed, during the nineteenth century America became at once much more heterogeneous as immigrants from three continents–Europe, Asia, and Latin America—reached its shores, and ever more devoted to schooling as a necessary component of social development and national cohesion. These two were vitally connected, something often obscured by the fact that American schools are locally based and their regulation within the domain of state power. This relationship is also complicated since schools were not created simply as a result of immigration. Nevertheless, the way schools developed and their strategic importance at particular times is inseparable from immigration and its powerful contribution to American nationality.

This intertwined development would continue throughout the twentieth century and assume a more urgent economic dimension as schooling became more manifestly bound up in the achievement of individual success. It is for this reason that as the twenty-first century unfolds the issue of schooling remains ineluctably connected to the continuing reality of immigration and its ever wider population sources. American nationhood is obviously more institutionalized and empowered in the twenty-first century than it was in 1850, but it remains culturally malleable and open-ended as the nature of its population evolves and as America's role in the world is redefined. It is for this reason, too, that when Americans seek to address the cultural, economic, or social issues that successive immigrations have raised, they have looked to the schools for assistance. Many of these issues—above all the identity, allegiance, and future of the second generation—have remained the same. Others have changed, but over the course of almost two centuries, ever wider and higher reaches of schooling—first "common" primary schools (1830–1880), then secondary education in high schools (ca. 1890–1950), and then finally colleges and universities (1960–present)—have been seen as vital and enlisted in this effort. While America is not unique in this upward expansion of educational resources, which is common to advanced societies, it has been historically the leader in this educational democratization, a leadership fundamentally connected to its early and steady exposure to issues introduced by immigration. Just as the Constitution propelled American imperial expansion into a continent while permitting the incorporation of incoming states on the same terms as the original colonies that thus together constituted the American realm politically, so has schooling provided the institutional mechanism through which the nation constitutes itself socially in the context of an almost continuous but ever changing immigration. While schooling has been under continuous pressure toward this end, its history can best be described and understood by examining three stages in its evolution from the early republic through the early twenty-first century.

Creating the Civic Realm: Education and Immigration in the Nineteenth Century

When the Constitution was adopted in 1789, the young republic's population had not yet reached four million. By the end of a century of explosive development and expansion, it was close to 75 million. Immigration contributed significantly to that growth. During the same period, schooling grew from an irregular, unsystematic, congeries of ad hoc arrangements that were either privately funded, publicly supported, or provided through charity, into an elaborate state-sponsored system that affected practically every child in America in some form of elementary instruction. The great majority of those students attended free public primary schools that were then seen as an expression of a vibrant American democracy. That system had also developed many upper and lower branches, including secondary education in public high schools and a network of state universities underwritten by national land grant legislation (the Morrill Act in 1862) as well as new public kindergartens for preschool children. For most of the nineteenth century, the central public policy issues looked to the lower levels of schooling. A much smaller parallel system of parochial (largely Catholic) schools was by then also quite vigorous and significant.

Immigrants were deeply involved in this vast growth of schooling. Their experience needs to be understood from two perspectives: how the schools developed in response to issues relating to immigrants; how immigrants experienced the schools. This dual interaction was complex and multivalent, not only because the issues meandered over a long nineteenth-century history, but because different groups in different places, not to say different individuals, could have quite divergent relationships and experiences with public education. During this century of national self-definition, schooling became an important expression of the development of state authority as the American nation and economy grew. Many prominent historians have pointed out that early nineteenth century schooling in the United States intersected in important ways with the growth of industry and the need for a disciplined, well-socialized labor force that the schools could provide. And certainly schooling permitted public oversight of the habits and manners of the young. Nevertheless, schooling itself should not be exaggerated either as an ingredient in that economic development or as an individual means for success. Indeed, schooling throughout most of the first century of American life expressed republican ideals of citizenship far more then it trained in skills necessary to either the individual or the society. By the end of the century those skills and the knowledge that schooling could provide became more significant and required more advanced schooling, which consequently grew in importance and moved to the center of policy discussions.

In the early years of the nation, much was said about the importance of schooling as an essential for republican life, not least by Thomas Jefferson, who proposed a system of graduated merit-based selection and advancement together with rudimentary training for the entire population. And Jefferson's vision has remained resonant through much of American history. But very little was actually done. American students, the children of immigrants among them, were schooled in either private or publicly supported institutions in most of the states, although the new western areas often lacked adequate facilities of any kind and were frequently traversed by zealous missionaries who advocated for schools. The immigrants to the early republic were mostly British, like those who dominated the peopling of the coastal colonies, and their education culturally and socially fell into familiar patterns. A small educated elite graduated from colleges and were highly educated in a classical format. Most Americans were literate and their knowledge and skills grew from a familiar complex of institutions—family, work, church, augmented by rudimentary formal instruction. This changed in important ways starting in the 1830s. The period from 1830 to 1860 was coincident with the first large and significant wave of immigrants to arrive into the United States, a time that also saw the development of a market economy and the earliest system of factory manufacture. It was in this context that the ideal of a public common school first took root in the United States, and it grew alongside other schemes that valued commitment to public improvements. That common school ideal was based in a "republican style" of education which Lawrence Cremin has summarized as composed of four commitments: "that education was crucial to the vitality of the Republic; that a proper republican education consisted of the diffusion of knowledge, the nurturance of virtue (including patriotic civility), and the cultivation of learning; that schools and colleges were the best agencies for providing a proper republic education; . . . that the most effective means of obtaining the requisite number and kind of schools and colleges was through some system tied to the polity."[2]

During these middle decades of the nineteenth century, educational development moved vigorously along all these routes. It established a host of academies and colleges for advanced instruction. It became a system tied to the state. But, most spectacularly it grew by expanding to larger proportions of the population, a population now strongly augmented by the migration of Irish, German, and Scandinavian immigrants whose cultural education could no longer be taken for granted. Immigrants were also believed to bring poverty and crime. In 1830, 35 percent of the population of those aged 5–19 were enrolled in school. This grew to 38.4 percent in 1840, 50.4 percent in 1850, and then to 57.7 percent in 1860. In 1870, after the Civil War, 61.1 percent of this broadly defined age group of American youth was enrolled in school. Enrollment should not be confused with attendance, but the very rapid growth testifies to the state's ability to enforce schooling as something for which children were required at least to register. By then the schools had been transformed from a hodgepodge of forms, types, and variously financed institutions into a systematic education that was publicly funded and publicly supervised. A common school regime, for which Horace Mann is remembered as a pioneer and toward which goal he had created an active reform society in the 1830s, described this ideal in a host of his reports and writings as an American necessity. By the last third of the nineteenth century, it had largely come into being. Mann had sought three things: to make a single school the common environment for all groups and classes so that the schools would "obliterate factitious distinctions in society";[3] that they be financed through public taxation; that they be centrally overseen in each state. For the most part, the schools that had developed in the North and the West had accomplished all three by the 1870s. After the Civil War, southern schools, which had lagged seriously behind, were also slowly brought onto this path.

For most immigrants, this meant that schools were an arena in which their children now learned American ways for at least the 3–4 years of attendance required of them. After the Civil War most states created laws that more effectively enforced attendance. While the importance of schooling for success in the nineteenth century should not be exaggerated, its significance as a means for creating an American identity cannot be overstated. Although there were a variety of exceptions, this meant that most children were instructed in the use of the English language, provided with a basic literacy, and required to see themselves as part of an American civic enterprise. Above all, they were exposed to a social institution not within their parents' control. The school as a source of alternative authority, rooted in an American identity and as an instrument of specific and latent instruction—a school "common" to all—was a powerful means by which the second generation (and less frequently younger members of the first generation) came to recognize how their experience differed from that of their parents. In this sense, the school's role was very different than other institutions such as the variously denominated churches, or the workplace with which the children of immigrants in the nineteenth century were all too familiar. Work was the means for survival and the potential route for success. And immigrants and their children trod the same path, with the children more often than not making either or both possible through their contributions to the family purse. School was the realm of childhood. In this arena, the child's separate fate and distinct destiny were inscribed.

The commitment to childhood as a special time and to schooling developed together in the nineteenth century. Both grew from a belief in an individualizing destiny. Childhood was romanticized in the nineteenth century, and as the century progressed, reformers sought more and more to protect and extend its length. The school became the primary site for this project. For immigrant children, this often resulted in considerable conflict as the goals of parents and those of the native guardians of the culture stood on different grounds. The American version did not always win, since so many factors affected how children related to this divergent authority. Still, the very existence of a conflict was already a victory for an American identity that the schools always brought with them—since schooling breeched the continuity of culture that the immigrant habits tried to preserve. In addition, language, habits, beliefs were deeply part of the routines of schooling. Habits of order, punctuality, cleanliness were often required and not infrequently used as a means of rebuke to homes where these practices were as foreign as the more explicitly "Protestant" values to which they were attached. For German Catholics and for the Irish who made up a large part of the mid-nineteenth-century immigrants, schools oriented toward all these goals introduced a number of issues of control which were only partially resolved.

Immigrants were hardly eager to give over authority regarding their children to the schools. Neither were the faith communities to which they subscribed happy to see their community's future confessional identities altered. Throughout the first half of the nineteenth century, despite the protestations of school reformers like Mann and Frederick A. P. Barnard that the education they envisaged was entirely secular, many immigrant spokesmen saw behind its face a Protestant vision. Thus, despite the general victory of the "common school," immigrants fought to permit different kinds of schools to survive which, by the late nineteenth century, continued to serve the specific needs of immigrants and their children. The Midwest especially became the site of innumerable German-language schools, some of them receiving state support, where continuity between generations could be maintained. Some of these schools provided hardly any English instruction, but taught history and mathematics as well as literacy in German. More encouraged learning in two languages with German language, history, and culture taught alongside the more conventional subjects. Innumerable small towns in Missouri, Wisconsin, and Iowa, as well as large cities such as Milwaukee and St. Louis, were homes to this compromise between national and immigrant cultural goals. Most of these schools would disappear by the end of the century, strangled by increasing nativist sentiment and laws such as the 1889 Bennet Law in Wisconsin.

More lasting, but with its roots in related issues, were the parochial school systems established by the Catholic Church to serve immigrant communities in cities throughout the country. The controversy with the Catholic Church broke into the public arena almost as soon as the public schools became part of the agenda, most notably in New York City. Here Bishop John Hughes debated with public school advocates over the legitimacy of alternative schools and for a share of the public purse. This debate was not marginal since Governor William H. Seward took the side of the parochial school advocates. His inaugural address in 1840 made clear how much was at stake in immigrant schooling: "The children of foreigners found in great numbers in our populous cities and towns . . . are too often deprived of the advantages of our system of public education, in consequences of prejudices arising from difference of language or religion. It ought never to be forgotten that the public welfare is as deeply concerned in their education as in that of our own children. I do not hesitate, therefore, to recommend the establishment of schools in which they may be instructed by teachers speaking the same language with themselves and professing the same faith. . . . Since we have opened our country and all its fullness to the oppressed of every nation, we should evince wisdom equal to our generosity by qualifying their children for the high responsibilities of citizenship."[4]

In the end, the parochial schools did not win access to public funds, but they did achieve a grudging acknowledgment of their role in the schooling of immigrant children. These schools took a long time to develop, but by the 1880s and 1890s, they were serving sizable portions (about 9 percent and often far more in specific places like Chicago), of a now growing number of children of foreign-born parents and an ever larger group of Catholics and others who chose a separate religious education for their children. By then, the change in the sources of immigration had become even greater, taking in larger and larger circles of non-Protestant Europe as the powerful forces of agricultural displacement, industrialization, and intolerance attracted a more diverse pool of immigrants to the United States.

It is worth observing that school planners addressed themselves almost exclusively to the children of white migrants of European descent who were seen as potential citizens and republican constituents. The children of the small migration from Asia that started in the middle of the nineteenth century, and was soon halted, was hardly a great concern. The schooling of African Americans was a wholly different matter. Almost all slave children were excluded from schools, and teaching them had become illegal throughout the South by mid-century. Free blacks in the North were sometimes schooled together with whites in common schools, and at other times placed in segregated Negro schools. Neither Africans nor Asians were, through much of the nineteenth century, a fundamental consideration in the evolving school regime, although freedmen and their children became the objects of elaborate, though temporary, schooling efforts modeled on the ideal of republican preparation for citizenship during Reconstruction under the auspices the Freedman's Bureau.

The non-English speaking or nonpublic schools are an important reminder that the schooling of immigrants has never been uniform, not during the common school era and not later as schooling took on new purposes and new power. American education remained locally financed and controlled and without central guidance, and different kinds of schools existed to serve its diverse population. At the same time, the existence of alternative schools was also a sign that the state now had the power to command that the young be schooled formally, and this power called forth imaginative compromises within the immigrant community as well as in American political ideas. These local community solutions to the potential for conflict over the second generation were overwhelmingly composed on American grounds. That would become clearer by the late nineteenth century as schooling became more important as an ingredient for successful negotiation of the American economy and when the, by then, large Catholic school system eagerly sought to imitate the innovations of the public schools in order to maintain the allegiance of its constituents. The immigrant-based nonpublic schools were always that—a response to the growing power of the state and the national identity that schooling had come to represent in the nineteenth century.

New Purposes, New Means, and New Students

In the late nineteenth and early twentieth centuries, schooling became a much more ambitious enterprise, more crucial to America's position as a growing world power, and a more significant feature of individual success and achievement. The nineteenth-century industrial transformation had created a corporate and commercial white-collar world that required higher levels of literacy and business know-how. So too, developments in industry put a premium on refined mechanical, metallurgical, and engineering skills. Even agriculture, which had been the common coin of the realm, was transformed into a business where higher levels of schooling paid. In the professions—law, medicine, architecture—new requirements and certifications replaced a previously laissez-faire situation in which casually reading law or practicing medicine in one of several ways had been a sufficient form of training. Schooling to which a few Americans had always looked for avenues to success became more central to status and mobility and a necessary means for acquiring the training, diplomas, and social skills required for economic success. And schooling also became a form of licensing as diplomas and degrees became requirements for placement or certification. At the same time, low-level industrial jobs, increasingly dependent on machines and machine processes, remained hungry for brute labor, a hunger that made America a golden portal for immigration. Thus the period saw two related movements meeting at the schoolhouse door—the drive for more and better schooling, and the new millions of immigrant children brought to or born in America whom the schools needed to incorporate into the nation.

The meeting was both fortuitous and uncomfortable. The need for skills and the presence of larger pools of greater varieties of immigrants (Poles, Magyars, Russian and Austrian Jews, Slovaks, Croats, Italians, Syrians, Greeks, Armenians) created significant pressures on the schools both to lengthen the time students spent in school so that a few years training in elementary school became inadequate, and to increase the rigor and organization of classroom learning. By the 1880s, bureaucratic drives had already made the school grade and school hierarchy important in primary schools in immigrant-swollen cities. By the end of the century, the old public high school was transformed toward these ends, and in the early twentieth century the new junior high school was created. Newer curricula emphasizing modern languages, science, and math rapidly superseded the older emphasis on classical languages and recitation for the academically inclined and college-bound. Older students, kept in school by increasing age of attendance requirements and the desire for advancement, forced high schools to deal with students who were neither academically inclined nor headed for college or professional schools. For them, school leaders and reformers began to design more practical courses of instruction in commercial or mechanical arts, or they expanded high school offerings through a watered-down version of the rigorous academic course. In the late nineteenth century, some cities, like Somerville, Massachusetts, maintained two high schools—one with a Latin-based curriculum for the college-bound and a newer school for those with non-college aspirations.[5] The many students who saw secondary schooling as an avenue for commercial and clerical success quickly made the latter school eclipse the former in size and educational importance. By the second decade of the twentieth century, these multiple tracks became increasingly familiar as alternatives in the new comprehensive high schools that sprouted in cities of every size in all parts of the nation, and somewhat later even in rural places, as the move toward school consolidation took over the countryside.

Immigration fed this process. As the number of immigrants moved past a million a year in the early decades of the twentieth century, and as their parents moved into the steel mills, meatpacking plants, construction sites, sweatshops, and vegetable stands of the major cities, the children found themselves in the newly invigorated and ambitious schools. School officials, eager for the growth of their own enterprises, welcomed them and were challenged and sometimes overwhelmed by the problems they brought: disease and bad teeth, inadequate English-language skills and behavior problems; and the irregular attendance that resulted from these problems and their parents' need for their assistance at home. The problems of poverty and displacement that the immigrant children brought were huge, but they were problems whose solutions would make an important contribution to school growth. During the first three decades of the twentieth century, schools at all levels, but especially high schools and junior high schools, evolved as modern institutions in part in response to these issues. Gymnasiums and nursing staffs, truancy departments and free lunch programs in new cafeterias, guidance clinics and academic testing—all became part of the vast institutional development of the school as a social institution and of the bureaucratization of school systems.

Only a few immigrant children initially went beyond the elementary school in the early years of the twentieth century, and those few were ethnically differentiated: far more Jews than Italians in the eastern cities, more Magyars and Czechs than Poles or Slovaks in the Midwest, more Japanese than Mexicans in the West. Many immigrant parents were simply baffled by the idea of physically grown children wasting their time in school when they could be helping their mothers at home or working alongside their fathers for the good of the family. As one Italian mother noted in exasperation at efforts to keep her adolescent children in school, "When girls at 13 or 14 wasted good time in school, it simply made us regret coming to America."[6] But the requirements stayed in place.

American views about children were increasingly at variance with those of many of the more traditional societies from which immigrants came. Adolescence, newly legitimated as a stage of life by G. Stanley Hall, was attached to childhood in American views as a period of transitional development and of social vulnerability. From the view of socialization, now widely adopted in the reform-minded schools, these were still tender years, which could make the difference between an effectively integrated adulthood and a maladjusted and socially dangerous one. Keeping adolescents in school, and especially the children of immigrants for whom the rocky transition between child and adult could lead to antisocial gang behavior, sexual precocity, and to a later life of crime, became all the more desirable and even necessary. Finding ways to occupy their time effectively so they could be kept there longer became a challenge.

By the 1920s the trickle into secondary schools that had begun earlier in the century became a flood of new high school enrollments, now often made up of the children of immigrants. The numbers tell the story well. In Providence, Rhode Island, in 1925, almost 70 percent of all children of Russian Jews had entered high school; so had more than 73 percent of the children of Irish immigrants; and even 33 percent of the children of the much more reluctant Italians. The Jews did best in graduating (66 percent), but almost one-half of the Italians who entered were also graduating at mid-decade.[7] It is likely that had Providence contained a significant number of students of Slavic background, their presence in high school would have been lower. But even then no fewer than 10 percent of Polish students would have likely graduated at this point, based on evidence from other cities.

The school people had succeeded, and they had built ever larger and more imposing buildings as a sign of that success. In many places, the high school became the biggest building in town, an anchoring symbol of modern democracy and economic opportunity. But, in those buildings, the immigrant children often led lives apart from the children of the native born while their destinies also diverged. High schools held out promises which were not always fulfilled since the vast expansion of schooling in the upper grades that took place in the context of immigration had been so rationalized and adapted to perceived student needs and skills that students in a comprehensive high school might have very different experiences and destinations.

Desirable as their presence was for school expansion, and necessary as it was perceived to be for purposes of socialization, the children of immigrants created problems in the schools and for their new programs. These problems were more and more viewed as matters of academic aptitude, rather than of home preparation or personal motivation. This perspective was underwritten by a growing commitment in American intellectual life to viewing differences among immigrants as biologically determined and to defining ethnic groups in racial terms. At the turn of the century, the problem of immigrant adaptation and poverty was usually understood by reformers, such as settlement house workers, as a result of environmental factors and subject to improvement. But immigrant issues by the second decade were often re-imagined as an intransigent effect of race, and the experience of the First World War, which increased national xenophobia, tended to confirm this perspective. So did the use of mental tests for intelligence during the war and the resulting reading of differences in scores as evidence for permanent group patterns of performance.

These same tests were adapted after the war by school systems across the country, which used them to sift the growing number of students into categories of higher or lesser potential for educated achievement. The extensive use of the "intelligence quotient" or IQ as it was now called, developed by Stanford psychologist Lewis Terman and interpreted by him as a stable and dependable measure of learning ability (native intelligence), increased the efficiency of the schools in allocating students to the different tracks they had been developing for the comprehensive high school. During the war, the army tests had already made clear that the "new immigrant" groups whose numbers had surpassed those of the older British, German, and Scandinavian groups sometime in the late nineteenth century, were consistently scoring lower on these tests than native groups and the so-called older immigration. And school officials were certainly not surprised when this proved to be the case for IQ tests as well. The IQ tests were a simple solution to a complex problem—how to arrange schools rationally so that all students could benefit to some degree and stay at school longer, at the same time that teaching these ever larger numbers could be organized not around the individual but around ability groups. The IQ could also rationalize different paths in life and different educational outcomes at a time when schooling was becoming more closely identified with social success. (See Chapter 2 in this volume.)

As a result, the vast expansion of secondary education and increased attendance of immigrants was an ambiguous democratic triumph. It certainly permitted some individuals to succeed in the terms of special merit that Jefferson would have approved. But it meant that for many students who were channeled into lesser programs, going to high school was far more a social experience than an academic challenge. The expanding American economy through most of the first half of the twentieth century was able to find comfortable places for these students, but the places they achieved hardly carried either the same status or the same potential rewards as awaited those who were channeled further into the colleges, the learned professions, and executive suites. The memory of this differentiation and the testing that served as its mechanism would last and was renewed during the second half of the twentieth century, when high school attendance or even graduation would no longer provide the places in the economy it once had.

If the high school distributed its academic resources and rewards differentially among the children of immigrants and natives, its social life was just as complex. Between the 1920s and 1945, a period when all immigration was reduced and immigration from Eastern and Southern Europe (the new immigration) practically ceased, the high schools became important arenas of Americanizing experience for the second and third generations, the children and grandchildren of those who had come earlier in the century. It was here, in the new cauldron of American life that had become a kind of adolescent rite-of-passage, that the ethnic complexity of America was most often brought home.

In most big cities, high schools could vary a great deal, some containing few ethnics, while others included a rich assortment of different groups. In New York—the premier immigrant city—these variations meant that social experiences differed a great deal. In New York, the highly selective Bronx High School of Science was composed overwhelmingly of one ethnic group—Jews. So was the very different Seward Park High School on the poor Lower East Side of New York. But at others, such as Evander Childs High School in the Bronx or George Washington High School in Manhattan, Italians, Irish, and Jews, and usually a few blacks, competed for prominence in extracurricular activities, prizing posts as newspaper editors and election to president of the student body as much as and sometimes more than academic honors. This competition often had ethnic dimensions. Even in activities where students did not compete, such as science clubs and glee clubs, they tended to make ethnically different choices that indicated that they were largely selecting their associations according to ethnicity. (See Chapter 3.) Despite the emphasis on immigrant socialization through public schooling, neither school organizers, nor principals and teachers could control the real social distinctions and forms of identity that long years of schooling encouraged among adolescents. Unlike elementary school students, those in high school were both more fully attuned to social nuance and more aware of its importance to them as they prepared to assume adult roles. Caught between the older world of their parents and the new world designed by the schools, they created a third way that was ethnically conscious within the schools. This rich social life drew them together with others with similar backgrounds, problems, and needs. Leonard Covello, the principal of Benjamin Franklin High School in the Bronx, who wrote an important book on the second-generation experience, understood this about his own life and about his students: "Here in America we began to understand . . . that there was a chance that another world existed beyond the tenements in which we lived and that it was just possible to reach out into that world and one day become part of it." That world could be reached through the school. But in the school, it could be imagined only with the help of others like oneself: "Whatever problems we had at school or in the street, we never took up with our parents. These were our personal problems to be shared only by companions who knew and were conditioned by the same experience."[8]

If the public high school was one place where this experience could be shared with others who led similar lives, another was the parochial high school. Although the Catholic Church's efforts to educate the children of immigrants was heavily concentrated at the lower levels of schooling, it became apparent early in the century that the secular success of its congregants would increasingly hinge on further and higher schooling. Impelled by the Third Plenary Council in Baltimore (1884) to create secondary institutions, the Catholic hierarchy in most large cities began to build diocesan schools. This was a slow and costly process. In 1922 there were still only 35 such schools anywhere in the country. But, by 1947 there 150 and the number continued to grow. The diocesan high school would allow the children of poor Catholics to reach higher without having to compromise their religious instruction or be forced into contact with students of very different backgrounds. Private Catholic academies had made this available through various religious orders to wealthier Catholics. It was the expansion of the diocesan high schools in the twentieth century that made it available to the Catholic masses. In these schools, secular subjects could be more safely taught by the religious teaching orders while home languages were maintained in religious subjects. Kept closer to home in all these ways, the Catholic high school nevertheless provided immigrant families with ways to allow their children to make social and economic progress in American life. This was a lesson that the Catholic hierarchy and Catholic parents also incorporated into the rapid development in the twentieth century of Catholic institutions of higher education, from Duquesne University in Pittsburgh to Catholic University in Washington, D.C.

Religion was only one piece of the immigrant background sometimes challenged by the public school that could be retained in parochial high schools of all kinds, Catholic, Jewish, as well as Lutheran. Other aspects of culture, such as holiday celebrations, foreign languages not taught in the public schools, views of authority, and intragroup dating that maintained marital endogamy were also more easily safeguarded. No matter how much students might stay with others like themselves, the public

schools tended to expose students to a greater variety of culturally accept-
able forms and more challenges to a uniform self-identity. Those parents
who chose religious schooling understood this well and tried to protect
their children from these challenges.

It was less possible to protect the young from the growing influence of
popular culture with its strong homogenizing and Americanizing trends as
the twentieth century progressed. Music, clothing, movies, teen magazines, slang, dating patterns—these were all ways in which the young
became another estate in America and through which immigrant youth
especially learned to adapt and become more like their peers from other
ethnic and native groups. While parochial schools could try to impede this
trend through the use of school uniforms and the blacklisting of movies
and books, they could hardly stop it completely. And popular culture
became an important component of the learning process by which the second generation became part of the American scene.

By the time of the Second World War and immediately after, many of
the challenges which had once defined the agenda of school expansion
had gelled into institutional form, most significantly in the guise of the
American public high school and its parochial school variants. Attached
to these institutions were all kinds of social trends that became associated
with youth culture in twentieth-century America. By then, too, most
immigrant groups had adapted to this new central American institution
while their young had used it to achieve a sense of themselves as American
youth, still connected to ethnic groups and ethnic friends in school and
out, but also very much part of a wider and expanding definition of
American culture.

Youth culture was only one of the issues the high school had brought
to the fore. The other was social mobility. In the nineteenth century,
schooling had served a few toward this end, but the overwhelming majority of Americans, including immigrants, carved out their place through the
expanding American economy. This began to change in the late nineteenth
century as certification and licensing made more education necessary for
success. The effects were already clear when high schools tracked students
with the understanding that high school achievements were related to success later in life. But this association was still somewhat muted since high
school graduation in and of itself remained a significant marker and a
desirable goal. This changed by the end of World War II. The strong modern association between education and social place had started to over-
whelm other ways in which status could be achieved in modern society, at
least for the vast majority not born to money or social position.

As we have seen, each new major current of immigration had contributed to the alteration of schooling and its purposes. In the early nine-

teenth century, problems of republican citizenship had empowered the schools to prepare the immigrants of the mid-century for their roles in the commonwealth. In the early twentieth century, immigration had transformed the schools into large, comprehensive social environments that were to compensate for the problems of immigrant groups while selectively preparing their children for the new economy. By the second half of the twentieth century, the role of schooling had become demonstrable and urgent for economic success. In that context, Americans looked ever upward as they sought to ensure that immigrants became successful Americans.

The Newest Immigration: Reaching Higher

The differential educational attainments and social mobility of the children of immigrants in the first half of the twentieth century resulted from cultural and economic differences among the groups as well as school policies. Thus Jewish students tended to go further in school than Poles for a variety of reasons relating to their parents' initial literacy, economic circumstances and ambitions, and the role of learning and achievement values. The Irish had used the parochial school system to much better effect than had the Italians because of their closer identification with the American Catholic church and its hierarchy as well as their drive for social place in America. School policies, as we have seen, often distinguished among students during their academic lives, facilitating or obstructing the potentials of some through limits imposed by testing or tracking. And almost everywhere, neighborhood poverty took its toll on school attendance and the provision of adequate educational facilities while home conditions made learning more or less possible. In higher education, quotas had been imposed on Jewish students in the first half of the century in professional schools (especially medicine) as well as in selective colleges, such as the Ivy League (most notoriously at Harvard and Dartmouth), because Jews were seen as overreaching their place or insufficiently refined for the high status these schools and achievements signaled. But these differences were the results of policies made at the local level or the toll of social discrimination.

Not until the Second World War, however, did the federal government discover the enormous national stake in schooling. The huge call-up of troops and the allocation of duties and responsibilities by skill and school level as well as the painful recognition of the cost of illiteracy in a modern technology-driven army was one part of this discovery. This led to an unprecedented extension of in-service literacy training during the war, training in mechanical skills, and higher levels of learning at university campuses for hundreds of thousands of men as the army helped create the manpower it needed. After the war, the experience resulted in the provision of further schooling for millions as part of the package of GI benefits. For the first time in history, the federal government was beginning to deploy its resources toward educating the American people.

Another critical result of the war experience was the recognition that investment in research and training at the very highest levels in science, math, and engineering as well as in foreign languages was a matter of national security. Americans had won the war not only because soldiers fought on the battlefields, but because scientists and professors who gathered on mountaintops and in laboratories developed new knowledge—in sonar and radar, in atomic weaponry, and in code-breaking. This experience had huge consequences for the postwar world as the government looked to the colleges and universities for the creation of new knowledge. National security matters were further brought home during the Cold War when the Soviet Union launched the first earth-orbiting satellite, Sputnik (1957), and then sent a man into space.

The consequences of these dual discoveries of the national stake in education were at first muted for immigrants and their children because immigration was not much of an issue until the major changes introduced by the reform legislation of the mid-1960s. Until then, the immigration policies of restriction of the 1920s were still in place, somewhat adapted at various points to accommodate postwar and Soviet-era refugees from Europe, including Jews, Germans, immigrants from the Baltic states, and other Eastern European countries.

This changed dramatically in the 1960s for three reasons. First, the levels of schooling required for success had shifted steadily upward. From the mid-1950s, informed by the experience of the war and subsequent Cold War, and the expansion created in higher education by the GI Bill, college going became a newly democratized objective, desirable for the nation's development and increasingly necessary to the maintenance or fulfillment of middle-class status. High school graduation was, for more and more Americans, no longer sufficient as a goal for their children. This view was encouraged by government policies as federal moneys poured into universities and other institutions of higher education from a multitude of agencies and departments to encourage research, which, in turn, expanded facilities and faculty. Second, the sources of immigration had begun to shift very notably and vigorously with the new legislation of the 1960s. American immigration issues had, until then, been overwhelmingly about European immigrants. The initial entrance of Asians in the nineteenth century had been successfully stanched by the first restrictive immigration policies in American history that targeted particular groups. The immigration of Mexicans had a different policy history but the same consequences since Mexicans had been largely treated as temporary workers rather than immigrants. Despite the long experience with Mexicans in the Southwest, where communities had existed since the nineteenth-century American expansion westward, the racializing of this brown population, and its relegation to a largely transient agricultural labor force, had made their schooling a local inconvenience rather than a central policy focus among educators. This now changed in dramatic ways as family reunification and the change in quota policies brought Asians and Latinos (including Cuban refugees) in large numbers to the United States. Finally, the civil rights legislation and temper of the 1960s brought matters of race to the forefront of social and political awareness. And it raised questions about equity, fairness, access, and mobility for groups hitherto marginalized, African Americans especially, but gradually other groups as well, including those from Latin America and Asia.

In the last thirty years of the twentieth century, this potent mixture once again brought issues relating to immigrants onto the educational agenda to become, for the first time, subjects for policy at the highest level of government. These issues of race, fairness, and higher education continue to reverberate into the twenty-first century. In addition, considerable numbers among the newest immigrants arrived with many of the problems of poverty, language, and conflicts in socialization and identity that had been part of the agenda of the schools since the late nineteenth century. Whether they came from isolated Vietnamese villages or large Latin American cities, the immigration of the late twentieth century brought children whose needs for basic schooling in citizenship was not less than that of the mid-nineteenth century Irish, and whose needs for socialization was similar to the early twentieth century Italians who preceded them. It could be argued that the most significant distinction between this newest immigration was less a matter of race (after all, the European groups had been described as races in the early twentieth century) than the result of the even greater range of dissimilarity in past experience that they brought with them, coming now from all parts of the known world. America was becoming, both abroad and at home, a global empire as people from everywhere created a population complexity probably never before seen in human society. Thus, older problems and more extreme heterogeneity now came together with newer concerns about civil rights in an elevated educational context that elicited much greater federal government attention to the education of its citizenry.

Questions about policy now affected schools at all levels and all immigrant and racial groups. Many of them were not new in the American context: among them questions of social services at school, high school ethnic particularism, and differential graduation rates. Others were genuinely innovative—above all affirmative action policies and federal mandates for local education. Some were more extreme versions of matters that had already appeared in earlier dialogues over schooling, such as bilingual education and the teaching of special ethnic subject matters.

Preschool education also falls into this last category. In the late nineteenth and early twentieth centuries, kindergarten advocates and teachers had adopted ideals of play with an almost missionary zeal, hoping to provide the children of the poor with a protected arena in which they could develop without the requirements of didactic instruction. Many denominations and settlements adopted kindergartens as part of the extension of social services to poor immigrants. Kindergartens emphasized socialization and expression and were meant to provide a few hours of elevated culture and beauty away from dreary home conditions. As an added benefit, they relieved overstressed mothers of their child-care obligations for a precious few hours. Kindergartens for those aged 5–6, before compulsory schooling kicked in, were expensive and only gradually incorporated into the normal public school regime over the course of the twentieth century. When they were, they became an arena for learning readiness rather than play, for the development of motor, memory, and behavioral skills to prepare students for more formal instruction.

It was this learning readiness that was central to the incorporation of new public preschool programs like Head Start that developed from Lyndon Johnson's Great Society programs in the 1960s. Growing from the era of civil rights, preschool became less a matter of protection than of preparation, and such programs were intended to compensate for inadequate home environments and to even out the disadvantages that some children brought with them to school. This was very much in line with the new emphasis on education as a means to correct social inequities that was common to the period and fundamental to the Great Society reforms. Concerned to address issues of inner-city poverty, especially that of children in African American communities, and to counteract its baneful effects, preschool and early childhood programs were adopted for their potential to care for and prepare children of the new and often very poor immigrants from Mexico, Latin America, and post–Vietnam War Asia. When other features of the Johnson "War on Poverty" were disassembled, this program was kept alive and expanded because it was a useful federal intervention in issues related to adequate preparation for schooling.

Much more contentious was the federally mandated bilingual education that resulted from both legislation and court decisions in the 1960s and 1970s (*Lau v. Nichols* 1974). This legislation also resulted from the new attitudes and views of the civil rights era, especially as Mexican Americans followed in the path of African Americans in demanding community self-determination and ethnic pride. Its advocates urged that children not be deprived of their home language and its associated culture. As Herschel T. Manual testified in hearings in 1967 in the United States Senate which was preparing to pass the first Bilingual Education Act (1968): "Although English is a basic necessity for the non-English-speaking child, as [for] every child, his native language should not be lightly cast aside. The home language of the child is an individual and community asset which the school should help develop from the child's first enrollment."[9] This emphasis on genuine bilingualism not just as a practical means toward English acquisition but as a resource for community and group identity was not new. The Germans had acted very much in the same way in the nineteenth century and used their political leverage in heavily German-populated communities in the Midwest. But it was new in the twentieth-century context, during which two world wars had created considerable fear and concern about subcommunity maintenance. Throughout the century, the acquisition of English had been assumed as a by-product of ever more vigorously enforced school attendance laws while socialization to a variety of American ways had been an objective. As a result, when the issue was reintroduced in the late 1960s, bilingual education was a very contentious issue. In many communities, especially in states with large and complex immigrant populations such as New York and California, despite federal financial assistance, it seriously raised educational costs when many different language communities had to be served often within the same school or school district. As with all new federal mandates, it also necessitated accounting and compliance procedures that were often resented by schools and local officials. Nevertheless, through most of the 1970s, 1980s, and 1990s, in the big cities that were home to diverse groups, the children of immigrants from China, Mexico, Vietnam, and Cambodia and many other places were often offered instruction in basic subjects in their native language at public expense. This trend has only now begun to decline, most significantly in California and Washington State because of popular referenda that have registered the electorate's view that such instruction is an impediment to English acquisition. In California, bilingual education, except as a temporary stopgap, has now been suspended. And in New York City, growing protest and unhappiness by Spanish-speaking parents at the inadequate progress of their children in acquiring English-language confidence, is putting that city's bilingual program in dispute.

Bilingualism is closely related to another issue that is both new and old in the public schools—ethnic cohesiveness. Many schools, especially high schools, are today seen as arenas marked by a nearly complete separation between students from different ethnic backgrounds even when they study side-by-side in the classroom. In the 1930s and 1940s it was not at all uncommon for students in high schools to associate largely with those like them, hanging out together in cafeterias and choosing the same extracurricular activities. But this was always done within a setting that emphasized integration and in many cases banned the speaking of foreign languages in the schools. The realm of extracurricular activities was imagined to be a continuation of the common school ideal and a stimulus to active democratic participation in the multitracked high schools. One advocate of these activities noted that they were "the one place where democratic ideals and objectives may function in a natural matrix. . . . Whether a student is notably dull, studious, rich, poor, handsome, or ugly he should have an equal opportunity to be a member of a school organization which ought under all circumstances to be organized upon a basis of democratic society."[10] By the 1970s and 80s, however, this view became suspect as unwelcome pressure toward assimilation and rejected as tending toward Anglo conformity. Instead, school life often became a battleground among different groups. In one survey, "frequent fights between race-ethnic groups" was seen as the most significant factor making students feel unsafe at school.[11] In many colleges, students not only associated by ethnic group but were allowed to live in separate dormitories and found a curriculum newly enriched with a variety of courses which permitted continuous identification with their ethnic cultures. All this was aggravated by the end of the century by the growing resegregation of schools, especially in places with large Latino populations, a trend that eroded the efforts begun after the great victory for integration and civil rights marked by the *Brown v. Board of Education* decision in 1954. Americanization efforts that had been very close to the surface in the early twentieth century, no matter what their success, were largely buried by the end of the century. As diversity became a byline of American culture, subgroup identity seemed less of a direct challenge. Indeed, the imposition of cultural uniformity by schools was viewed in the late twentieth century as unworthy of a democratic multicultural society.

Except in one area. In matters relating to material success and opportunity, the schools have more than ever been enlisted in the project of immigrant incorporation. If in the nineteenth century the polity was considered the heart of American citizenship and in the early twentieth century social and cultural habits were seen as the core of an American identity, by the late twentieth century Americans began to embrace a more pluralistic cultural vision. Instead of an older emphasis on political participation or cultural unity, social policies substituted active and contented economic activity as the mainstay of social solidarity and national stability. While this economic and consumer emphasis was already solidly in place in the much more culturally homogeneous 1950s (and anticipated even in 1850), it was amplified by the commitments of the civil rights era that followed. At a time when multiplicity in cultural tastes and lifestyle choices dominated approved social perspectives, equal access to economic resources became the dominant objective in a consumer-based society.

In the second half of the twentieth century, the mobility that had been offered as a by-product of schooling in the early twentieth century became in the second half the sine qua non of a successfully functioning school system. This was in part the result of the growing importance of consumerism to the American economy and to the close identification between the acquisition of material symbols of success and social worth. In this context, college going and its economic placement value became a necessity. By the 1980s, these patterns were deeply etched, making competition in and through schooling a central focus of social policy. In fact, the findings of various studies such as the 1983 report "A Nation at Risk," that American schoolchildren were not holding their own compared with students elsewhere, became the subject of national policy concern. Affirmative action, initially a strategy for the better integration of African Americans into American institutions of all kinds, including higher education, became a football in this process.

Certainly not all of the new immigrant groups were either included in or needed the extra boost that affirmative action policies in college admissions offered. The huge diversity of immigration since the 1960s had included groups such as the Chinese and Koreans who were extremely successful academic performers and whose college-going rates were higher than those of natives. Some groups, such as Indians from South Asia, came from families whose educational and skill levels were already very high and who encouraged their children's achievement. And globalization was making the presence of binational students from Asian societies familiar at colleges and universities throughout America. These groups were, like the Jews before them, soon to be found in very large numbers at institutions of higher education, especially in California. But other groups prominent in the new migration, such as Mexicans and the Hmong people of Indochina, came from cultural backgrounds in which education was not highly emphasized and from homes that were marked by material deprivation. During the 1980s these groups were increasingly included in affirmative action policies at schools that began to provide some extra advantage in the admissions process to those who had succeeded against the odds. Often these policies were seen as a means to increase racial diversity at college, since most of the people joined African Americans and

Native Americans in being described as people of color or underrepresented minorities. This coalition has become a new feature of life at institutions of higher education, where it has also often been accompanied by various efforts to increase the diversity of faculty and the subjects of study to help inscribe the multicultural perspective into the university curriculum. The California colleges and universities, among them the University of California and Stanford University, have led in these efforts.

Since the new immigration is enormously diverse, that perspective has not always been welcomed by other groups, such as the Koreans, whose ascent has been unassisted and self-motivated. As in the past, the experience of different groups, and of different individuals, has hardly been uniform, and the issues remain contentious and complex. As of this writing, affirmative action has been upheld as a result of two divergent decisions by the United States Supreme Court in 2003, both resulting from admissions policies at the University of Michigan. In the first, *Gratz et al. v. Bollinger et al.,* the court rejected the automatic recalculation of admissions requirements that the university had used in evaluating applications by minority candidates and called for a much more individual approach to the admission of undergraduate students. The second, *Grutter v. Bolinger et al.,* upheld the carefully framed concept of affirmative action that had been introduced in the landmark Bakke decision in 1978, a decision that rejected a numerical quota but allowed the University of California to take race into account in admissions (*Bakke v. University of California*). In judging that the University of Michigan Law School could continue to include race among its admissions criteria, the Supreme Court clarified its position, which had been under dispute, in various subsequent federal court rulings and by popular referenda (ballot propositions) in California and Texas in the 1990s.

The most influential recent study of the long-term consequences of affirmative action, a study by two past Ivy League university presidents, Derek Bok and William Bowen, suggests that affirmative action policy operates successfully in creating a more diverse college-educated professional group among those previously deprived. The graduation rates of those who came to college with an extra boost differed hardly at all from those who did not, and they have now become an anchor of a newly diverse middle class. From the point of view of social policy, affirmative action has created a more fully incorporative society. The study confirms the larger social issues which underlie the federal government's growing role in educational issues. At the same time, from the point of view of competing students eager for the benefits that entry to the very best schools and professional programs can provide in a highly competitive educational market place, issues of personal injustice and unequal treatment are often keenly felt.

While these matters have dominated education at the top, the question of education lower down and its relationship both to successful social and economic integration and to affirmative action have remained a powerful political issue. In California, among other places, the children of Mexican immigrants continue to graduate from high school at much lower rates than others, and only about half make it through. This has been a concern at all levels of policy in the state. But the issues have now developed a national face. Indeed, for the first time in American history, presidential candidates have developed educational proposals as among their primary campaign themes, most recently in President George W. Bush's "Leave No Child Behind" campaign. Bush, a former governor of the state of Texas, a state with a very large Mexican American population, understood that the successful schooling of the newest immigrants as a matter of both politics and equity is a fundamental national objective. Part of this effort resulted in a renewal of demands that national standards and tests be used to make sure that all children receive a basic education that will fit them for participation in a modern, technologically driven, and globally competitive economy. As in the past, the children of immigrants are very much in the minds of those who have launched this campaign, as they are in the minds of those who oppose it as a shallow and inadequate response to a significant problem. The schooling of immigrants has finally been elevated from the local to the national level at a time when schooling at all levels, from preschool to professional school, is a subject of national policy and debate.

Since the first half century of American life, schooling and immigration have been fundamental matters in national self-definition. While the issues were first left at a fairly rudimentary level and involved largely local commitments, the last 150 years have seen the two become more and more central to American culture, politics, and economic life. Today the question of schooling as it relates to a society still being redefined by immigration is a fundamental one from the lowest to the highest levels of politics and policy. It also remains an issue close to the heart of every immigrant family eager to keep its children close to their roots in a different past while propelling them onto the road to American success.

Notes

This essay was published in *A Companion to American Immigration* (New York: Blackwell, 2006), edited by Reed Ueda, and is reprinted here with permission of the editor and of Blackwell Publishers.

1. Quoted in Oscar Handlin, "Education and the European Immigrant, 1820–1920," in *American Education and the European Immigrant, 1840–1940,* ed. by Bernard J. Weiss (Urbana: University of Illinois Press, 1982).

2. Lawrence A. Cremin, *American Education: The National Experience, 1783–1876* (New York: Harper, 1980), 148.

3. Quoted in Carl F. Kaestle, *Pillars of the Republic: Common Schools and American Society, 1780–1860* (New York: Hill and Wang, 1983), 91.

4. Quoted in Cremin, *American Education,* 167.

5. See Reed Ueda, *Avenues to Adulthood: The Origins of the High School and Social Mobility in an American Suburb* (New York: Cambridge University Press, 1987).

6. Stephen Lassonde, "Should I Go, Or Should I Stay?: Adolescence, School Attainment, and Parent-Child Relations in Italian Immigrant Families of New Haven, 1900–1940," *History of Education Quarterly,* 38 (Spring 1998): 37–60, 52. *See also* Stephen Lassonde, *Learning to Forget: Schooling and Social Life in New Haven's Working Class, 1870–1940* (New Haven: Yale University Press, 2005).

7. For Providence, see Joel Perlmann, *Ethnic Differences: Schooling and Social Structure among the Irish, Italians, Jews and Blacks in an American City, 1880–1935* (New York: Cambridge University Press, 1988).

8. Leonard Covello (with Guido D'Agostino), *The Heart Is a Teacher* (New York: McGraw-Hill, 1958), 39, 47.

9. Quoted in Francesco Cordasco, *Bilingual Schooling in the United States: A Sourcebook for Educational Personnel* (New York: McGraw-Hill, 1976), xvi.

10. Charles R. Foster, quoted in Paula S. Fass, *Outside In: Minorities and the Transformation of American Education* (New York: Oxford University Press), 76–77.

11. Alejandro Portes and Rubén G. Rumbaut, *Legacies: The Story of the Immigrant Second Generation* (Berkeley: University of California Press, 2001), 203.

BIBLIOGRAPHY

Alba, Richard, and Nee, Victor. *Remaking the American Mainstream: Assimilation and Contemporary Immigration.* Harvard University Press, 2003.

Berg, Ellen. "Citizens in the Republic: Immigrants and American Kindergartens, 1880–1920." Ph.D. dissertation, University of California at Berkeley, 2004.

Bodnar, John. "Schooling and the Slavic-American Family, 1900–1940." In *American Education and the European Immigrant,* ed. by Bernard J. Weiss. University of Illinois Press, 1982.

Bowen, William G., and Bok, Derek. *The Shape of the River: Long-Term Consequences of Considering Race in College and University Admissions.* Princeton University Press, 1998.

Bowles, John, and Gintis, Herbert. *Schooling in Capitalist America.* Basic Books, 1976.

Brilliant, Mark. *Color Lines: Civil Rights Struggles on America's Racial Frontier, 1945–1975.* Oxford University Press, forthcoming.

Caplan, Nathan, Whitmore, John K., and Choy, Marcella H. *The Boat People and Achievement in America: A Study of Family Life, Hard Work, and Cultural Values.* University of Michigan Press, 1989.

Chapman, Paul Davis. *Schools as Sorters: Lewis M. Terman, Applied Psychology, and the Intelligence Testing Movement, 1890–1930.* New York University Press, 1988.

Cohen, David K. "Immigrants and the Schools." *Review of Educational Research,* 40 (1970): 13–27.

Cordasco, Francesco. *Bilingual Schooling in the United States: A Sourcebook for Educational Personnel.* McGraw-Hill, 1976.

Covello, Leonard (with Guido D'Agostino). *The Heart Is a Teacher.* McGraw-Hill, 1958.
———. *The Social Background of the Italo-American Child: A Study of the Southern Italian Family Mores and Their Effect on the School Situation in Italy and America,* ed. by Francesco Cordasco. Brill, 1967.

Cremin, Lawrence A. *American Education: The National Experience, 1783–1876.* Harper, 1980.

Daniels, Roger. *Coming to America: A History of Immigration and Ethnicity in American Life.* HarperCollins, 1990.

Dinnerstein, Leonard. "Education and Advancement of American Jews." In *American Education and the European Immigrant, 1840–1940*. University of Illinois Press, 1982.

Fass, Paula S. *Outside In: Minorities and the Transformation of American Education*. Oxford University Press, 1989.

Freedman, Samuel G. "Latino Parents Decry Bilingual Programs." *New York Times,* July 14, 2004, A21.

Handlin, Oscar. "Education and the European Immigrant, 1820–1920." In *American Education and the European Immigrant, 1840–1940*. University of Illinois Press, 1982.

Jefferson, Thomas. *Notes on the State of Virginia,* ed. by William Peden. Norton, 1954.

Kaestle, Carl F. *Pillars of the Republic: Common Schools and American Society, 1780–1860*. Hill and Wang, 1983.

Katz, Michael B. *The Irony of Early School Reform: Educational Innovation in Mid-Nineteenth Century Massachusetts*. Beacon Press, 1968.

———. *Reconstructing American Education*. Harvard University Press, 1987.

Lassonde, Stephen. "Learning and Earning: Schooling, Juvenile Employment, and the Early Life Course in Late Nineteenth-Century New Haven." *Journal of Social History,* 29 (Summer 1996): 839–70.

———. "Should I Go, Or Should I Stay?: Adolescence, School Attainment, and Parent-Child Relations in Italian Immigrant Families of New Haven, 1900–1940." *History of Education Quarterly,* 38 (Spring 1998): 37–60.

———. *Learning to Forget: Schooling and Social Life in New Haven's Working Class, 1870–1940*. Yale University Press, 2005.

Olneck. Michael, and Lazerson, Michael. "The School Achievement of Immigrant Children, 1890–1930." *History of Education Quarterly,* 18 (Fall 1978): 227–270.

Perlmann, Joel. *Ethnic Differences: Schooling and Social Structure among the Irish, Italians, Jews and Blacks in an American City, 1880–1935*. Cambridge University Press, 1988.

Portes, Alejandro, and Rumbaut, Rubén G. *Legacies: The Story of the Immigrant Second Generation*. University of California Press, 2001.

Ravitch, Diane. *The Great School Wars: New York City 1805–1973*. Basic Books, 1974.

Rumbaut, Rubén G. *The Immigrant Experience for Families and Children,* Congressional Seminar, June 4, 1998, Spivak Program in Applied Social Research and Social Policy, American Sociological Association, Washington, D.C., 1999.

Sanders, James W. *The Education of an Urban Minority: Catholics in Chicago, 1833–1965*. Oxford University Press, 1977.

Suárez-Orosco, Marcelo M., Suárez-Orosco, Carola, and Qin-Hilliard, Désiree. *Interdisciplinary Perspectives on the New Immigration, vol. 5: The New Immigrant and American Schools*. Routledge, 2001.

Tyack, David B. *The One Best System: A History of American Urban Education*. Harvard University Press, 1974.

———. *Seeking Common Ground: Public Schools in a Diverse Society*. Harvard University Press, 2003.

Ueda, Reed. *Avenues to Adulthood: The Origins of the High School and Social Mobility in an American Suburb*. Cambridge University Press, 1987.

———. *Postwar Immigrant America: A Social History*. Bedford Books of St. Martin's Press, 1994.

Wechsler, Harold S. *The Qualified Student: A History of Selective Admission in America*. John Wiley and Sons, 1977.

Weinstein, Rhona S. *Reaching Higher: The Power of Expectations in Schooling*. Harvard University Press, 2002.

2

The IQ
A Cultural and Historical Framework

It is doubtful whether so much public interest has been aroused since Darwin propounded his theories about the descent of man.
> —Harlin Hines, *Measuring Intelligence* (1923)

Over the last 50 years, IQ testing has become a highly significant, though largely informal, social instrument lying at the very core of the American educational system. But its once automatic use in the schools and our present, almost equally automatic, tendency to deflate its significance obscures its very real historical importance as a product of American culture. The IQ[1] was, and remains, far more than an educational tool. It is a way of seeing, a method for organizing social experience, and a cultural concept whose history is critically intertwined with the turbulence of the late nineteenth century and the specific order of the twentieth to which it gave way. In the half-century from 1870 to 1920, American society was caught in a whirlpool of movement and dislocation which profoundly altered every aspect of personal and social life. Within the vortex of the late-nineteenth–early twentieth-century world, two related processes—immigration and education—emerge as especially dynamic social forces. For, just as mass immigration was a symbol for— even the embodiment of—cultural disruption, education became its dialectic opposite, an instrument of order, of direction, of social consolidation. The IQ evolved from the interplay between disorder and direction; its nature determined by the problems immigration represented and the solutions education offered; its form and meaning determined by the needs of the society for which it provided solutions, explanations, and ultimately its own future problems.

It is my intention in the following essay to discuss the historical context in which IQ emerged in the United States to become such a powerful organizing principle. The essay proposes a loose suggestive framework rather than a fully elaborated demonstration. I am certainly aware that neither the community of psychologists from which IQ testing emerged, nor the educators who adopted it, or especially the public which accepted it ever completely agreed about the merits of IQ. Nevertheless, IQ did become an American activity, indeed almost an American industry, for 50 years, and it must be asked what it was about American culture and society at this time that made IQ so attractive despite the repeated challenges that surrounded it from its inception.[2] Thus I am discussing IQ, not to engage in a debate over its validity as a measurement of intelligence, but as a mirror for the culture that adopted and believed in it. In so doing, I am assuming that IQ, like all cultural inventions—scientific, institutional, mythical, or ideological—serves a certain purpose in the society within which it is developed, and that to understand the invention permits us better to understand the culture. And while my interests have less to do with the history of science than with the history of social ideology, IQ must first be introduced through its scientific beginnings.

"Mental testing," as the measurement of intelligence was universally called throughout its early development, was rooted in various currents of nineteenth-century European science, and resulted from what one early historian of testing called "the convergence of four strains of scientific development: German, French, English and American."[3] Its foundations lay in the laboratory techniques of German Wundtian psychology, which was concerned with the precise measurement of discrete physio-mental functions like memory, reaction time, and sensory discrimination. Powerfully augmented by the development of statistical methods in England by Karl Pearson and Charles Spearman, heirs of Sir Francis Galton, the specific form and content of mental testing finally bore the indelible signature of the French psychologist Alfred Binet. Concerned with the identification and education of feebleminded children, Binet removed tests from the domain of pure experimentation and statistical graphs to that of the school and the child. It is interesting to note that in each of these cases, the German, English, and French contributions reflected the highly evolved scientific-intellectual orientation of the contributing culture. But the European background of the tests need not detain us.

In the United States, mental testing first surfaced in a relatively minor way in the 1890s, as part of the then dominant German laboratory tradition, in a report by the pioneer psychologist James Cattell.[4] But this early interest among psychologists and a few educators was nothing compared with what was soon to follow. For it was only as the French concern with personality and abnormality and the English preoccupation with individual and group differences, as measured in aggregates and norms, were superimposed on the older German emphasis on laboratory testing of specific functions that mental testing as an American science was born. Despite its European ancestry, testing became a major preoccupation only in American psychology, where, in the words of an early historian of testing, during the second and third decades of the twentieth century the "movement has swept everything else before it."[5] As is so often the case, the American penchant or tolerance for intellectual eclecticism resulted in something quite new.

What was new, however, had little to do with the specific intellectual content of the psychology which resulted. Rather, what was new and significant about this movement was the incorporation of mental testing—this hybrid American psychology—into the mainstream of American culture where it exercised an influence which was not only scientific but social. Mental testing is important in the United States not because it dominated American psychology for a generation, although this is interesting, but because it crystallized the interests and needs of a whole culture. It provided Americans with a powerful organizing principle, a way of ordering perceptions, and a means for solving pressing institutional and social problems.

The Americanization of mental testing began in 1911 when Lewis Terman, the Stanford psychologist, translated Alfred Binet's age-mentality scale designed to sift the feebleminded from the French schools and adopted it to test, sort, and classify American schoolchildren. Terman was not the first American to use Binet's tests, but he was the first to use them with normal children.[6] With Terman's adoption of the Binet scale and his subsequent modification and introduction of the concept of intelligence quotient in 1916, the history of IQ testing in America properly begins. But the context for what would subsequently become the IQ craze had emerged much earlier. Its roots lay not only in the psychological laboratory, but in the schoolroom, the city ghetto, and above all in that disorderly society of the first two decades of the twentieth century for which historians have never found an adequate label, but the response to which has invariably been called progressivism.

There is no need to repeat here the familiar story of the Progressive era: the concern to renovate, reinvigorate, and reform American democracy to meet the new challenges of industrialism, urbanism, and statism. It was, in fact, the whole layout of a rapidly changing society—its population, its landscape, its institutions, and its direction—that stimulated American policy makers, professionals, and philosophers of the early century. The challenge this posed was met everywhere by a recourse to education: education through the ballot, education in the social settlements, education in the agricultural stations, education through muckraking, education through a wide array of professional and reform societies. And, of course, education through the schools.

It was perfectly fitting that the towering figure in progressive thought was an educator. John Dewey is still remembered primarily as an educational reformer, and while most of his philosophy has been discarded, his theories of education remain to inform and direct our action. Through a long life, Dewey appropriately maintained his primary affiliations with institutions of education. While it may be too large a claim that Dewey was the progressive par excellence (progressivism was too many things and Dewey was too many things), it is certainly true that in many ways Dewey's concern and interests were an especially refined expression of American progressivism generally.

Dewey's educational theories are popularly, and mistakenly, remembered today only for their advocacy of the open-classroom approach to learning and the freeing of the individual from the rigors of traditional academic discipline. But Dewey's interest was, in fact, with the problem of education in its broadest social sense: with how best to educate the whole child, and how to organize instruction in such a way that the child's mind and talents would be free to grow and adapt in an infinitely changing universe. Dewey never intended to free the child from social responsibilities or from the burden of his role and place in life. Rather, he sought to liberate education so that each child's abilities and talents could find their high-water mark and each individual could make his contribution to a society whose vitality required it to use all available talents and resources for the common good. If Dewey was interested above all in education as a method, his deepest concern was with democracy, with how, in the midst of change, democratic goals could be maintained by democratic means.[7] Dewey's ideas were part of a tradition at least as old as Thomas Jefferson, newly tuned to a nation changing more rapidly than Jefferson would have ever dreamed of or wanted.

Dewey's dilemma, how to translate an expansive liberal philosophy into a method of mass instruction which required organization, direction, and systematization, has become familiar to historians. Since Richard Hofstadter's pointed attack on Dewey, historians have tirelessly noted that, in the name of Dewey, progressive education became something quite different from the free and open growth which Dewey advocated; that, in fact, education became a means of mass control and conformity rather than of individual liberation.[8] Whatever Dewey's contribution to the specific denouement of these institutional problems may have been, it was certainly John Dewey who most provocatively addressed the broader social context within which education functioned and challenged the schools to undertake a resolution of the problems confronting that society. And it is within that broader context, and the roles the schools assumed within it, that IQ must be understood.

First, Dewey focused attention on the pivotal issue of mass education and of the relationship between education and democracy. Specifically, he emphasized the role of education as a means of control and direction in a changing society. Despite Dewey's vagueness about organizational detail, he was always crystal clear that education was to be the primary channel for democratic evolution. Second, Dewey zeroed in on a related issue that dominated educational discussions for decades—"individualized instruction" in the context of democratic society. [9] As Dewey interpreted this issue, it required both the fullest education for each child and a just solution of the problems facing democratic social life. This educational issue is most familiar to us in the various guises of the impulse toward meritocracy—the just and equitable distribution of training and rewards according to individual abilities. In the early twentieth century, educators understood that the school would become the strategic agency in this process as the allocation of rewards became more formalized, routinized, and less personal in the society as a whole. Here, on this crucial issue, Dewey presented an almost absurd challenge to education, for he called for instruction organized around a kind of Socratic teacher-pupil relationship in which learning would result from a free interaction over time. While the implementation of such views was impossible in the context of the evolving realities of schools and school systems in the early twentieth century, the underlying issue as it was interpreted by educators led to a more differentiated instruction for which, as we shall see, the IQ provided what seemed to be the fairest and the most practical, as well as the most culturally felicitous, organizing principle.

Although Dewey was not responsible in any simple way, for IQ testing in the schools,[10] he was responsible for at once raising the expectation of what the schools could and must achieve, and for inspiring schoolmen with a vision of a more effective educational regime. So too, Dewey's educational philosophy, with its emphasis on individual potential and child-tailored instruction, provided a context which legitimated the use of IQ testing. Thus, Dewey both reflected the pervasive faith in education and stimulated the search for innovative procedures that would serve the needs of the child and the society. These procedures were especially necessary as the size and scope of education changed in the early twentieth century.

Mass education was certainly not new in the twentieth century. Before the twentieth century, however, education had been neither as important nor as complicated a matter as it was subsequently to become. It was not as important because work, status, and one's role in society had been the product of many factors. Formal education was only one of these, providing literacy for most students and professional training to a select few. It was not until the twentieth century, however, that education, professionalization, and technical competence became the primary means by which an individual's niche in society was determined. By the twentieth century, the promiscuous and informal training of the nineteenth century was institutionalized, rationalized, and centralized in the schools. Similarly, with all the rich variety of nineteenth-century American life, it was not until the twentieth century with its dense cities, polyglot ghettos, and unending migrations that the diversity of American culture was transformed from a pride into a problem.

Most Americans, and the progressives especially, were fully aware that in this new context education for those who were to succeed, as well as for those who were merely to survive, was an imperative. Education became, above all, a way of managing the new society, and the schools became necessarily social organizations which would direct and define: direct the mass toward responsible behavior and define the individual's role in society. Toward that objective, the democratic tradition behind mass education, best exemplified by Dewey, was joined by another equally puissant force emerging from the disorders of the late nineteenth and early twentieth centuries. For while they treasured their traditions of democracy, Americans, and the progressives specifically, had also grown to respect and even to revere a newer tradition—science, scientific thinking, and its accompanying technical experts with their numbers, charts and statistical averages. The collector of statistics had become a central actor in the progressive drama. He was first of all an educator who investigated and provided information about a wide range of social problems. Most progressive legislation was preceded by elaborate and precise surveys which still today give us some of the best information we have about the way Americans lived at the turn of the century. Like education, science and the collecting of numbers became a way of organizing, of defining, and ultimately of mastering change, for the progressives' interest in science went beyond its potential as a form of data collecting. Science was also to provide a method and an orientation for solving social problems and making social policy.[11]

Thus, when at the climax of the Progressive era, America found itself fighting a war to save democracy and was forced to organize its heterogeneous democratic army into an efficient fighting force, a committee of scientists offered to contribute to the war effort by constructing a series of tests. Initially designed to eliminate the unfit, the tests were quickly adapted to select leadership from the ranks and to make work assignments on the basis of ability.[12] The members of that committee came from the new scientific discipline of psychology: a hybrid calling which was part biology, part philosophy, and in good part linked with the evolving profession of education. Indeed, testing seemed to be raising the stature of both psychology and education by making each seem more "scientific."[13] It is with that committee, whose personnel would continue to dominate the testing field and the army tests which they designed, that the story of IQ testing in the American schools properly begins.

Intelligence tests had been developed by a number of individuals since the early years of the century. By 1916 Terman had regularized the concept of intelligence quotient and standardized the Binet scale with his Stanford revision. But these tests had hitherto been used only with small experimental groups, in mental institutions like Vineland, New Jersey, where H. H. Goddard had been using the tests since 1908, as well as with selected groups of schoolchildren, as Terman was doing in California.[14] Since the Binet tests required expert administration on an individual one-to-one basis, they had not generally been used on a large scale and never with the intention of sifting a mass population into rungs or positions according to relative merit. Before the army tests, these difficulties of administration (and of evaluation) had prevented their large-scale application. Psychologists, newly self-conscious and jealous of their scientific expertise, were careful that the instrument not be abused by those inadequately equipped and insufficiently knowledgeable.[15] But, while the American army in 1917 was nothing like a controlled laboratory, neither were the times normal. An emergency situation called for extraordinary measures.

Although the army tests were based on and still linked to the individual Binet scale, the army test was a "group test" organized and routinized around pen and paper exercises which required only one administrator to provide general instructions to a large group. Over 1.7 million men were eventually tested in this way. The army tests demonstrated the feasibility of this kind of mass testing.[16] As one textbook on testing noted, "The possibility of measuring an individual's intelligence by a short and simple test has captured the imagination of school people and of the general public."[17]

While in the long run the army tests were a significant administrative breakthrough, the contemporary interest and headline grabber involved the results. The early discussions of the army tests revolved around a pseudo-issue—the apparent fact that almost half the American draftees had scarcely the mentality of 13-year-olds.[18] Doomsayers and gloomsayers quickly latched on to this "fact" to add fire to the many forecasts about the decline of American civilization to which the period was prone.

Walter Lippmann, in a now famous essay, handily disposed of this issue by noting that, in their haste, the testers had failed to translate into adult terms an age-grade scale which had originated with the testing of school-children.[19]

Neither Lippmann nor other critics were able so easily to dispel another feature of the results that would have long-lasting social consequences. For, as they proceeded to refine the test results in the early twenties, psychologists went beyond comparing and ranking individuals within a large population. They also correlated differences in scores with social categories like region, education, race, and country of origin of the draftees.[20] And while there were marked differences within all categories, those that focalized attention concerned the markedly lower scores registered by blacks and the recent immigrants like Italians and Slavs who did less well than native white Americans on both tests administered to those literate in English (Alpha) and those not literate or non-English speaking (Beta). The army tests made the crucial link between mental ability and race, not for the first time, but on a mass scale and in the full glare of public attention.

What had begun as a way of eliminating the feebleminded, then proceeded to a ranking of individuals according to talent, finally became a means for ordering a hierarchy of groups. Mental testing as a measuring device was a defining and sorting instrument, a way of distinguishing and differentiating which, given the cultural concerns of the time and in the context of the growing use of statistical techniques like normal distributions, correlations, mean and factor analysis, led predictably to racial comparisons. In so doing, of course, intelligence testing sharpened and accelerated the cultural awareness of individual and group differences.[21] An instrument whose purpose was to differentiate helped to direct and accent a culture's attention to the fact of differences. Since Americans were, in the first 30 years of the twentieth century, inundated by dozens of immigrant groups who were so radically different first from "Americans" and then from each other, the emphasis on differences now measurable by scientifically validated tests was translated from the realm of the senses to that of statistics. This made the differences seem firmer, sharper, and also more controllable. At a time when democracy seemed threatened by heterogeneity, counting, sifting, and ranking provided a form of order and containment.

All of this was true regardless of whether the mentality that the tests were measuring was innate or learned. In fact, as far as the needs of the army were concerned, it mattered not at all whether the tests measured ability or achievement, whether they reflected what an individual could learn or had learned. The army had been interested in finding suitable leadership talent. What they needed was an objective means to locate talent and to make assignments. Their concern was suitable to an organization drawn from a democratic mass which was to be organized for maximum efficiency.

It did, of course, matter very much that mental tests purported to measure innate ability rather than learning, but it mattered less for what the army functionally needed than for what it reveals about American interests at the time. For what the American designers and promulgators of intelligence tests proposed was that they could arrive at an absolute measure of potential and not merely a relative way of discriminating among individual abilities. By the time of the army tests, American testers, especially Lewis Terman, were eager to demonstrate the infallibility of the tests as absolute yardsticks.[22] In so doing, they emphasized the constancy of intelligence, the fact that once measured, an individual's intelligence would thereafter remain measurably the same. In part this reflected, as we shall see, the specific needs of education which, once the tests were used with sample "normal" children, obviously became the primary field for the future application of tests and was so recognized even before 1917.[23]

This stress on the IQ as an absolute measure of an unchanging quality was more than a response to the needs of American schools. It was especially attractive to Americans because it necessarily brought the whole issue of inherited endowment into sharp relief. Alfred Binet had never been overly concerned with defining tests as a measure of native capacity or of distinguishing between test performance which resulted from innate as opposed to environmental factors. Nor had he drawn a sharp line between these. Binet firmly believed that "intelligence" could be improved by training. But this made him no more an "environmentalist" than it made him a "geneticist." Rather, it demonstrated both his lack of interest in the distinction and his firm conviction that neither environment nor native endowment could be expressed apart from the other, and that each was meaningless in isolation.[24] Throughout Europe, researchers using the Binet tests were finding strong correlations between performance and sociocultural factors like class, and noted the marked academic inclination of the tests. One group of Italian psychologists particularly attacked the view that Binet's scale could ever measure "pure intelligence" outside of a specific social milieu, and others were arguing that the validity of test results could never be more than group specific.[25]

In the United States, Binet's tests were greeted with an enthusiasm which they failed to arouse anywhere else including his native France, probably because Binet's tests, as distinct from Binet's views, provided the possibility of measuring innate mentality and, therefore, an absolute and unchanging potential.[26] Most psychologists were usually careful to phrase the issue in such a way that they could always claim that they had not excluded environment as part of actual performance on the tests.[27] But the clear direction of American interpretation and the construction of experiments with tests were toward the view that intelligence tests were measuring something that was pure and inborn. If still imperfect, the hope was that the tests could eventually measure the innate, untutored capacity of the individual.[28]

If the society and the schools of the early twentieth century needed some objective means to identify the skills and aptitudes of the population, American psychologists, educators, and the public they served, which turned enthusiastically toward them for guidance, wanted something more than a relative way to distinguish among individuals. They wanted a precise and stable way of sorting and a method which could be used extensively, practically, and quickly. This the tests provided. So too, education as it was being redefined or reformed under Dewey's aegis was turning away from measuring "learning" as the product of former knowledge toward issues of potential educability and variable social needs. It was Dewey, after all, who passionately rejected the view that education was the acquisition of the accumulated wisdom of the past and urged instead that the unfolding of a child's (and the society's) future potential be the mission of education. Here, as in so many areas relating to IQ, there was a structural congruence between Dewey's educational purpose and the promise of IQ. And again, while Dewey was not responsible for IQ testing specifically, his philosophy of education, which so pointedly highlighted the concerns of the time, provided the fertile ground within which IQ took root. At the same time, educators and Americans in general also carried with them into the twentieth century a continuing deference to individualism, not to comparative evaluations, but to the individual as his own measure. This complex of cultural concerns—the need to sort and order a racially and ethnically mixed population, the orientation to future education, and the emphasis on individualism—defined the context in which IQ was developed and understood.

"Mental age," Kimball Young, an early tester and historian of the movement observed, "was after all a qualitative concept. The notion of intelligence quotient, however, took a step decidedly toward the quantitative expression of the individual performance with the scale."[29] The intelligence quotient, or IQ, publicized by Terman was both more than and different from a number which compared the individual to his peers. It compared him first to a norm, established apart from the specifics of time and place, and then expressed the results as a wholly personal ratio. In arriving at an IQ, age norms were derived by testing a representative sample population, and were thus statistical determinations based on average performance. A norm was an agreed-upon level at which some proportion (usually 75 percent) of children of a certain age could be expected to answer various kinds of questions correctly.[30] Each individual's performance was, in fact, compared to that norm which was stabilized or regularized as a yardstick for an age group. This established one standard for all children of a certain age regardless of the environment in which the child existed or the time the examination was taken. Thus, although performance on an IQ test was in fact comparative,[31] it was abstracted from a specific population and the test measured an individual against an absolute, asocial, and abstract constant. This idea of age-mentality norms had been introduced by Binet.

In the United States, Terman (borrowing from the German psychologist William Stern) transformed the age-mentality scale, which was still a form of comparison, albeit to an abstract norm, into IQ. The IQ was not expressed as a percent or percentile, which implied comparative performance, but as a function relating two personal qualities—mental age/chronological age. This completely personalized the measure, eliminating, at least on the surface, all comparative social components. It made the IQ appear timeless, asocial, and individual specific. The special quality of mental tests and their difference from ordinary tests was thus assured by testers in the expression of their results—first by comparing performance to an absolute standard rather than to a specific temporally and socially defined population, then by framing the results in terms of an individual ratio. Expressed in this way, intelligence looked absolute, changeless, and abstract.

The IQ is, in fact, a very strange number: a complete abstraction and a wholly statistical product. Unlike more familiar ratios, like miles per hour, dollars per unit, or, more appropriately, correct answers per total answers, IQ is not expressed in any recognizable units. It is self-defined; that is to say, an individual is defined in its terms. Of course, this quality is precisely what makes the IQ so absolute. It seemed to have an existence apart from the measuring instrument. This appropriately exaggerated the appearance that IQ described constant innate qualities which were not so much a measure of individual performance on a specific test as an abstract expression of the individual himself. In a society which was becoming national in scope, changing rapidly, and seeking to control change by measuring and counting, but which still revered the individual and insisted that rank and position reflected personal virtue, the IQ provided a numerically precise and timeless measure of the individual.

The form in which intelligence was measured both reflected and affected American social concerns. This was especially significant in two areas, race and education, which were from the beginning most crucially intertwined in its evolution. It could effectively be argued that, had Americans not been racially oriented and educationally obsessed, neither the enthusiasm for mental testing nor the specific form of its evaluation would have arisen. I have already noted how the social concern with differences made testing to measure differences attractive. To this it need only be added that an evolving racial consciousness (in the early twentieth century attached to white immigrants as well as black natives) tended to look for and emphasize inborn qualities to explain those differences. The search for a biological means to explain differences in character and habits was not new in the twentieth century.[32] Americans had measured skulls in the nineteenth century. But the presumption that what distinguished groups as well as individuals was not only some innate potential but an unchanging quality invulnerable to environmental modification was not entirely developed in the United States by the time American psychologists began to work on mental tests in the early twentieth century, nor even once the tests became a national obsession after the world war. This incipient search for a racialist explanation for differences informed American perceptions of the usefulness of testing and, perhaps more significantly, helped to determine what the tests would be interpreted to mean. For if Alfred Binet could not have cared less whether intelligence tests measured inheritance or environment, Americans could not have cared more.[33]

American testers spent years, in fact, the entire decade of the twenties and beyond, trying to eliminate the possible social components which might mar the test results as measures of unvarnished innate capacities.[34] Literally hundreds of sample populations were tested in the twenties to determine whether and how much various social factors like occupation, rural-urban residence, class, and language affected the tests as objective measuring devices.[35] Testers developed elaborate statistical procedures to determine exactly what the contribution of each of the factors was and how they could be eliminated from the absolute determination of mentality. The very process of searching for, identifying, and quantifying variables augmented the presumption that innate and learned factors could somehow be distinguished. And, if Binet was generally unconcerned with attaching some invariant number to general intelligence, Americans eagerly sought a number as precise and abstract as possible. As Kimball Young appropriately explained, "The grip which apparent exactitude in numbers has upon us ought not to need mention to psychologists. One of the strong appeals to educational and psychological workers using tests . . . is undoubtedly the fact that an array of averages and correlations gives them a sense of definiteness and finality."[36]

Once American needs and perceptions framed the form in which test results were expressed and explained, the two gave a powerful boost to a racism hitherto lacking scientific precision. Where nineteenth-century evolutionary science had provided Americans with the presumption that some races were superior to others, the IQ provided an absolute calibration and a ranked hierarchy as demonstrated by performance differences on tests. The intelligence tests also sharpened the division between environment and heredity as a significant form of understanding and explanation by providing a device oriented to distinguishing between them. In turn, American researchers worked on refinements of that instrument in order to find more effective ways to measure the discrete contribution of the now differentiated factors. As the IQ became ever more refined by the search to eliminate social components, the belief that environment and heredity were separable and that the IQ could eventually test only inherited capacity was increasingly confirmed. Racialist perceptions thus helped initially to organize the search for a measure of innate intelligence, and the IQ in turn exacerbated racism by providing it with a precision hitherto lacking. In the context of the American search for a basis for evaluating racial differences, the newly developed science of statistics provided psychology with the gift of numerology.[37]

This self-perpetuating cycle of perception and explanation had very specific social results. Nearly every study of group differences in IQs during the early twenties was introduced or concluded by a scholarly *obiter dictum* on immigration policy.[38] Americans, and psychologists among them, were profoundly concerned with the effect that uncontrolled immigration was having on democratic institutions, values, and the moral fiber of the nation. With the introduction of intelligence testing, Americans also became obsessed with mentality. This had been foreshadowed by the panicked headlines surrounding the results of the army tests. While the racial conclusions that accompanied intelligence testing were not the cause for immigration restriction, testing provided measurable evidence that greatly enriched and sharpened the alarmed context in which the immigration exclusion legislation of the 1920s took place. Americans did not need the test results, but the numbers and graphs helped to clarify the danger, and Americans used them.

It would be a mistake to conclude as a result of this instrumental function of IQs that they were merely a way to support a racially informed social policy. As we have seen, race influenced the development of mental testing in far more complex ways. Racial exclusion was a by-product of a whole manner of thinking, of perceiving, and of ordering which the IQ organized into a science and helped to stabilize.

The most significant effect of IQ testing was, quite foreseeably, in the schools, which are our most potent cultural translators. Here the IQ became an instrument of profound and continuing importance. For in defining intelligence in terms of a constant potential (IQ) rather than in variable social terms (comparative and time-linked performance), intelligence testing provided both a functional and densely cultural organizing principle in a school system plagued by an ever-enlarging and increasingly heterogeneous population, the growing demands that education adjust to a changing social environment, and the challenge of John Dewey that education cultivate individual potential.

One of the truly remarkable aspects of the early history of IQ testing was the rapidity of its adoption in American schools nationwide. In the twenties, the IQ tests were taken from the psychological laboratory, where they were still being tested, retested, and modified, and were fast on the way to being an entrenched part of educational administration. By 1922, one Detroit educator could boldly state in the *Yearbook of the National Society for the Study of Education* that "the adoption of the group method [of testing] by hundreds of school systems is now an old story."[39] Immediately after the war, the same group of psychologists who had constructed the army Alphas developed the National Intelligence Test. Over 575,000 copies were sold within a year of its issuance and 800,000 copies in the following year, 1922–23. By 1922, it was competing with numerous other tests of a similar kind. In 1922–23, over 2.5 million intelligence tests were sold by just one firm which specialized in their development and distribution. Forty different group intelligence tests were by then available on the national market.[40] Many more were rapidly being produced to satisfy an expanding demand. Indeed, tests were being rushed into press before they were adequately evaluated; some were a hodgepodge of different forms completely unintegrated and uncoordinated.[41] Psychologists suddenly found themselves in a lucrative business with skills very much in demand. The schools and their administrators adopted the products, quickly disregarding the still officially cautious attitude of the psychological community.

While the rapidity with which IQs were adopted was remarkable, it was not really surprising. The IQ grew out of the many issues and concerns facing American society in the early century. It was almost inevitable that it be adopted by the schools, which were the arena in which these problems were played out and which were also expected to solve them. The IQ established a meritocratic standard which seemed to sever ability from the confusions of a changing time and an increasingly diverse population, provided a means for the individual to continue to earn his place in society by his personal qualities, and answered the needs of a sorely strained school system to educate the mass while locating social talent.

Since the mid-nineteenth century, American education had been confronted by a central difficulty of democratic schooling—how to educate the mass without losing sight of the individual. Americans, unlike Europeans, could not depend on an exclusive elite class with its system of tutors and private schools which channeled and nurtured individual talent from the nursery through the university. In Europe, educating the masses normally meant educating them up to a certain level of competence, fitting them to industrial tasks, and filling them with a proper respect for the values and institutions of the society. Talent could and did rise out of the ranks, but that was not the school's most pressing concern. The American school was also intended to provide a basic education in literacy and social behavior and certainly functioned from the earliest days of the republic as an instrument of social control. At the same time, however, the schools were theoretically and actually the talent pool from which social leaders would be drawn. American private school education, except perhaps for the antebellum South, was never a reliable or exclusive basis for social advancement. Throughout the nineteenth century, the schools were simply not that important. What was important was the tradition of education as a democratic sieve, a tradition passed on to the twentieth century when the schools assumed a new prominence both as control and as channel.[42]

As schooling grew in importance, public education in the high school rather than in primary school moved to the center of educational discussion in the twentieth century.[43] The switch in orientation reflects not simply expectations about rising educational levels for the mass of the American population. It also suggests that training in skills and a socially relevant curriculum were now at the forefront of attention. The attention given to high school education in the twentieth century also meant that educators became, for the first time, deeply involved with specifically administrative issues of school organization, integration, and system. All of this required a new attention to the systematic ordering of education as a long-term process for the individual and the organizational details that accompanied institutional complexity. The democratization of high school education, which began very slowly at the turn of the century, accelerated before the First World War, and then exploded in the twenties, signals the coming-of-age of modern American education.

In the midst of these developments, John Dewey egregiously compounded the problem for the schoolmen and women. With a broadly democratic and liberal appreciation for the diversity of mankind, and a totally relativistic philosophical orientation, Dewey proposed that education be thrown wide open to, and in fact encourage, never-ending change. It would not be a parody to describe his aim as the opening up of the limitless potential of each individual to the limitless opportunities of social evolution. Hence, the gauntlet that he threw down to the schools, that they become leaders in a changing society by encouraging democratic forms which would provide maximum education to release the potentials of each child. This made the schools even more important than they already were. By shifting the charge to the schools away from the traditional one of instilling an agreed upon body of knowledge, to an active development of knowledge pegged to individual talent and instrumental in a changing society, Dewey helped to make some instrument like IQ a probability. For the schools needed first, to find a means for discovering each individual's potential, and second, to develop, organize, and systematize a learning process which could educate that potential. They needed, in short, to find a mechanism for selection and a basis for curriculum development. In order to do so, the schoolmen had to first find some way to stabilize Dewey's highly relativistic universe endlessly spinning around the strategic axis of the school.

The IQ was just the organizing principle needed to fulfill all these goals.[44] It established a stable educational center by assuming an unvarying constant within each child—his inborn capacity—and was based on a simple testing method designed to discover that potential. Finally, it permitted the development of a curriculum tailored to the potential the IQ described, which would be an orderly progression of learning suitable to children within a certain IQ range.[45]

That this ultimately predefined children so that students would thenceforth learn only so much as they were at the outset judged able to learn and ironically limited the function of the school by establishing the primacy of innate ability was in many ways a blessing. For in dealing with an increasingly heterogeneous population, the schools needed, or thought they needed, some way to evaluate individuals in order to arrange, organize, and subdivide the classroom and grade system, to "individualize" instruction and to make it more effective, even before learned performance was measured and compared. As one rather judicious authority on tests, Frank Freeman, observed, "The usefulness of measures of intellectual ability depends in part upon their stability and the possibility of predicting the individual's future intelligence from the measure of intelligence made at a given time. If the purpose of the test is, for example, to classify pupils so that the demands made upon them may be adjusted to their abilities it is necessary that their abilities shall remain more or less constant."[46]

The growth of American education and specifically the requirements of educational administration, like the American sensitivity to racial differences, meant that whatever the instrument of selection used, it should provide a constant measure of some inherent and unvarying potential. And just as the immigrant presence was crucial to the cultural network that created IQ as a form of organizing perceptions, so the presence of vast numbers of immigrant children in the schools was basic to the educational situation which seemed to make IQ testing an instrumental necessity. The problems facing the schools—the need for better organization, selection, and a curriculum at once more fully tailored to the individual and more socially alert—was not entirely the result of the presence of new immigrants. But the pressures on education to expand beyond the three R's, the stricter school attendance laws, and the concurrent child labor legislation which vastly expanded school populations cannot be separated from problems associated with immigration during this period. If immigration exclusion was one response to the alien presence, Americanization, remedial socialization, and vocational training, all of which were school centered, were others. Immigration made the schools grow exponentially both in scope and in size. At the same time, it made the schools' problems vastly more complicated.

It would be unfair and mean-spirited to argue that educators used IQs to cut across the problem and to exclude the newer immigrants from the lines of advancement which the schools now promised. It was never so simple. The schools continued to be theoretically and actually a force that facilitated immigrant access to society's rewards both as an agency incorporating immigrant children into the mainlines of the culture and as a lever for social and occupational advancement for individuals. At the same time, educators were certainly not surprised when immigrant children scored significantly and consistently lower on the examinations. They had, after all, been well prepared for these results by the army tests and by a whole battery of tests often administered at the very wharfs of Ellis Island.[47] They certainly did little or nothing to guard against the conclusions the tests offered. "If the stream of immigration from Southern and Eastern Europe continues to inundate us," Kimball Young declared, "the schools must take into account the mental abilities of the children who come from these racial groups. . . . The present situation is already causing a revamping of the curriculum and the general educational policy in many school systems."[48] Initially, at least, immigrant children were often channeled into programs which either stopped before the high school door, or, if they entered, ended in technical and vocational programs which provided little basis for effective social mobility through education.[49] Since their earliest application, IQs had been used to guide students to programs suitable to their "needs" and "talents," and as early as 1923, one popularizer of testing warned that "Many administrators . . . have expanded this idea of vocational guidance through the use of the test results until, if it were generally accepted, we would have nothing short of a type of Prussian control."[50] Immigrants were especially vulnerable to this kind of channeling.

Immigration helped frame the educational context for curriculum development, but the tests were not aimed at immigrants alone. They were a convenient necessity to the schools because they made possible the development of a learning process tailored to individual potential, organizable by classes, while still allowing for a progression of instruction by age. The best way to describe this network is a "track." Just as age subdivides schools horizontally and permits instruction to be developed according to progressive levels of advancement, the track subdivides the system vertically and channels and differentiates instruction more precisely as determined by individual abilities. The organizational grid that results from the intersection of age and ability allows instruction to be technically more individualized. If IQ is a ratio which compares age and ability, the tracked class and school system is the map that is projected from that concept.

One of the primary concerns of educators was with how the schools could best serve each child's needs and talents, and the early proponents of the use of IQs in the schools used this argument constantly. If the school system was not to swamp the individual in a monolithic curriculum which intimidated slow learners, held back fast learners, and failed to take into account future jobs and needed skills, factors like personal potential, ability, and interest should be taken into account. The vertical track could do just that. It was the peculiar virtue of the IQ that it could at once provide the organizing mechanism around which a complex school system could be built, while purportedly protecting the individual against the impersonality of that system. As the educator Carleton W. Washburne explained in 1925, tracking or "ability grouping" "is but a step toward individualization—a step which makes individual instruction easier both to initiate and to incorporate . . . ability grouping is one of the best first steps toward individual instruction."[51]

The track was a much more efficient way of personalizing instruction than the individual-specific education espoused by Dewey. The track brought together a group of individuals of similar IQ and tailored instruction to the group. But the IQ-determined ability group limited the definition of what was significant in that instruction. Where Dewey was concerned with the education of the whole child, the track brought together children within a similar IQ range. Since the IQ tested only selected forms of ability or accomplishment as expressions of general intelligence—and this was admitted by even the most vociferous proponents of testing—the track not only switched the orientation from Dewey's individual to a group, but related that group by the specific qualities tested in the IQ.[52] In the process, it transformed Dewey's ever-malleable child into one with a constant and determinate IQ capacity and translated the open-ended and constantly changing environment into a narrow-channeled curriculum.

In many ways, IQ tracking was an administratively workable but also enlightened and progressively informed way of answering Dewey's challenge to education. In order to personalize instruction and to organize the school, it would have been possible to use a very different form of evaluation—motivation, interest, even physical size; or indeed, color, sex, ethnicity. School grades could have been subdivided into classes by any one of these or a number of other criteria. But where motivation, interest, or physical size can vary over time, the IQ presumably did not. That was its glory. It could provide just what American schools needed—an infallible tracking system. As infallible and easily administered as one based on sex, color, or ethnicity, but it would be a track based on personal merit and not ascriptive status. As Americans interpreted it, IQ was as absolute, biologically determined, and constant as sex or color, without having their inherently antidemocratic characteristics.

The IQ was an instrument of differentiation which had all the qualities race and sex lacked: scientifically established; numerically exact; an expression of individual learning potential defined by performance, not ascription; and an age orientation around which modern schools had evolved and in whose terms educators were accustomed to thinking. It was the perfect ordering and selecting mechanism for the democratic school.

It may seem strange that in a rather lengthy discussion of intelligence testing, nothing should have been said about what intelligence was understood to be. The historical record is certainly full of ideas about intelligence. But the record is notable for two things: first, the complete absence of agreement on a precise definition; and second, the practical lack of importance attached to the disagreements. In 1921, the *Journal of Educational Psychology* thought it might be useful to ask the "17 leading investigators" in the field of mental testing to describe "What I conceive 'intelligence' to be, and by what means it can best be measured by group tests."[53] The question, of course, implied that whatever intelligence was, it could somehow be measured. The resulting symposium yielded as many different definitions as the number of respondents: 14. The answers ranged from definitions so broad they could easily be made to include plant tropisms (adaptations to the environment), to the most exclusive forms of intellectualization (abstract and symbolic thinking). The range of definitions provided by psychologists all working in the field of mental testing do not suggest, however, that this was a particularly important debate or research problem, but that here precision and agreement were simply not necessary.[54] Although discussions about the definition of intel-

ligence continued throughout the twenties and thirties, so did the imprecision and disagreements. In fact, most proponents, willy-nilly, agreed on a
working hypothesis: intelligence was what intelligence tests tested.[55] The
definition of the object inhered in the form and the fact of its measurement.

In this, they were correct, historically. The significance of intelligence
testing lies not in some intellectual formulation with a specific content,
but in a methodology with instrumental results. In the course of creating,
elaborating, and refining a method to evaluate the undefined, those who
worked in the field of testing, those who used the tests in the schools, and
the public, which welcomed the answers it provided, fashioned an instrument which would thenceforth define what intelligence was. They had
translated the culture's perceptions, and its needs, into a method for
ordering, selecting, and directing its own evolution. For, as the IQ became
part of American education in the twentieth century, the continuation of
the concerns, interests, and ordering incorporated in its origin was
assured. Thenceforth, even the debate that periodically accompanied its
implementation would be strictly confined by the terms set by the concept
of IQ.

NOTES

This essay was first published in *The American Journal of Education*, volume 88, no. 4,
August 1980, pp. 431–58. Copyright 1980 by the University of Chicago Press. It is
reprinted here with permission.

The research for this essay was completed during a leave in 1976–77 made possible by a
Rockefeller Humanities Fellowship. I would like to thank the Rockefeller Foundation for its
generous assistance. I would also like to acknowledge, with thanks, the kindness of Henry
May, Lawrence Levine, Winthrop Jordan, Leon Litwack, John Lesch, David Tyack, Robert
Middlekauff, and Richard Abrams for their helpful comments on various versions of this essay.
These individuals and institutions are, of course, in no way responsible for its conclusions.

1. Throughout this essay, I use the term "IQ" to represent both the procedure of mental
testing and what talent tests were understood to describe (the intelligence quotient). I do
this not in order to confuse, but rather to suggest that for the testers the procedure and the
object of investigation became more and more closely allied, and that for the general public,
performance on the test increasingly came to stand for what was commonly perceived as
intelligence.

2. See, for example, N. J. Block and Gerald Dworkin, eds., *The IQ Controversy: Critical
Readings* (New York, 1976); Florence L. Goodenough, *Mental Testing, Its History, Principles and Application* (New York, 1949).

3. Kimball Young, "The History of Mental Testing," *Pedagogical Seminary*, 31 (March,
1923), 4; for other early discussions of historical antecedents, see Frank N. Freeman, *Mental Tests: Their History, Principles and Applications* (Boston, 1939, originally published in
1926), and Joseph Peterson, *Early Conceptions and Tests of Intelligence* (Yonkers, N.
Y.,1925).

4. Peterson, *Early Conceptions and Tests*, pp. 78–83, 93–94; Young, "History of Mental
Testing," 30–33.

5. Young, "History of Mental Testing," 1.

6. Peterson, *Early Conceptions and Tests,* p. 230.

7. See John Dewey, *Democracy and Education: An Introduction to the Philosophy of Education* (New York, 1944), and *The Child and the Curriculum* and *The School and the Society,* combined edition (Chicago, 1976); originally published as *The Child and the Curriculum,* 1902; and *The School and Society,* 1899.

8. Richard Hofstadter, *Anti-Intellectualism in American Life* (New York, 1962), pp. 299–390. For other criticisms of progressive education, see, e.g., Arthur Zilversmit, "The Failure of Progressive Education, 1920–1940," in *Schooling and Society,* edited by Lawrence Stone (Baltimore, 1976), and Sol Cohen, "The Industrial Education Movement, 1906–1917," *American Quarterly,* 20 (Spring 1962), 95–110.

9. See, for example, National Society for the Study of Education, *The Twenty-Fourth Yearbook,* Part II, *Adapting the Schools to Individual Differences* (Bloomington, Illinois, 1925).

10. Dewey never explicitly rejected mental testing as a procedure, but he did publicly refute the more extreme claims made on behalf of the tests. See John Dewey, "Individuality, Equality and Superiority," and "Mediocrity and Individuality," *New Republic,* 33 (1922), 35–37, and 61–63.

11. For progressivism and science, see Robert H. Wiebe, *The Search for Order: 1877–1920* (New York, 1967), pp. 111–95; Samuel P. Haber, *Efficiency and Uplift: Scientific Management in the Progressive Era* (Chicago, 1964).

12. Franz Samuelson, "World War I Intelligence Testing and the Development of Psychology," *Journal of the History of the Behavioral Sciences,* 13 (July 1977), 274–82; Daniel J. Kevles, "Testing the Army's Intelligence: Psychologists and the Military in World War I," *Journal of American History,* 55 (December 1968), 565–81.

13. Harlan Cameron Hines, *Measuring Intelligence* (Boston, 1923), p. 82; Samuelson, "World War I Intelligence Testing."

14. For Goddard's contribution to testing, see Peterson, *Early Conceptions and Tests of Intelligence,* pp. 226–29.

15. Lewis Terman included the following rejoinder in his preface to *The Measurement of Intelligence* (1916) which introduced the world to the Stanford-Binet tests: "It cannot he too strongly emphasized that no one whatever his previous training may have been, can make proper use of the scale unless he is willing to learn the method of procedure and scoring down to the minutest detail" (p. xi). See also Peterson, *Early Conceptions and Tests of Intelligence,* pp. 232–33.

According to Harlan Hines, who wrote a popularizing introduction to tests in 1923, "Put into the hands of untrained examiners, intelligence tests are dangerous tools." (*Measuring Intelligence,* p. 70.)

16. Freeman, *Mental Tests,* pp. 2–3; Young, "The History of Mental Testing," pp. 39, 40.

17. Freeman, *Mental Tests,* p. 3.

18. Freeman, *Mental Tests,* p. 127.

19. See Lippmann's essays and Terman's replies in Block and Dworkin, eds., *The IQ Controversy,* pp. 4–44.

20. See Robert M. Yerkes, "Psychological Examining in the United States Army," *Memoirs of the National Academy of Sciences,* vol. 15, Washington, D.C., 1921; C. C. Brigham, *A Study of American Intelligence* (Princeton, N.J., 1923). See also the discussion of the army test results in Freeman, *Mental Tests,* pp. 404–30.

21. As one tester, Rudolph Pintner, noted, "That there are differences in intelligence and in other characteristics between races has been assumed by many anthropologists and psychologists." He then appropriately describes the tests designed to elucidate those differences (*Intelligence Tests: Methods and Results,* revised edition [New York, 1923], pp. 448–67).

22. As early as his first published discussion of his use of the Binet tests in 1911, Terman insisted, "I believe that by its use it is possible for the psychologist to submit, after a forty-minute diagnostication, a more reliable and more enlightened estimate of the child's intelligence than most teachers can after a year of daily contact in the schoolroom." This was particularly significant in the context of Terman's statement that "Everything else is relative

to intelligence. " Quoted in Peterson, *Early Conceptions and Tests of Intelligence,* p. 231. In 1916, Terman compared intelligence testing to another fundamental "scientific" measurement, by noting that the tests are "destined to become universally known and practiced in schools, prisons, reformatories, charity stations, orphan asylums, and even ordinary homes, for the same reason that Babcock testing has become universal in dairying. Each is indispensable to its purpose." Lewis Terman, *The Measurement of Intelligence* (Boston, 1916), p. 35. Terman was prone to sweeping claims for intelligence testing. One among many was his assertion that invention of the age-mentality scale, IQ, "ranks, perhaps, from the practical point of view, as the most important in all the history of psychology." Terman, *Measurement of Intelligence,* p. 41.

23. In his 1916 introduction to Terman's *Measurement of Intelligence,* Ellwood Cubberley, probably the most influential educational spokesman of the time, noted, "The present volume appeals to the editor of this series as one of the most significant books, viewed from the standpoint of the future of our educational theory and practice, that has been issued in years." He added "it is the confident prediction of many students of the subject that, before long, intelligence tests will become, as much a matter of necessary routine in schoolroom procedure as a blood-count now is in physical diagnosis." In Terman, *Measurement of Intelligence,* pp. vii, viii. The comparisons made between intelligence testing and other scientific procedures (Babcock, blood count) are notable.

24. Peterson, *Early Conceptions and Tests of Intelligence,* pp. 274–75. See E. J. Varon, "Alfred Binet's Concept of Intelligence," *Psychological Review,* 43 (1936), 32–58.

25. Young, "History of Mental Testing," 19–24.

26. Americans tended to draw opposite conclusions from the class correlations found by European investigators. Terman, for example, in discussing the European studies both underplays their significance and concludes, "the common opinion that the child from a cultured home does better in tests solely by reason of his superior home advantages is an entirely gratuitous assumption. Practically all of the investigations which have been made of the influence of nature and nurture on mental performance agree in attributing far more to original endowment than to environment. Common observation would itself suggest that the social class to which the family belongs depends less on chance than on the parents' native qualities of intellect and character." (Terman, *Measurement of Intelligence,* p. 115.) C. C. Brigham, in reporting on and analyzing the army results, used precisely the same words to deny the significance of environmental factors; see Brigham, *A Study of American Intelligence,* p. 182. Even a careful and judicious investigator like Clifford Kirkpatrick, after first noting that "nature never exists apart from nurture," explained that heredity was a factor that could be separately investigated by careful research designed to eliminate or keep environment constant and that ultimately, "High germ plasm often leads to better results than high per capita school expenditure. Definite limits are set by heredity, and *immigrants of low innate ability cannot by any amount of Americanization be made into intelligent American citizens* capable of appropriating and advancing a complex culture." Kirkpatrick, *Intelligence and Immigration,* Mental Monographs, serial no. 2 (Baltimore, 1926), p. 2 (my italics).

Although American tests generally assumed that environment and heredity could be separated, it needs to be noted that there were some voices heard that questioned the advisability of comparing racial (ethnic) groups by results obtained on the same test. The problem of language differences and disabilities and its possible influence on test results troubled some of the psychologists. See, for example, Rudolph Pintner and Ruth Keller, "Intelligence Tests of Foreign Children," *Journal of Educational Psychology,* 13 (1922), 214–22; Stephen S. Colvin, "Principles Underlying the Construction and Use of Intelligence Tests," in *The Twenty-First Yearbook, National Society for the Study of Education* (Bloomington, Illinois, 1922), pp. 11–25, and Kirkpatrick, *Intelligence and Immigration,* pp. 87–90, 105.

27. See, for example, Guy Whipple's response to William Bagley, the most vociferous opponent of testing: "No psychologist that I know of pretends that we are measuring intelligence directly. . . . We cheerfully admit that many other factors besides that of general intelligence do influence the progress of pupils in our schools." In Hines, *Measuring Intelligence,* p. 118.

28. According to William C. Bagley, a self-proclaimed educational "democrat" who waged a long and vocal battle against the testers, "The sanction which mental measurements apparently give to educational determinism is based, not upon the facts that measurements reveal but upon the hypotheses and assumptions that the development of the measures has involved." That it was "for all practical purposes . . . 'safe to predict a child's future at the age of twelve.' . . . With his instruments of selection admittedly faulty, with his instruments that measure something that no one yet has been able to define, the determinist proposes this policy and seeks to justify his proposal on the high ground of social welfare and especially of social progress." *Determinism and Education* (Baltimore, 1925), pp. 11, 22.

29. Kimball Young, "History of Mental Testing," 39.

30. See, for example, Pintner, *Intelligence Testing,* pp. 448–67.

31. "Tests," Frank Freeman noted, "whether they be mental tests or educational tests, are both relative. That is, the score which results from the application of the test has significance only by comparison with scores which are made by other individuals. The score serves as a comparatively exact numerical method of indicating the rank of the individual in a group." Freeman, *Mental Tests,* p. 19.

32. For the growing interest in hereditarian explanations, see Charles E. Rosenberg, "The Bitter Fruit: Heredity, Disease, and Social Thought in 19th Century America," *Perspectives in American History,* 8 (1974), 187–235.

33. See William H. Haller, *Eugenics: Hereditarian Attitudes in American Thought* (New Brunswick, N.J., 1963); Kenneth M. Ludmerer, *Genetics and American Society: A Historical Appraisal* (Baltimore, 1972).

34. As Kimball Young noted, "The scientific problem is that of eliminating from the tests used as measuring instruments those particular tests which demonstrably measure nurture, and to measure with genuine tests of 'native intelligence' random or impartial samples from each race throughout the entire range of its geographical and institutional distribution." Young, "Mental Differences in Certain Immigrant Groups," *University of Oregon Publications,* 1 (July 1922), 194–95; see also Kirkpatrick, *Intelligence and Immigration,* pp. 7–14.

35. Among the numerous studies that could be cited beginning in the teens, the following is a small chronologically organized sample: Joseph Weintraub and Raleigh Weintraub, "The Influence of Environment on Mental Ability as Shown by the Binet-Simon Tests," *Journal of Educational Psychology,* 3 (1912), 577–83; Robert M. Yerkes and Helen M. Anderson, "The Importance of Social Status as Indicated by the Results of the Point-Scale Method of Measuring Mental Capacity," ibid., 6 (1915), 137–50; A. W. Kornhauser, "The Economic Standing of Parents and the Intelligence of Their Children," ibid., 9 (1918), 159–64; S. I. Pressey and Ruth Ralston, "Relation of the General Intelligence of School Children to the Occupation of Their Fathers," *Journal of Applied Psychology,* 3 (1919), 366–73; Luella Winifred Pressey, "The Influence of (a) Inadequate Schooling and (b) Poor Environment upon Results with Tests of Intelligence," ibid., 4 (1920), 91–96; Ada Hart Arlitt, "On the Need for Caution in Establishing Race Norms," ibid., 5 (1921), 5, 179–83; Kwot Tsuen Yeung, "The Intelligence of Chinese Children in San Francisco and Vicinity," ibid., pp. 267–74; Gilbert L. Brown, "Intelligence as Related to Nationality," *Journal of Educational Research* 5 (1922), 324–27; Rudolph Pintner and Ruth Keller, "Intelligence Tests of Foreign Children," *Journal of Educational Psychology,* 13 (1922), 214–22; D. L. Geyer, "Reliability of Rankings by Group Intelligence Tests," ibid., pp. 43–49; May Bere, *A Comparative Study of the Mental Capacity of Children of Foreign Parentage,* Contributions to Education, Teachers College, Columbia University (New York, 1924); Bertha M. Boody, *A Psychological Study of Immigrant Children at Ellis Island,* in Mental Measurements Monographs, serial no. 3 (Baltimore, 1926). For the best summary of research in the field, see National Society for the Study of Education, *Twenty-Seventh Yearbook, Nature and Nurture* (Bloomington, Illinois, 1928).

By the thirties, the studies were more precise and recherché. Their intention now became to isolate very specific environmental variables. See, e.g., H. E. C. Sutherland, "The Relationship between IQ and Size of Family in the Case of Fatherless Children," *Journal of Genetic Psychology,* 38 (1930), 161–70; F. H. Finch, "A Study of the Relation of Age Interval to Degree of Resemblance of Siblings in Intelligence," ibid., 43 (1933), 389–404; Arthur

L. Benton "Influence of Incentives upon Intelligence Test Scores of School Children," ibid., 49 (1936), 494–97; Otto Kleinberg and Dorah B. Lithauer, "A Study of the Variation in IQ of a Group of Dependent Children in Institution and Foster Home," ibid., 42 (1933), 236–42; Arthur E. Traxler, "Reliability, Constancy, and Validity of the Otis Intelligence Quotient," *Journal of Applied Psychology,* 18 (1934), 241–51.

36. Kimball Young, "History of Mental Testing," 47.

37. It needs to be noted in this context that in England, the very methodology of statistics as developed by the followers of Francis Galton grew from the attempt to define differences among individuals. As in the United States, the sharp differentiation between heredity and environment was elaborated and hardened as numbers and correlations became more precise. See Haller, *Eugenics,* pp. 8–14.

38. For example, Brigham, *A Study of American Intelligence,* pp. 110–17, 155–78, and the foreword by Robert M. Yerkes. Brigham also acknowledges his debt to the two most potent racial analysts of the period, Madison Grant and William Z. Ripley (pp. xvii–xviii). See also Young, "Mental Differences in Certain Immigrant Groups," 3, 72–84; Pintner, *Intelligence Testing,* pp. 466–67; Bere, *A Comparative Study of the Mental Capacity,* pp. 90–98; Kirkpatrick, *Intelligence and Immigration,* pp. 105–16.

According to Young, "Mental Differences in Certain Immigrant Groups," 83: "Our American policy of immigration should revolve around an appreciation of the significance of mental differences rather than economic. Two new points of view on the part of the public opinion and the legislative bodies of this country must come into being. The first concerns a changed attitude from quantity of immigration to quality, the second, the control of immigration in the interest of real national welfare and not immediate and partisan (e.g., economic) exploitation. Restriction of immigration should go on in terms of capacity of the immigrants and not of their cheapness as laborers."

39. Warren K. Layton, "Group Intelligence Testing Program of the Detroit Public Schools," in *The Twenty-First Yearbook, National Society for the Study of Education,* p. 123. See also Paul Davis Chapman, *Schools as Sorters: Lewis M. Terman, Applied Psychology, and the Intelligence Testing Movement, 1890–1930* (New York, 1988).

40. Freeman, *Mental Tests,* p. 3; see also Guy M. Whipple, "An Annotated List of Group Intelligence Tests," in *The Twenty-First Yearbook, National Society for the Study of Education.*

41. Peterson, *Early Conceptions and Tests of Intelligence,* pp. 232–33; Hines, *Measuring Intelligence,* pp. 60, 108; Freeman, *Mental Tests,* pp. 14–16.

According to Edward Thorndike, the preeminent psychologist of the generation, "In the elementary schools we now have many inadequate tests and even fantastic procedures parading behind the banner of educational science. Alleged measurements are reported and used which measure the fact in question about as well as the noise of the thunder measures the voltage of lightning. To nobody are such more detestable than to the scientific worker with educational measurements." Quoted in Hines, *Measuring Intelligence,* p. 113. Thorndike was prone to use richly practical language. For Thorndike's role in testing and the evolving science of psychology, see Geraldine Joncich Clifford, *The Sane Positivist: A Biography of Edward L. Thorndike* (Middletown, Conn., 1968).

42. Rush Welter, *Public Education and Democratic Thought in America* (New York, 1962); Lawrence A. Cremin, *The Transformation of the School: Progressivism in American Education* (New York, 1961).

43. Alexander J. Inglis, "Secondary Education," in *Twenty-Five Years of American Education,* edited by I. I. Kandel (New York, 1924); George Sylvester Counts, *Secondary Education and Industrialism* (Cambridge, Mass., 1929); Lawrence A. Cremin, "The Revolution in American Secondary Education, 1893–1918," *Teachers College Record,* 56 (March 1955), 295–308; Theodore R. Sizer, *Secondary Schools at the Turn of the Century* (New Haven, 1964); Edward A. Krug, *The Shaping of the American High School,* 2 vols. (Madison, Wisconsin, 1969); Martin Trow, "The Second Transformation of American Secondary Education," *International Journal of Comparative Sociology,* 2 (September 1961), 144–61.

44. "The educational significance of the results to be obtained from careful measurements of the intelligence of children can hardly be overestimated," Ellwood Cubberly noted in his preface to Terman's *The Measurement of Intelligence.* "Questions relating to the choice of

studies, vocational guidance, schoolroom procedure, the grading of pupils, promotional schemes, the study of the retardation of children in schools [meaning children not advancing in grade according to age], juvenile delinquency, and the proper handling of subnormals on the one hand and gifted children on the other all alike acquire new meaning and significance when viewed in the light of the measurement of intelligence as outlined in this volume" (pp. vii–viii).

45. One authority on testing, Kimball Young, observed, "The curriculum is the crux of the matter. . . . The principles of curriculum making must take into account the need of children for proper economic life activity in accordance with their abilities." Young, "Mental Differences in Certain Immigrant Groups," 69.

46. Freeman, *Mental Tests*, p. 345.

47. For example, Boody, *Psychological Study of Immigrant Children at Ellis Island.*

48. Young, "Mental Differences of Certain Immigrant Groups," 65–70; see also Robert Alexander Fyfe McDonald, *Adjustments of School Organization to Various Population Groups,* Contributions to Education, Teachers College (Columbia University, 1915); Selma Berrol, "Immigrants at School: New York City, 1900–1910," *Urban Education,* 4 (October 1969), 220–30.

49. George Sylvester Counts, *The Selective Character of American Secondary Education* (Chicago, 1922); Cohen, "The Industrial Education Movement"; Marvin Lazerson and W. Norton Grubb, "Introduction," *American Education and Vocationalism: A Documentary History,* edited by Lazerson and Grubb (New York, 1974); David K. Cohen, "Immigrants and the Schools," *Review of Educational Research,* 40 (1970), 13–27.

50. Hines, *Measuring Intelligence,* p. 134; see also Hines's defense of instruction organized to suitable vocational aims, pp. 93–97.

51. National Society for the Study of Education, *The Twenty-Fourth Yearbook, Adapting the Schools to Individual Differences,* p. xiii; see also National Society for the Study of Education, *The Twenty-First Yearbook, Intelligence Tests and Their Use.*

52. See Hines, *Measuring Intelligence,* p. 53, and p. 111, citing Haggarty, and Pintner, *Intelligence Testing,* pp. 45–71, for examples of how claims for IQ were qualified.

53. E. L. Thorndike et al., "Intelligence and Its Measurement: A Symposium," *Journal of Educational Psychology,* 12 (March, April, May 1921), 123.

54. In his textbook on intelligence testing (revised edition published in 1931) Rudolph Pintner noted that "we have been speaking of the measurement of general intelligence, without having attempted in any way to define the meaning of this term, and it is not easy even at present to do so. As a matter of fact general intelligence has rightly been assumed to exist and psychologists have gone about the measurement of an individual's general ability without waiting for an adequate psychological definition" (*Intelligence Testing: Methods and Results,* p. 45). He also admitted, "Many definitions of intelligence have been proposed by psychologists, and these vary greatly according to the standpoint from which the psychologist views this problem. Although they differ greatly, they are not therefore contradictory" (p. 47). Terman noted in 1916, "To demand as critics of the Binet method have sometimes done that one who would measure intelligence should first present a complete definition of it, is quite unreasonable" (*The Measurement of Intelligence,* p. 44). William Bagley was one of those unreasonable opponents who questioned the use of "a scale to measure the undefined." Bagley, *Determinism and Education,* pp. 14–15.

55. Freeman, *Mental Tests,* p. 17. Overall, Freeman's judicious presentation of the issues in intelligence measurement presents a practical and useful discussion of the middle positions in mental measurement.

3

Creating New Identities

Youth and Ethnicity in New York City High Schools in the 1930s and 1940s

In the early years of the twentieth century, educators moved vigorously to expand and rationalize schooling, and to extend the age of attendance well beyond childhood into adolescence. "The period of adolescence," the famous progressive educator, Elwood Cubberly, noted, "we now realize is a period of the utmost significance for the school."[1] This period, newly encoded as a life stage and coincident with high school age, was increasingly viewed as a strategic period for socialization as well as education.[2] The new emphasis on adolescent schooling was in good part a response to the immense growth of the immigrant population in cities and the social issues this presented. The possibilities that schooling offered for assimilation were not new, of course, but in the first two decades of the twentieth century schooling was newly viewed as the solution to various social problems, making its urgency among immigrant youth seem ever more obvious and necessary. As schooling expanded to incorporate the children of immigrants during their important transition from childhood to adulthood, indeed as it helped to create this transition,[3] a genuinely new kind of educational environment was created, one in which young people contended within schools for control over student behavior, allegiance, and identification. By the 1930s, and certainly by the 1940s, the attendance at high school of large numbers of the progeny of the great early twentieth-century migrations marked the arrival of a new common school era. In contrast to its nineteenth-century predecessor, the common school era of the early twentieth century concerned adolescents, not children, and in large cities it replaced the pious air of Protestant respectability with a complex cosmopolitanism.[4] In cities like New York and Chicago, the high schools, like the neighborhoods in which they flourished, became ethnic (often multi-ethnic) enclaves. In this context, the high school as a fundamental agency of socialization became both more important and different than its planners had anticipated.

By the 1920s and 1930s, educators looked to the developmental significance of adolescence, especially to the special aptitudes for self-direction and the clannishness of youth as a potent force for citizenship and assimilation, and with this in mind they tried to construct a broadly conceived school program. Integral to their new programs was a range of activities in which students, although under adult auspices, exercised their own forms of self-direction in social, civic, athletic, and academic affairs. Through these extracurricular activities, Earle Rugg of Columbia's Teachers College noted, "The school may well make itself the laboratory for training pupils for efficient citizenship." Various informal school activities had existed at the fringes of the academic curriculum since the nineteenth century, but it was not until after World War I that educators made a concerted effort to align them with the expanded concerns and "progressive" developmentally oriented pedagogy of the modern school. "Largely within the past decade, and wholly within the past two," Elwood Cubberly noted in 1931, "an entirely new interest in the extra-curricular activities of youth has been taken by the school. In part this change in attitude has been caused by the new disciplinary problems brought to the school through the recent great popularization of secondary education."[5] That popularization, it hardly needed to be said, now included vast numbers of young people from neighborhoods and urban enclaves who scarcely dreamed of attending school some decades earlier.

Educators and school administrators who hoped to adopt extracurricular activities to the purpose of socialization had to walk a fine line that balanced adult supervision with student initiative. Although they hoped to use the activities for their own purposes, too much control would undermine the usefulness of the activities as theaters for training in genuine citizenship and voluntary cooperation. The activities were thus both an obvious and tricky realm for educational efforts. It is clear, moreover, that school systems and individual schools differed in their treatment of the activities, especially in the degree to which they were directed by adults and integrated into the curriculum.[6]

With this variation fully in mind, it is still possible to reconstruct certain dimensions of students' social experience as registered in their participation in extracurricular activities. In fact, as an area of youth semi-autonomy, the activities had the potential to be pivotal locales in which the plans of school officials and the social needs of students clashed. In light of the assimilationist aims of the schools, the extracurriculum also provides us with an unusually important vantage for observing how immigrant youth became Americans during the strategic decades of the thirties and forties, and how their school experiences affected this process.

The following analysis is based on the extracurricular participation of fifteen thousand New York City high school graduates between 1931 and 1947 as these experiences were recorded in high school yearbooks.[7] It was my aim to determine if and how ethnicity influenced extracurricular choices in order to evaluate the place of ethnicity among students in high school. Obviously, partly because my tabulations are based on name identification and because all activities were self-reported, these conclusions are only near approximations of what took place. The results may also have been skewed by the fact that all the students were seniors, and the different ethnic groups were unevenly represented in graduation rates. The seeming precision of numbers should not be allowed to obscure the imprecision of the method. Still, given how underexamined schools have been as lively arenas of youth culture and how very difficult it is to peer into the process of Americanization from below, even this kind of inexact portrait can begin the serious process of understanding how youth culture intersected the historically critical issue of Americanization.

New York was in no way a representative environment, but it was the preeminent immigrant city and an investigation of the city's schools is especially illuminating. Students in New York came from a very wide variety of nationality groups; I have selected six for analysis—native white, Irish, German, Italian, Jewish, and black.[8] The schools varied greatly in ethnic, class, and even gender composition and in their neighborhood setting. These differences mattered. Wherever possible, therefore, I have based my conclusions not only on the overall pattern but on the behavior of groups within specific schools, and I have defined ethnic tendencies only when there were compelling similarities among several schools.[9]

For the high school graduates of the thirties and forties, extracurricular activities had become a regular part of their school experience.[10] Four-fifths of all students participated in some club or activity, although the extent of their participation varied from a high of 99 percent at Bay Ridge High School to a low of 56 percent at Theodore Roosevelt, and women were everywhere more active than men. Given that these were seniors, this high rate is not surprising, since seniors, as the most successful of all students, were probably most involved in all aspects of school life. But certain groups were more active than others and engaged in a wider range of activities. Jews and native white students were the most active. Table 3.1 summarizes the experiences of the various groups.

TABLE 3.1. *Participation in Some Activity by Sex and Ethnicity*
(Each box signifies overrepresentation in designated school)

	Men						Women					
	1	2	3	4	5	6	1	2	3	4	5	7
Jewish	X	X	—	X	X	X	X	X	X	X	X	X
Italian	—	—	—	—	—	—	—	—	—	—	—	X
Black	—	X	X	X	a	—	—	—	X	—	—	X
Irish	—	—	b	X	X	—	—	—	—	X	X	X
German	—	—	X	X	—	—	—	—	—	X	—	—
Native	X	—	X	X	—	X	X	X	—	X	X	—

Note: School Key
1. George Washington High School
2. Evander Childs High School
3. Seward Park High School
4. Theodore Roosevelt High School
5. New Utrecht High School
6. High School of Commerce
7. Bay Ridge High School

a. No blacks at Utrecht High School
b. Not enough Irish at Seward Park to be meaningful.

A student's ethnicity clearly influenced the extent of his or her participation in the extracurricular world of high school. More significantly, ethnicity had a powerful effect on the kind of activity a student was likely to elect. Sometimes the ethnic variations depended on a specific school environment, but at other times there were uniformities across schools that suggest strong ethnic preferences.[11] Taken as a whole, the yearbooks point to the strategic role of ethnicity in determining student choices among extracurricular offerings and help to define the continuing significance of ethnicity in the lives of high school students.

Members of some ethnic groups rarely or never joined in certain activities. Irish men only rarely joined science clubs or participated in the orchestra or in dramatics. Jews and blacks participated in religious clubs very infrequently. Indeed, blacks were the most consistently absent from a wide range of activities;[12] they almost never participated in dramatic clubs or in the sciences; no black woman or man was ever elected president of the senior class or the student body; no black was ever editor in chief of the newspaper. The fact that blacks were the group most frequently absent from a range of activities suggests a strong exclusionary bias against them. Blacks joined only certain activities and almost never others; no other group was absent in so many categories in so many schools. Blacks who were eager to participate in school activities—and three-quarters of blacks did participate—chose carefully and judiciously, consistently sidestepping activities in which they either had no interest or were clearly not welcome.

In one activity, black men were dominant in an unparalleled way. In every school with a meaningful population of black men, they conspicuously chose the track team. Indeed, track was the activity most consistently associated with blacks: almost one-third of all black men in the entire population were on the team. At George Washington High School, where blacks were scarcely 5 percent of the male population, eleven of forty-four track men were black. At Seward Park, where blacks constituted slightly more than 1 percent of the male population, three of thirteen runners were black in a population of only thirty-one black men. Half of all black men at Evander Childs (six of twelve) and one-sixth (ten of sixty) of all black men at the High School of Commerce were on the track team. Although these were small numbers, because the number participating in track was small and because the number of black seniors was small, it was stunningly clear that the chances of a black man electing track as one, and possibly his only, high school activity was very great.

The same concentration of black men was present in no other sport. Although black men were also active in basketball, they almost never played football and rarely participated in other sports. These sports were dominated by white natives, Italians, and Germans, and, to a lesser degree, the Irish. Jews, like blacks, were not drawn to football. When Jews participated in sports, they strongly favored basketball. Italians showed the opposite tendency, choosing basketball only rarely, but inclining strongly toward football. Native whites participated most heavily in football and in the "other sports" category, but very infrequently in track.

The pattern in sports choices is clear and illuminating. Members of different ethnic groups made significant distinctions among the sports offered at school. They divided the sports among themselves as each group chose several of the sports categories and bypassed the others. We can only guess at how these preferences were established. Track, a highly individualistic sport that required little team cooperation or body contact, may have served as an ideal outlet for blacks against whom discrimination would preclude strong group involvement. Native white men may have been particularly drawn to football with its collegiate aura. It is possible that the example of some sports hero, like Jesse Owens or Red Grange, helped to orient different groups to sports in a selective manner. Once the preferences were set, however, they most likely defined a clear status and prestige hierarchy and created ethnic associations that, in turn, differentially attracted members of various groups. The strong symbolic meanings that divided men among the sports apparently did not affect women. Sports never played the ethnically differentiating role for women that they did for men. In the end this may mean that women simply did not invest sports with the same social meaning as men.

In general, even though ethnic patterns were less sharply etched for women, certain preferences were notable. Jewish women tended to elect literary activities of all kinds in all schools. Wherever women were edi-

TABLE 3.2. *Participation of Jewish High-School Women in Literary Activities by School and Activity*

School	Total No. Jewish Women	% of Women Who Are Jewish	Activity*			
			Editor (%)	Other News (%)	Other Publications (%)	Yearbook (%)
George Washington	(525)	40.4	(2) 100.0	(19) 38.3	(4) 80.0	(9) 20.0
Evander Childs	(858)	46.8	(2) 66.7	(23) 57.5	(20) 58.8	(31) 57.4
Seward Park	(770)	75.9	—	(29) 85.3	(25) 86.2	(20) 76.9
New Utrecht	(1026)	60.7	(1) 100.0	(73) 79.3	(33) 73.3	(55) 76.4
Theodore Roosevelt	(575)	43.4	(3) 100.0	(21) 63.7	—	(41) 50.0
Bay Ridge	(88)	6.4	(1) 16.7	(8) 13.3	(4) 18.2	(15) 9.7
All Schools	(3842)	44.8	(9) 60.0	(173) 56.0	(86) 63.2	(171) 39.5

*In each column, the number in parentheses represents the number of Jewish women in the activity in each school during four years of my sample. The percentage is the proportion of all women in each activity who were Jewish.

tors of the student newspaper, they were almost certain to be Jewish. At Theodore Roosevelt, all three female editors were Jewish; at George Washington, both women were Jewish; at New Utrecht, the one female editor was Jewish, and at Evander Childs two of the three women editors were Jews. Only at Bay Ridge High School, where Jewish women were a very small group in an all-female school was there a much broader ethnic distribution. Overall, Jewish women were 60 percent of all female editors but only 48 percent of the female population, a disproportion that would have been far greater if the special case of Bay Ridge were excluded. (See table 3.2.) In the 1930s and 1940s in New York high schools, literary activities for women took on a distinctly ethnic cast. German and native white women were also quite active on the school newspaper, but Italian, black, and Irish women were consistently underrepresented, as they were in the "other publications." Jewish men were active in literary activities as well, but far less consistently than Jewish women.[13] The yearbook was an exception to the ethnic patterns in literary activities. Jewish women were not as conspicuous on the yearbook staff while Irish and native women were far more heavily represented in this than in other literary activities. Native women and especially native men tended to be disproportionately active on the yearbook. Irish men also expressed a unique interest in the yearbook, contrary to their usual reticence to join publications activities. A major reason for these differences was due to the fact that the yearbook was a political tool. In documenting senior class activities, the yearbook played a strategic role as the publicity vehicle of dominant senior personalities.

In fact, student politics attracted a different constituency than literary activities. Overall, Irish men were the most disproportionately represented among presidents of the senior class and student body. Eleven percent of all male presidents were Irish, although the Irish made up only a little more than 4 percent of the male seniors. Native men were also very active, and German men, usually the least active of all the groups, appear to have been especially drawn to student politics. Native and German men were nearly twice as likely to be presidents than their population would warrant. Jewish men were somewhat underrepresented, and Italians had fewer than one-half of the presidents warranted by their numbers. No black ever achieved this coveted position.

The strong showing of the Irish is somewhat misleading. In fact, it was the natives, not the Irish, who usually dominated presidential offices. Whenever native whites composed a significant part of the school population, they disproportionately controlled presidential offices, except at the High School of Commerce. It was the presence of three Irish presidents at Commerce, in the absence of any native presidents, that exaggerated the Irish presence. Elsewhere, though the Irish were very active in politics, as shown by their frequent election to "other political" offices, it was natives who were most frequently elected to the highest offices. At George Washington, four of five presidents were natives, although natives were only one in five senior men. At Evander Childs, where natives composed one-sixth of the male population, two of six presidents were native. At Theodore Roosevelt, one-half of all male presidents were native, but natives were less than one-fifth of the male population. If we think of the president as a symbol of aspiration, the conspicuous position of natives among presidents becomes more explicable and significant. Only at Seward Park and New Utrecht, in each of which Jews were more than 50 percent of the population, were Jewish men consistently chosen. All the male presidents at Seward Park were Jews and at New Utrecht, located in a heavily ethnic neighborhood which grew from the outmigration of Jews and Italians from the Lower East Side, four of the five male presidents were Jewish. In these two schools, the president was of course a direct expression of electoral realities. But if the presidency was also symbolic, as I have suggested, then the pattern at these schools indicates an alternative social environment and another ideal. Both Seward Park and New Utrecht were heavily ethnic schools, with Jews the dominant ethnic group. Within an overwhelmingly ethnic setting, Jews set their own standard of success, as natives did in schools which were middle class and status was defined by native whites.

The Irish were very heavily involved in the lesser offices. Fifteen percent of all Irish men held some political office, compared with slightly more than 10 percent of the Jews, natives, and Germans. Irish men, not especially active in the clubs generally, tended to gravitate toward political

TABLE 3.3. *Celebrity Status by Sex, School, and Ethnicity (in percentages)*

| | Jewish | | Italian | | Irish | | Native | |
	Pop.	Celebrities	Pop.	Celebrities	Pop.	Celebrities	Pop.	Celebrities
Men								
George Washington	39.2	40.9	4.0	4.5	4.8	0.0	21.0	45.5
Evander Childs	39.7	50.0	19.5	0.0	4.8	0.0	16.7	0.0
Seward Park*	—	—	—	—	—	—	—	—
New Utrecht	55.9	73.7	24.2	21.1	1.2	0.0	7.8	0.0
Theodore Roosevelt	32.9	31.8	23.3	13.6	5.3	4.5	17.3	45.5
Commerce	20.2	29.3	17.8	14.6	11.7	2.4	18.6	29.3
Totals	44.9	40.4	17.4	12.8	4.4	1.8	13.4	29.3
Women								
George Washington	40.4	27.3	4.3	9.1	2.8	22.7	20.1	18.2
Evander Childs	46.8	14.3	15.1	0.0	1.5	0.0	20.0	57.1
Seward Park*	—	—	—	—	—	—	—	—
New Utrecht	60.7	47.4	15.7	10.5	0.7	0.0	9.9	31.6
Theodore Roosevelt	43.4	20.0	20.5	5.0	2.9	10.0	14.5	30.0
Bay Ridge*	—	—	—	—	—	—	—	—
Totals	44.8	29.4	15.9	7.3	2.7	10.3	16.4	29.4

* At these schools, celebrities were not indicated in the yearbook.

activities in high school, choosing political office over many other kinds of endeavors. Irish women were likewise more frequently elected to political office than either Jewish or native women. Neither Italians nor blacks were represented up to their proportion of the population.

Students interested in politics were forced to seek and to get general peer approval. Native men seem especially to have benefited from this, at least at the highest political level. One other measure of popularity and esteem was contained in the category "celebrity status," which was not strictly an activity, but an expression of school prominence. A celebrity could be the man or woman chosen most likely to succeed, prettiest, handsomest, best athlete, best musician, etc. Although some of these designations suggest special talent, they all depended finally on prominence in school affairs and required peer approval.

Among female celebrities, Irish and native women were far ahead of women from all other groups, while Jewish women were frequently selected at only one-half of their proportion in individual schools, and were represented at just 66 percent of their population overall. This was the case despite the strong involvement of Jewish women in a wide range of extracurricular clubs and activities. Black women were *never* chosen. Among men, natives found the most approval with twice the proportion

TABLE 3.4. *Participation by Men in Science, Other Academic Clubs, and Arista by Ethnicity, across all Schools*

	Chemistry (%)	Physics (%)	Other Sciences (%)	Other Academic (%)	Arista (%)	% of All Men
Jewish	(46) 54.8	(30) 60.0	(58) 52.7	(288) 52.7	(273) 56.4	44.9
Italian	(6) 7.1	(3) 6.0	(11) 10.0	(81) 14.8	(59) 12.2	17.4
Black	(0) —	(0) —	(1) 0.9	(4) 0.7	(3) 0.6	2.0
Irish	(2) 2.4	(0) —	(0) —	(10) 1.8	(11) 2.3	4.4
German	(4) 4.8	(2) 4.0	(5) 4.5	(22) 4.0	(16) 3.3	5.3
Native	(14) 16.7	(8) 16.0	(17) 15.4	(72) 13.2	(62) 12.8	13.4

of celebrities as the native population and they were especially conspicuous in three schools. Jewish men did better than Jewish women, but lagged behind native whites. Italian men, like Italian women, were favored in only one school, while Irish men, unlike Irish women, were uniformly underrepresented. Two black men made the list.

The discrepancies between male and female celebrities, most obvious between Jewish men and women and the Irish, are revealing. Men appear to have been accorded celebrity status for their achievements, such as sports, politics, and editorships, which explains the fairly good showing of Jews and even the special instances of black success. Women appear to have been differently evaluated; often, in light of the preferred celebrity categories, on measures of beauty, grace, popularity. Irish, native, and to some degree German women, not Jews, Italians, or blacks most consistently embodied idealized versions of these attributes. In other words, if this designation was anything more than a quirky and humorous yearbook game, Jewish men appear to have better approximated peer criteria of success than Jewish women. Irish and German women did far better approximating a female ideal. But, overall, native men and native women were the most popular. (Table 3.3 compares the celebrity status of four ethnic groups.)

The achievement of Jewish men in the extracurricular realm was impressive, but they were especially prominent in academically related activities. Most conspicuously, Jewish men dominated the science clubs. The pattern in the sciences was repeated with only small variations in the category of "other academic clubs." Native men also participated substantially, while the Irish, Germans and Italians were only weakly involved. Black men were least active.

A glance at the representation of men in Arista, the National Honor Society, brings the academic pattern home. Arista was not a voluntary activity; students were honored by election to Arista on the basis of school record. But the parallel between academic standing and personal choice among the activities makes clear how cogent the club choices of high school students could be. Only Jews were elected to the honor society disproportionately to their numbers in every school and by very wide margins. (See table 3.4.)

Whatever it was that drew Jewish men toward the science and other academic clubs—college and professional ambitions, cultural preferences, or association with members of their own group—did not do so to nearly the same degree for their sisters. The number of women in the physics clubs was very small, but Jewish women failed to participate strongly in either physics or chemistry, and they showed only a weak interest in the "other science" clubs. Irish and native women showed a strong interest in chemistry and also made an impressive showing in the other sciences. Jewish women were also far less active than Jewish men in the "other academic" clubs. Italian women, on the other hand, made the strongest showing overall, and the special interest of Italian women in academic clubs, in sharp contrast with Italian men, requires some explanation. That explanation may lie in the selective attendance (and graduation) of Italian women in the 1930s and '40s. Unlike other groups, such as the Jews and the Irish, who began to send female children to school much earlier and kept them there longer, Italian preconceptions about women's place and the limited expectation of women's ambitions meant that only the most academically inclined and ambitious attended high school at all, and fewer still graduated.[14] Those who did may have chosen academic clubs as a further expression of their seriousness of purpose and possibly even to legitimate their extracurricular participations to themselves and to their parents.

Men and women often behaved differently. Native women were much more likely than Jewish women to join Jewish men in the chemistry club. Jewish women were not drawn to academic clubs to the same degree as Jewish men or Italian women. Ethnicity at school was often differently expressed by men and women, and this suggests that whatever culture students brought to high school, it was shaped and refashioned in gender-specific ways. In general, however, when we look at each school individually, men and women from the same ethnic groups tended toward the same choices among the performance clubs—orchestra, glee club, and drama. In fact, the similarity in the school-specific choices of ethnic men and women appear more striking than any marked consistency in ethnic choices across schools. This was probably because dramatic and musical performances were social events as well as arenas for aesthetic expression, and the strong resemblance between men's and women's choices suggests that these clubs and activities provided important occasions for heterosexual socializing.

The service category was the weakest ethnic differentiator and, not coincidentally, this was the activity least dependent on peer acceptance or approval. Service did not require a heavy commitment of time or a demonstration of strong interest. Usually rendered during a free period in the regular student schedule, work in the dean's office, on the projector squad, or any one of the myriad other services students performed was least peer intensive and peer dependent. Since Jews engaged most extensively in extracurricular activities in general, it is not surprising that Jewish men and women were the most active in service in most schools, but every group of men and women was overrepresented in service in at least one school. Blacks often made quite a good showing in service, and this strongly confirms what might have been expected: in their desire to participate in school affairs, black men and women often chose just those activities that involved few group events, little team work, and few potentially exclusionary practices by other students.

The absence of a strong relationship between service activities and ethnicity places the other patterns into even sharper relief. Certain of these patterns are especially notable. Despite the generally high level of Jewish participation, Jews did not gravitate equally to all parts of the extracurricular network. Instead, Jewish men moved into literary activities, science and academic clubs, and to service. The opposite tendency is evident among the Irish, who were rarely engaged in scientific, literary, or academic clubs, except the yearbook, but very active in politics, religion, and many of the sports. Italians also chose religion, but much more rarely politics. They were much more selective among the sports, choosing football above all. The Germans were less selective than the Irish, participating more broadly in literary and academic clubs without marked prominence, but like the Irish they chose politics frequently. Black choices were the most limited of all—track, basketball, service, and to some extent the orchestra. Native men were least restricted in their choices and were very frequently over-represented in a wide range of clubs and activities, but they were particularly conspicuous in the most prominent positions and those that were socially most strategic—the presidencies, editorships, and the yearbook. And they were most often chosen as school celebrities.

The pattern among women was less sharp but still revealing. Jewish women were almost as active overall as Jewish men, but far less prominent among the celebrities. Despite their disproportionate election to Arista, Jewish women bypassed the academic and science clubs to choose literary activities consistently. Native women also chose literary clubs, but not to nearly the same degree. When they did, they chose the yearbook. Native women were also very active in the performance clubs and in social activities, which may explain their special prominence among the celebrities. Weakly involved in most areas, Italian women made a clear and specific decision to join academic clubs and religious activities. Irish women were far more dispersed among the activities than Irish men, but like Irish men they chose politics and religion very frequently. Unlike Irish men, they were active in the science clubs. Whatever the reason for these strong and clear expressions of preference, men and women from various ethnic groups made definable choices in selecting extracurricular activities, choices that describe a complex and busy social system in which ethnicity affected what students did and how they viewed each other.

It is important to remember that ethnicity, which we reconstruct with some difficulty today, was at the time visible, palpable, and meaningful for young men and women. It helped them to define who they were, where they belonged in the extracurricular world, and where others were in that world. It not only set groups apart but provided individuals with effective networks of peers, establishing a competitive universe with hierarchies of power and status that provided tangible lessons in Americanization. This was, in many ways, the core of high school assimilation, a process defined not merely by incorporation and cultural diffusion but through the very process of differentiation, stratification, and group identification.

Overall ethnic patterns provide only partial insight into the lively social environments youth peers created at high school. A fuller and more focused view results when we examine the ethnic patterns at specific schools. A closer look at the environments in which the second and third generations learned about America and an understanding of the consequences of their diversity offer an important means for understanding the multivalent nature of assimilation. The seven schools can be crudely described as illustrating three different paths to assimilation: schools where native patterns dominated; schools in which one ethnic group was especially powerful; and finally schools in which there was vigorous contention among ethnic groups. While this tripartite division only begins to suggest the intricacy of school life as it was lived, it provides a significant basis for grasping how the societies young people created influenced their experience of Americanization in the 1930s and 1940s.

Manhattan—symbolic center of New York's urban primacy—contained a variety of vocational and academic high schools all through the twentieth century. Two of the borough's comprehensive schools, Seward Park High School and George Washington High School, illustrate the enormous range of the borough's social and ethnic experiences. Situated at the very top of Manhattan Island, George Washington was located in a luxurious building in a solidly middle-class neighborhood of prosperous and up-to-date apartment buildings, although the school drew from a larger and somewhat more heterogeneous area.[15] Yearbook pictures documented the well-to-do appearance of students who were usually elegantly dressed and many of whom wore fashionable furs even during the depression decade. Paul Robeson, Jr., was among the 120 blacks who graduated from George Washington in this period, and black students, like students from other groups, were among the most economically privileged of their community. Seward Park, on the opposite end of the island, was unlike George Washington in almost every respect. Drawing its students from the tenements and alleys of New York's Lower East Side, the classic American ghetto-slum, students at Seward Park could also depend on the similarity in the economic circumstances of their families whatever their ethnic origins. Poor Italians, poor Jews, Germans, and others attended Seward Park in the twenties and thirties, and gradually in the forties and after, more and more blacks and Puerto Ricans.[16]

The most heavily Jewish of the seven schools (74 percent), Seward Park was in many ways a Jewish city. No other group had even 10 percent of the remaining population. Instead, at Seward Park, Germans, natives, Italians, and blacks contributed only small spices to a homogeneous stock. At Seward Park, black men played football, as well as basketball and track, held minor political offices, and were even duly represented in "social activities." They seem to have been welcomed to an extent that was unusual in New York schools in the thirties and forties. Black women were even more widely involved in activities; proportionately they were the most active group of women. Unlike black men, who were totally absent from academic activities, sciences, and Arista, black women were represented to some degree in each of these. For black women certainly, Seward Park proved to be a hospitable environment for the expression of a broad range of interests and talents.

The experience of blacks at Seward Park is illustrative of the mixed ethnic character of the activities. Most clubs were ethnically heterogeneous, although, of course, most were also overwhelmingly composed of Jews. Despite their ubiquity, however, Jews seem not to have participated as strenuously at Seward Park as in most other schools. The one exception was politics. Jews were politically very much in control at Seward Park. Their numerical superiority showed itself in this one activity which explicitly represented power and which required election by peers. In a Jewish school, Jews could depend on other Jews for very large voting majorities. All presidents, male or female, at Seward Park were Jewish. Of all male groups, only Jews were disproportionately represented in political office holding.

It is worth thinking about the lackluster performance of Jews at Seward Park in the context of the record Jews made elsewhere. Bearing in mind that Seward Park catered to an overwhelmingly working-class population (those poorest members who had not yet made the trek to satellite areas of Brooklyn and the Bronx), it is still revealing that where the Jews were most at home, they were least competitive. Jews could assume their social acceptability (and political control) at Seward Park, and in that context they seem to have exerted themselves least. At the same time, their overwhelming presence did not exclude other groups, including blacks, from active participation in the extracurricular life of the school.

Jewish experience at George Washington was very different. Jews were disproportionately active in general and especially conspicuous in certain areas, orchestra, drama, "other political" offices, and the whole range of academic clubs. But the strenuous involvement, which seems on the surface a demonstration that Jews had arrived, may well have been the reverse. If Seward Park provides a yardstick of Jewish activity in a largely Jewish context, then Jewish hyperactivity at George Washington may suggest a kind of restlessness produced by a lack of manifest status and assured social position. Significantly, Jewish men were underrepresented as presidents and as editors of the newspaper, the most prominent positions a student could hold. In both, Jews took second place to native men, who captured far more presidencies and editorial chairs than was warranted by their numbers. Unlike Seward Park, where Jews were the occupants of these positions but were not conspicuously active in most other activities, Jews were active participants at George Washington, but failed to capture the positions with the most power and prestige.

Native men held these positions to a very marked degree. They did well in general at George Washington, but they were even more prominent than is apparent from a quick perusal of their overall level of participation, since they were especially strong in certain areas of strategic and visible importance—presidencies, editorships, yearbook staff, news staff, football—and they contributed almost one-half of all "celebrities." The conspicuousness of native men in these areas, despite the fact that they were only half as large a group as the Jews, suggests a great deal about the relationship between ethnicity, prestige, and power at George Washington.

Jewish restlessness and achievement in extracurricular life as well as in academic activities seems to have been especially strong at George Washington. In part, this was a function of the largely middle-class composition of its student body—it was full of students whose parents had already gained considerable economic success. This may also explain the strong showing made by Italians. Usually a quiescent group elsewhere, Italian men at George Washington were unusually active. Their choices were selective to be sure, but the elevated level of activity by Italian men is notable nevertheless and underscores how social class affected participation. Italians completely, and uncharacteristically, ignored football at George Washington. Instead, they concentrated on social activities, as well as socially related activities, the yearbook, orchestra, glee club, track, and "other sports." Italian men and even Italian women avoided the academic clubs, where Jews were extremely dominant. The weak showing made by Italian women in academic clubs may well have reflected the great prominence of the Jews. Academics, formal and informal, at George Washington were even more than elsewhere an arena for Jewish achievement.

The social texture of student life at George Washington is best understood in the fact that while all groups participated actively, power and status belonged to native whites. It is worth considering the possibility that "native" names at George Washington may have hidden ethnic roots, that is to say the parents of ethnic students changed their names with their own increasing prosperity. This would only underscore the conclusion that at George Washington, native standards defined student culture. George Washington illustrated an archetypical pattern of assimilation in which standards were set by native whites who held the most visible campus offices and were selected as representatives of student values and ideals.

The experience of students at Seward Park is less easily definable. Most students at Seward Park were Jewish. That they were not unduly active in most clubs hardly affected the social environment of these activities or the school since Jews were influential by their sheer numbers and they did hold the important political offices and run the newspaper. The Jewish presence did not seem to dampen the enthusiasm of other groups for participation, but it did mean that Jews, not natives, set the standards for other Jews and probably for other groups. The behavior of the eighty-nine senior natives (in four years) could not have meant much in a place like Seward Park. But Seward Park also represented a form of Americanization, although one in which it was possible for Jewish men and women to go through adolescence and graduate from high school without making significant contact with students outside their own ethnic group, either in class or out. As significantly, for non-Jews at Seward Park, Jews, not natives, defined the host society. For students at Seward Park, American urban culture and assimilation was a very different experience than for those who attended George Washington. Both, of course, were thoroughly exposed to American values and ideals in the classroom, but neither the meaning of those values nor their practice in the context of daily school experience was the same for students from the two schools.

George Washington and Seward Park capture two different geographic and economic corners of Manhattan. Evander Childs in the Bronx and

New Utrecht in Brooklyn were suburban. Overwhelmingly white and lower middle to middle class, New Utrecht in Bensonhurst and Evander Childs in the Pelham Parkway section of the Bronx serviced two of the many satellite immigrant communities growing up all over the greater city in the 1920s and 1930s.[17] At Evander Childs, Jews and Italian newcomers (44 percent and 17 percent of the senior classes), met a large contingent of natives (19 percent) in an area previously dominated by native whites. Also present were small groups of Germans, Irish, and an even smaller number of blacks. New Utrecht was less complex and more Jewish. It had no blacks, few Irish, and less than 10 percent native whites. The Jews were a substantial majority with 58 percent of the population; the Italians the largest minority with 20 percent.

The Jews were very active in both schools; but while they dominated at New Utrecht, they were far less prominent at Evander Childs. Italians also had different experiences at the two schools. At New Utrecht, Italians were underrepresented in the social world of politics, dramatics, publications, and the yearbook, which was controlled by Jews. Italian men tended to cluster in the glee club, religious clubs, and football, and they showed an unusual interest in academic clubs. They were joined in these activities by Italian women, who also joined religious clubs and academic clubs in very disproportionate numbers, and substituted "other sports" for the male interest in football. This patterning of extracurricular clubs effectively describes a social world in which Jews exercised power and enjoyed prestige, although Italian men, and especially Italian women, did join Jews in some activities. Italian and Jewish separation suggests both marked distinctions in choices and the probable exclusion of Italians from the most sensitive political and social areas. This conclusion is amplified by the fact that natives had less trouble joining Jews in politics, the newspaper, and on the yearbook. Not surprisingly, Jewish men at New Utrecht dominated the "celebrity" categories. Even at New Utrecht, however, Jewish women were denied "celebrity" status commensurate to their numbers while native women, here as elsewhere, represented ideals of beauty and popularity.

Italians also showed no special prominence at Evander Childs, but they engaged more extensively in sensitive areas and were the most disproportionately active of all groups in the category of social activities. At Evander, Italian men also held one of three editorships and one of six presidencies. They were disproportionately represented on the yearbook staff. Blacks, on the other hand, were almost invisible at Evander Childs. Besides service and track, which absorbed three-quarters and one-half of all the black men, respectively, they were scarcely represented in the extracurricular world of Evander Childs. While blacks were physically absent from the New Utrecht population, blacks were effectively socially absent from Evander Childs's as well.[18]

In contrast, native men were everywhere at Evander Childs. They were especially active in all publications, the presidencies, other sports, football, Arista and other academic clubs, editorships, and in social activities—their involvement was both far-ranging and intense. Jews also fanned out into most activities, but they rarely dominated them as they did at New Utrecht. As was true at George Washington, Jews were bested by native whites in the most prestigious posts, the presidencies and editorships. Even though there were more than two times as many Jewish as native men at Evander Childs, there were twice as many native presidents and as many native editors.

Jewish women at Evander took first place in a long list of activities, including Arista, "other science" clubs, editor in chief, social activities, "other publications," and "other news." As they had at George Washington, Jewish women did relatively better than Jewish men and they did so in a similar social setting, a middle class school with a substantial native population. In this context, native men tended to capture and hold strategic positions, while Jewish and native white men appear to have been in continuous competition with their interests similarly focused. While Jewish and native white women were also active in similar activities, Jewish women were usually more active and more readily assumed prominent posts. Despite these achievements, native women overwhelmed Jews in "celebrity" status.

The differences in the experiences of Jews and Italians at Evander Childs and New Utrecht seems to have had less to do with the economics than with the demographics of the schools and their surrounding neighborhoods. Evander Childs, like its Pelham Parkway neighborhood, was more recently developed and changing rapidly as it became increasingly populated by newer ethnic groups.[19] Between 1933 and 1945, the proportion of native whites in the senior class at Evander was cut in half, from 26 percent to 14 percent, while the proportion of Italians more than doubled from 10 to 23 percent. This growing Italian presence may help to explain the substantial participation among Italians. Sensing their developing role in the school, Italian men moved more smoothly into the social life of Evander Childs than they could or were allowed to at New Utrecht, where Italians were a constant minority, with Jews in the majority. The other groups were too small to matter. In that context, Italians were an outgroup and their status in the activities expressed that position. While Italians were active in a broad range of clubs, status and influence was exercised by the Jews. Seventy percent of all male celebrities at New Utrecht were Jewish. At Evander Childs, Jews had to compete with a large and active native group and a growing Italian population. In that context, Italians were not an outgroup, but only one of several minorities. This kind of complex and changing ethnic situation was also part of Americanization in the city's schools. It affected not only the experience of growing up in the neighborhoods but the structure of social relationships in the schools. Young men and women from the city's ethnic groups often reacted as much to each other in their development as they did to any certain and stable native norm.

At Theodore Roosevelt High School in the Bronx, Jews experienced an even sharper set of constraints than at Evander Childs. An ethnically mixed school with a substantial Jewish minority, Theodore Roosevelt had very clearly defined patterns of ethnic participation. Despite its relatively small Irish population (4 percent), its location in the old Irish bailiwick of Fordham Road (directly across the street from Fordham University) meant that the extracurricular world at Theodore Roosevelt reflected the specific ethnic pressures of its location. During the 1920s, 1930s, and 1940s, parts of the old Irish neighborhood rapidly filled with Jews and Italians, and the whole area was witness to the heightened friction between the Irish and Jews in the context of the depression and the special pressures of the city's political coalitions. Antisemitism became a familiar experience for Jewish youths who were frequently harassed by the Irish on the streets. Even the churches became embroiled in the controversies.[20]

At school, too, Jewish men appear to have been on the defensive. At Theodore Roosevelt, Jewish men were far less prominent in the extracurricular realm than elsewhere. Again and again at Roosevelt, the small group of Irish men and the larger group of native men made a remarkable showing in the activities.[21] The strength of their combined influence may have intimidated Jews, or more likely, the Irish and natives in control of strategic areas of the extracurricular realm actively excluded Jews from participation. It is significant that so many Irish and a good many native white men belonged to religious clubs at Roosevelt. Elsewhere, religious clubs were largely female preserves, but at Roosevelt, one-fifth of all the Irish men and one-tenth of all native men were members, as well as almost one-third of all Irish women. Italians, though they were Catholics, did not participate significantly. Religion may have become especially important at a school like Theodore Roosevelt as the Irish were forced to define themselves in the context of a growing group of new immigrants.

The Irish and natives were the most active groups in general, and both groups were especially prominent in politics. Native men were three times as likely to be presidents as was warranted by their population and twice as likely to hold other political offices. The yearbook staff, which as I have suggested had strong social and political possibilities, also had a large disproportionate Irish and native presence. The Irish were unusually active on the newspaper staff as well as in dramatics clubs, a situation unlike that of most other schools, where Jews tended to be dominant in both these activities. Election to the presidency highlighted the pattern: the Irish and natives together controlled two-thirds of the male presidencies but scarcely one-fifth of the population.

Although the pattern of ethnic exclusiveness and separation is not as clear for women as for men at Roosevelt, there remain strong indications of a prestige hierarchy in which the Irish and natives were dominant. The only woman ever to be elected president was native, and other political offices were disproportionately in the hands of Irish women. But even here, the strong tendency for Jewish women to elect literary activities was evident and sharply distinguished them from Jewish men. All three women who ever became editor in chief of the newspaper were Jewish, and Jewish women were much more prominent than Jewish men on the news staff. Although not quite so consistently or strongly as men, Jewish, Italian, and German women tended to cluster in activities not interesting or important to Irish and native women. Overall, however, Jewish women were more active than Jewish men. Jewish men, far more than Jewish women, apparently were overpowered in influence and prestige by natives and Irish in the school's extracurricular world.

High schools exist within the broader context of the neighborhoods they serve. In the 1930s and 1940s, they reflected not only the economic realities of those locations but also their special social and cultural pressures. At Roosevelt, the Irish made a much stronger showing in activities just as they were a powerful presence in the community. Schools do not operate in isolation from the other pressures young people experienced at home and in the streets, and the young often brought these into the school. This was the case despite and possibly even in response to the assimilationist emphasis exercised by the planned school program.

New York City was also full of special schools, defined not by neighborhood but by vocational or other goals. Some of these were sexually restricted. Bay Ridge High School and the High School of Commerce were two such schools. Although quite different from each other, both were sexually exclusive; Bay Ridge was a woman's academic school in Brooklyn, while Commerce, as its name implies, emphasized business. During the war, Commerce became coeducational but throughout the thirties and most of the forties it was exclusively a men's school.[22]

Located in Brooklyn's southwest corner, Bay Ridge High School drew its students from a wide geographic area. Though it was noted for its academic excellence in the 1930s and 1940s, Bay Ridge's most prominent feature was social: as a woman's school, Bay Ridge was considered "safe," a factor of some consequence for parents, many of them first- or second-generation immigrants who hoped to protect their daughters from daily association with men.[23] This seems to have been especially important to Italians, who sent large numbers of their female children to Bay Ridge. Italians with 31 percent and natives with 26 percent (the school was situated in a heavily native enclave) were the two largest population groups. There were far fewer Jews, only 6 percent.

At Bay Ridge, Italian women participated more widely and actively in extracurricular activities than elsewhere, a fact that explains why Italian women were reticent to participate in coeducational schools and restricted their participation largely to academic clubs. It may also reflect the sheer size and greater confidence of the Italian population. At Bay Ridge, Italian women were unusually active in politics, winning four of the presidencies. Italian women also landed two of the editor's posts; two others went to natives and one each to an Irish and a Jewish woman. At the same time, and despite their small portion of the population, Jewish women were very active in a large number of activities and especially prominent in literary activities. Indeed, Jewish women appear to have expressed their literary interests regardless of specific environment. Italian women, on the other hand, were not especially drawn to any of the literary activities—yearbook, news staff, or other publications. Native women at Bay Ridge were also very active, but it was the Italians, not the natives, who dominated the social activities.

Bay Ridge was hospitable to all the ethnic groups. Indeed, its most prominent characteristic was the extraordinarily high, practically universal, participation of students in extracurricular activities. Despite having clear preferences for certain activities, the groups seem less marked for their differences than for universal participation. This is well illustrated by the experience of blacks. The number of black women was small, only four, but they were involved in a surprisingly wide range of activities, in sharp contrast to the experience of the small numbers of black men at Evander Childs and Theodore Roosevelt. Bay Ridge appears to have provided a uniquely mixed environment. Ethnically heterogeneous, the school provided all groups with substantial access to the activities and encouraged different groups to mix in the clubs. It is significant that Bay Ridge had only women students. Women, as we have seen, tended to demonstrate fewer sharply defined ethnic patterns. In addition, at Bay Ridge, the social functions of the extracurricular clubs in the dating-and-rating games of adolescence was missing, and therefore some of the reasons for ethnic associations were absent. The very high level of participation also suggests that clubs at Bay Ridge were probably closely monitored by faculty who encouraged universal involvement and may well have discouraged too much ethnic clustering.

The High School of Commerce, like Bay Ridge, was a unisex school, in this case male, and it had an even more ethnically balanced population. Of the 1138 senior men, 20 percent were Jewish, 18 percent Italian, 5 percent black, 12 percent Irish, 7 percent German, and 19 percent native white. Unlike Bay Ridge, Commerce was a vocational school, one of the many located in Manhattan. The extracurricular pattern at Commerce demonstrates and amplifies the tendency for Jews and native whites to take the lead in student activities. Except for sports, the orchestra, and social activities, Jews were almost always the most active group. Most surprising was the Jewish absence in the science categories. The tiny number of science club members and the business orientation of commercial students probably explains this. Jewish students with clear academic and professional interests went elsewhere than to Commerce. Among the other groups, the Irish showed considerable activity. In addition to their control of one-third of the presidencies, the Irish were heavily involved in "other political" offices, the yearbook, other news, and all the sports. But the Irish did poorly on various measures of academic interest—Arista, "other academic" clubs, "other publications." Indeed, Irish interests and avoidances in general are well illustrated at Commerce. Wherever the Irish attended in any number, they concentrated in sports, politics, and the yearbook staff, as well as in social and religious clubs. They rarely took an interest in the sciences, "other academic" clubs, and usually made a poor showing in Arista. This pattern was no doubt related to the peculiar pattern of attendance of Irish Catholics at public high schools in the 1930s and 1940s, when the most ambitious and academically talented attended Catholic rather than public schools. Indeed, the unusually large proportion of Irish at Commerce already points to this, since the less academically oriented were often enrolled in the city's vocational programs.[24]

The Germans, like the Irish, were very selective among the activities at Commerce as they were in most schools, and they tended to cluster very markedly. They were lowest ranked of all the groups in general activity level and in service. Though completely absent from basketball, they were especially active in "other sports." Germans ignored the orchestra, but chose the glee club and especially drama. For Germans at Commerce, this marked clustering seemed more significant than the choices themselves.

Native whites joined Jews at Commerce to take the lead in campus activities. Jews and natives were designated "celebrities" to about the same extent at Commerce, an unusual pattern in schools with a substantial native population where natives elsewhere invariably took a strong lead. Above all, natives were largely absent from the newspaper staff, had no editors and no presidents. In these categories of symbolic prestige, the absence of natives is curious. Perhaps the most reasonable explanation for this anomaly lies in the different ambitions of students attending the High School of Commerce from those attending the usual comprehensive high school. Unlike most high schools, Commerce had fewer students with college plans, and thus the extracurricular world did not serve as leverage for college entrance. To some extent extracurricular participation everywhere reflected the different college-going ambitions of various ethnic groups. At a time that college admissions committees were beginning to evaluate students according to nonacademic or marginally academic criteria, the college-oriented were far more likely to participate and especially to strive for the plums of the extracurricular arena like editor in chief of the newspaper or a presidency.[25] In this context, the special propensity for extracurricular participation of Jewish students and those of native background at most schools becomes more comprehensible since they were most likely to have college plans or ambitions. Their prominence in the choice positions of the extracurricular world as well as their prominence on the Arista rolls substantiates this.

It would be a mistake, however, to attribute the complex patterns in extracurricular activities to selective college-going ambitions of different ethnic groups alone. These ambitions could intensify the pattern and might explain certain features, but would be inadequate to explain the many patterns we have been finding. Far more students participated in activities than could or would attend college. Moreover, the diversity in school experiences and the specificity of choices made by different ethnic groups cannot be understood by reference to college ambitions. One example will suffice. Although both editorships and presidencies were prominent and attractive positions, native men were much more likely to be presidents, while Jews were more frequently editors. The elaborate patterning of extracurricular participations in New York high schools must be understood at least in part as the effects of ethnic preference and evidence for the continuing significance of ethnic group association at school.

As the child of immigrants, Leonard Covello understood how much school life was a shared group experience. "Whatever problems we had at school or in the street, we never took up with our parents. These were our personal problems to be shared only by companions who knew and were conditioned by the same experience."[26] Certainly the lives of the children were unlike those of their parents, but they shared that life with others of their own group, and high school students still existed in a world strongly shaped by ethnic bonds and identities. Even at school, where assimilation was an educational objective, and among adolescents who could be expected to view their parents' old-fashioned world with disdain, or with pain, ethnicity was a significant fact of social experience.

The ethnic experiences of high school students were not like those of their parents. Indeed, that experience differed even for students of the same group among the different schools in the city of immigrants. A Jew at Theodore Roosevelt did not have the same experiences as one at New Utrecht or at George Washington. An Italian at Evander Childs had different American school experiences than an Italian at New Utrecht or at Bay Ridge. The specific mix of ethnic groups, the neighborhood context, the size of the native population, as well as traditions specific to the school's history all influenced the nature of high school extracurricular and social life. So too, ethnicity often affected men and women differently. Women often made different choices than their ethnic brothers. Italian women placed a heavy emphasis on academic clubs, a choice much more rarely made by Italian men. Jewish women chose literary activities more consistently than Jewish men but hardly ever joined Jewish men in the science clubs. Irish women chose science clubs while Irish men almost never made the same decision. These were strong variations, and they remind us that ethnicity, like culture in general, is not homogeneous but operates in a socially differentiated universe strongly marked by gender. Ethnicity seems also not to have been as consistently expressed by women as by men, and one sees the ethnic patterns across schools and within schools much more clearly by looking at men only. Male ethnics divided their activities more regularly among themselves, as each group emphasized different kinds of interests. Participation in extracurricular activities and successful competition especially may have had status resonances and possibly relationships to future goals that appear not to have influenced women to the same degree as men. Some of this was no doubt the result of differences in college-going plans between men and women. But women may have been more accepting of other groups and less exclusionary in general.

The class composition of a school population also mattered. Except for service activities, the ability of students to engage in many extracurricular activities was dependent on the time available to students after school hours. Some groups, like Italians and blacks, probably had less leisure, because they were poorer. At a prosperous school like George Washington, Italians and blacks were far more active across the board than at a lower-middle-class school like New Utrecht.

It is also important to remember that even where activities were ethnically stratified, students from different groups did meet. That mixing was most notable at a school like Bay Ridge but it was true almost everywhere that, except for blacks, students from different groups had overlapping interests in a range of activities. Since I have made conclusions about ethnic participation on the basis of group disproportions, it is easy to overlook or discount the degree to which individuals from all the groups made contacts with those from other groups in the social life of the school. Even at Theodore Roosevelt, Jews met Irish as well as Italians, Germans, and natives on the yearbook staff. These exchanges were mediated by considerations of status, prejudice, and even hostility, as well as shared interests and friendship, but that only meant that the activities reflected the larger realities of American society.

In this sense, the high schools and the social and extracurricular activities exposed students to various critical features of American social and civic life. This was certainly what theorists and administrators had in mind when they developed the activities as allies in socialization and Americanization. But Americanization and assimilation were never neat or uniform. At different schools, students began to grasp the complex features of the society differently. While they met students from other groups, they did so in ways that were mediated by ethnic bonds and stratifications. The prestige of natives, the ambition and drive toward success of Jews, the exclusion of blacks were variously experienced, and these experiences introduced students to the broad features of American urban life in which ethnicity was as much a part as voting, caucusing, and the ability to change one's name. The cliquing and selection of friends, the preferences for certain activities, and the inclination to attribute power, popularity, even beauty to some and not to others was a fundamental experience of adolescents in school and out. Those who theorized about the potential of the extracurricular activities in socialization were correct to this extent.

In the end, however, one is left with the sharp and clear impression of a high school society divided along ethnic lines of which assimilation-minded educators would not have approved. On the simplest level, this meant that it was more likely for men and women of the same group to associate together in performance clubs and social activities at individual schools. Beyond that, groups became identified with different talents and characteristics. Some groups, notably the native whites and Jews (and the Irish in politics and sports), usually captured the limelight and strategic posts. Certain activities, like science, track, and football for men and literary clubs for women, were disproportionately selected by members of some ethnic groups over others. Wherever females were appointed editors, they were almost certain to be Jews. In schools with a native white population, males of this background were most likely to be elected to high office. The track team was likely to contain a good portion of the male black population. And almost everywhere, Jews were the academic achievers.

While the data provide us with provocative and compelling patterns, they are less yielding in giving insights to the causes of this variation. It would be tempting but unwise to ascribe the differences to cultural traditions pure and simple. It is also important to avoid stereotyping the groups as they adapted to American circumstances that can be read into the Jewish interest in science and the Irish fascination with politics. It is probably safe to conclude, however, that extracurricular life and student society at school generally encouraged continued reliance on group bonds.

Beyond this, the regularity of certain patterns across schools suggests that student society helped to create new American identities, identities which resulted from a strategic interaction between inherited traditions which shaped perceptions initially, functional patterns of adaptation, and forces of imitation in a youth environment which rewarded imitation. If imitation of natives was important, as I believe it was in light of the extraordinary popularity of natives registered in celebrity status, the dispersal of natives among almost the full range of extracurricular activities (they were far more dispersed than other groups) meant that various groups attached themselves to different areas of the school's social world in the process of imitation. Once they did, however, each group created coherent and meaningful ethnic patterns at school, patterns strongly mediated by ethnic peers. In other words, youth society shaped ethnicity for the second and third generation. This peer-mediated ethnicity provided an important form of differentiation in the schools of the thirties and forties, and it was a potent ingredient in the status and prestige hierarchy among students at most schools. Despite the rhetoric and plans of educators who hoped to loosen students from their ethnic pasts, students refashioned their immigrant traditions into American identities. Throughout the most significant period of Americanization, ethnic peers continued to provide students in high school with a source of group bonds within the mass culture and the massive impersonality of the schools.

NOTES

This essay, based on chapter 3 of my book, *Outside In: Minorities and the Transformation of American Education* (New York: Oxford University Press, 1989), was revised as "Creating New Identities: Youth and Ethnicity in New York City High Schools in the 1930s and 1940s," for *Generations of Youth: Youth Cultures and History in Twentieth Century America,* edited by Joe Austin and Michael Nevin Willard (New York, New York University Press, 1998). Copyright Paula S. Fass, 1998.

1. Editor's Introduction to Elbert K. Fretwell, *Extra-Curricular Activities in Secondary School* (Boston: Houghton, Mifflin, 1931), vi.

2. For adolescence, see Joseph F. Kett, *Rites of Passage, Adolescence in America. 1790 to the Present* (New York: Basic Books, 1977). The development of the high school is discussed in William Reese, *The Origins of the American High School* (New Haven: Yale University Press, 1995); Edward A. Krug, *The Shaping of the American High School*, 2 vols. (Madison: University of Wisconsin, 1964, 1972); Theodore R. Sizer, *Secondary Schools at the Turn of the Century* (New Haven: Yale University Press, 1964); Lawrence Cremin, "The Revolution in American Secondary Education, 1893–1918," *Teachers College Record*, 56 (March 1955), 295–308.

3. For an important discussion of the role of schooling in creating new age categories among immigrants, see Stephen Lassonde, "Learning and Earning: Schooling, Juvenile Employment, and the Early Life Course in Late Nineteenth Century New Haven," *Journal of Social History*, 29 (Summer 1996), 839–870.

4. As early as 1911, almost 50 percent of the secondary school students in 37 of the largest cities were of foreign-born parentage. See Francesco Cordasco, *Immigrant Children in American Schools: A Classified and Annotated Bibliography of Selected Source Documents* (Fairfield, N.J.: A. M. Kelly, 1976), 27.

5. Earle Rugg, "Special Types of Activities: Student Participation in School Government," *Twenty-Fifth Yearbook of the National Society for the Study of Education* (Bloomington, Illinois: Public School Publishing Co., 1926), 131; Cubberly, "Editor's Introduction," v. For a brief history of the activities, see Galen Jones, *Extra-Curricular Activities in Relation to the Curriculum*, Contributions to Education, Teachers College, Columbia University (New York: Teachers College, 1935), 13–29. See also the discussion in Elbert Fretwell, *Extracurricular Activities in Secondary Schools*. Fretwell was a premier exponent of the extracurricular activities and socialization.

6. Fretwell, *Extracurricular Activities*. Some have argued that by the 1920s, the aim of most educators was toward maximum control; see Thomas W. Gutowski, "The High School as an Adolescent-Raising Institution: An Inner History of Chicago Public Secondary Education, 1856–1940," (Ph. D. diss., University of Chicago, 1978), 221–238.

7. For a discussion of how the data were developed, see *Outside In*, Appendix I, 237–239.

8. Native white was defined for the purposes of this study to include all students whose surnames were either British (exclusive of Ireland), Dutch, or French. I have included these non-British groups in this category because historically both the French and Dutch were long settled in New York. It is certainly true that some Germans, Jews, and Irish were also long established in the city, but their numbers were small compared to the large migrations of the late nineteenth and early twentieth century. Obviously, those students of French or Dutch ancestry who were part of the newer immigration would have been included among the natives.

Because many individuals of Irish descent have native-sounding names (for example, White), there was probably some undercounting of Irish students. This was probably greatest at Theodore Roosevelt High School, where the proportion of Irish was lower than might have been expected from the demographics of the neighborhood.

All German surnamed individuals, except those who were most probably Jews, were included as Germans. The "other" category was composed of a very large variety of individuals, including Hispanic surnamed, Scandinavian, Russians, and Poles who were, obviously, not Jews, Chinese, Japanese, and Middle Eastern.

9. Readers are directed to Appendix 2 in Fass, *Outside In,* 240–253, for the tables detailing the evidence for the following discussion.

10. Gutowski argues that in Chicago, extracurricular participation had become almost a requirement by the 1930s because it was a strenuous part of the whole way in which high school education was conceived by educators. Moreover, some extracurricular participation was necessary to election to the honor societies. See "High School as an Adolescent Raising Institution," 211–221. While participation among seniors in New York was generally very high, it was not uniform across schools and therefore does not appear to have reflected across-the-board policy. At the same time, individual school principals may have made participation almost obligatory.

11. For the purpose of analysis, student activities were divided into twenty-three categories. Although these did not exhaust the range of activities available to students in all schools, they were generally comprehensive of the most important activities in which students engaged.

12. The reader should note that small population groups, like blacks and Irish, may be absent from some activities within a school more commonly than larger population groups like the Jews or Italians.

13. Only at Seward Park were black women overrepresented in "other publications," but this was a statistical fluke, since only one black woman was in fact involved. (See Fass, *Outside In*, Appendix II, Table H, 247.) In literary activities, Jewish men were in fact less conspicuous than native men. This is best seen by looking at the editors. Of twenty-one male editors, thirteen were Jews, although Jews were only 45 percent of the male population. But native men held four of the twenty-one editorial chairs and were more disproportionately represented (13 percent of the male population). Indeed, the apparent success of Jewish men among editors was inflated because of their control of the editorial posts at New Utrecht, where all editors were Jewish.

14. For the attitudes of Italians toward women, see Virginia Yans McLaughlin, *Family and Community: Italian Immigrants in Buffalo, 1880–1930* (Ithaca, N.Y.: Cornell University Press, 1977), 147, 149–151 and passim.

15. Students were admitted to high schools in New York in the 1930s and '40s technically on the basis of open admissions, that is, students could choose which school they wished to attend. In practice, however, except for those who elected to go to the academically exclusive schools like the Bronx High School of Science, where admission was by test, most students attended high schools in their general area.

16. For the remarkable ethnic diversity in today's Seward Park, see Samuel G. Freedman, *Small Victories: The Real World of a Teacher, Her Students and Their High School* (New York: Harper and Row, 1990).

17. See Deborah Dash Moore, *At Home in America: Second Generation New York Jews* (New York: Columbia University Press, 1981).

18. In a memoir of Evander Childs during the depression, Shirley Jacoby Paris notes that black students were hardly noticed at Evander Childs because "They were students, integrated with the rest, meeting the same standards as the whites, and given neither adverse nor preferential treatment." "Evander Childs High School," *The Bronx County Historical Society Journal*, 21 (Spring 1984), 5. In fact, whatever their equality in the classroom, blacks were unnoticed in the busy club and activity life because they were so largely absent from these. Blacks probably came to Evander Childs from outside the neighborhood.

19. Moore, *At Home in America*, 24, 66.

20. See Ronald H. Bayor, *Neighbors in Conflict: The Irish, Germans, Jews, and Italians of New York City, 1929–1941* (Baltimore: Johns Hopkins University Press, 1978).

21. Some of the natives may in fact have been Irish with English surnames. The high proportion of natives in religious clubs makes this likely as does the low number of Irish at the school.

22. I tried to use the June 1947 class at Commerce, which was coed, in order to get a glimpse of the patterns when the school contained women, but the numbers were simply too small and the range of activities women engaged in too limited to be very useful.

23. At Bay Ridge, the secretaries in the principal's office, who had themselves attended the school in the forties, made clear that parents usually chose to send their daughters to Bay Ridge because it was an exclusively female school and considered safe. This, they told me, was especially true for Italians. Many Catholic families may have used Bay Ridge as a substitute for parochial schools.

24. Fass, *Outside In*, chapter 6.

25. See Harold S. Wechsler, *The Qualified Student: A History of Selective College Admissions in America* (New York: John Wiley and Sons, 1977).

26. Leonard Covello and Guido D'Agostino, *The Heart Is the Teacher* (New York: McGraw-Hill, 1958), 47.

PART II

Children in Culture

Introduction to Part II

By the late nineteenth century, childhood, as a special period of life, had been made precious in the United States and in other societies in the West. Reformers sought to remove children from adult arenas, especially the world of work, but also from street activities associated with adult vice and immorality. As they acted to keep children in school for longer periods and to extend upward the age of female consent to sexual activity, such reformers as Jane Addams and Felix Adler, and organizations like the Societies for the Prevention of Cruelty to Children in various states, succeeded in extending the period of childhood upward into adolescence in the attempt to protect more and more children from the hazards of industrial and urban life. In extending the sentimental visions of childhood that was a Victorian middle-class convention to all children and adolescents, many Americans hoped that the twentieth century would truly become the Century of the Child, in Swedish feminist Ellen Key's compelling phrase.

Culturally, an expanded and isolated childhood in the twentieth century turned out to have its own hazards. One of the constant themes of twentieth century culture has been the belief that succeeding generations of children are out of control and that families are less and less able to responsibly contain and direct their children's behavior. Where middle-class reformers once condemned immigrants and slum dwellers for mistreating and inadequately supervising their children, in the twentieth century this criticism was turned inward. Respectable families, including the most privileged, seemed to have lost the ability to pass on their own beliefs, values, and ideals. This plaint was first heard loudly and clearly in the 1920s, as "flaming youth" invaded the colleges and the living rooms of America. It was repeated thereafter regularly for the rest of the century when the bobby-soxers gave way to the rock 'n' roll generation of the 1950s, and the rebels of the 1960s gave way to the generation Xers of the 1980s. There was something about the very nature of a cosseted and pampered youth that created a cultural urge to self-condemnation. In the following three essays, I explore different aspects of this modern cultural phenomenon.

No two "boys" better represented the problem of "spoiled children" than Nathan Leopold, Jr., and Richard Loeb, whose outrageous crimes of kidnapping and murder inflamed the nation in the mid 1920s. The essay republished here (Chapter 4) first appeared in the *Journal of American History* in 1993. Part of the essay was subsequently included, in an altered form, in my book *Kidnapped: Child Abduction in America* (1997). In examining how a crime and its publicity operated culturally, I have tried to look at this particular episode for what it tells us about the growing role of the media as a cultural interpreter and how dynamic psychology began to penetrate American conceptions of childhood.

In the nineteenth century, child protection was assumed to be largely a family responsibility, and child rearing its supreme duty. It was only if the family failed to provide such protection that the state intervened. And it was widely assumed that respectable families could take care of their own. This changed in the twentieth century because the state became actively involved in protecting children from the hazards of work, from abuse and neglect by parents, and because divorce became an acid of middle-class family stability. The law and the courts became part of the lives of even respectable people. While the rise in divorce was already noticed in the 1920s, it was not until the 1960s that divorce became a familiar middle-class way of life and its effects on children a serious subject for discussion and cultural concern. This was nowhere more acutely registered than in the odd interest and focus on "parental kidnapping," which became a serious genre in women's magazines and in American books (even for children) in the 1980s. In Chapter 5, based on a chapter in *Kidnapped* and revised as an essay first published in *All Our Families* (Oxford University Press, 1999), I discuss parental kidnapping historically and note how its depiction was transformed over time, from its first appearance in the late nineteenth century to its haunting explosion in the late twentieth, into a symbol of the untrustworthiness of modern families. If we read the cultural texts, the family in the last decades of the twentieth century seemed to have become a treacherous institution, unstable, unreliable, and dangerous to its own children. In the twentieth century, the relevant literature concerning the family was, as these two essays suggest, often legal, and court cases became part of popular culture and popular representations. Psychology and psychiatry were often brought in as witnesses to the family as a site of personal and social problems.

It is this troubled family and its unreliable children that is the subject of the last essay in Part II. Written for *The Columbia History of the United States: 1945–2000,* it explores the last fifty years of intergenerational relations. What role children play for parents has become as important in modern cultural discussions as the role that parents were supposed to play for children was in the late nineteenth and early twentieth centuries, and this essay ends by considering this question. The twentieth century has witnessed a fraught relationship between parents and children at just the point when children became most emotionally precious. Today, when we have been given the opportunity (not invariably successful) to choose our children, the choices we make are legitimately the subject of cultural self-reflection. What happens when parents get to choose their children will certainly help to set the agenda for our discussions in the twenty-first century. I end this essay with some reflections on our increasing drive personally to control our children, and the declining social investment in childhood.

4

Making and Remaking an Event
The Leopold and Loeb
Case in American Culture

The act which created a stir far beyond this country is so frightful,
psychologically so incomprehensible, so singular in its unfoldment
that, if Poe or a writer of detective stories wished to unnerve his
readers, no better tale could be invented; no harder knot to unravel;
no events could follow each other more effectively than life, or rather
disease, has here woven them together.

> —Maurice Urstein, *Leopold and Loeb:*
> *A Psychiatric-Psychological Study,* 1924

What a rotten writer of detective stories Life is!
> —Nathan Leopold, *Life plus 99 Years,* 1958

From the instant it broke on public awareness in 1924, the
Leopold and Loeb case was enveloped by the mass media. In fact, journalists gathered critical evidence that helped crack the case. And two news-
men on the *Chicago Daily News,* James Mulroy and Alvin Goldstein,
eventually shared some of the reward money as well as the Pulitzer Prize
for helping to connect Nathan Leopold, Jr., and Richard Loeb to the
abduction and murder of Bobby Franks. As they pursued leads, rumors,
and suspicions, journalists not only helped solve the crime, but gathered
materials for stories that became the basis for public knowledge of the
presumed events. Journalists and storytellers continued their active
involvement with the case throughout the twentieth century as the
Leopold and Loeb affair maintained a hold on the American imagination.
Journalists, novelists, and screenwriters interpolated fictions into the facts
of Loeb's murder in prison, testified at Leopold's parole hearings, and
fictionalized the case in novels and movies. When Meyer Levin published

Compulsion in 1956, this process of story creation not only culminated in a new form of historical fiction but also occasioned a notable court ruling about the boundaries between public and private, fact and fiction. Through their stories, the media actively offered Leopold and Loeb as subjects for a process of social interpretation, which began in 1924 and continues today, as the two have become characters in an avant-garde film with a very contemporary focus.

I began to study this case while writing about child kidnapping, and I gradually became convinced that the tangled mystery at its heart—why two rich, gifted boys would commit a murder embedded in the form of a ransom kidnapping—had a Dostoevskian quality that made it at once compelling and unsolvable. Leopold and Loeb may have been aware that they were playing at the boundary of human consciousness where analytic intentionality blended with irrational passion, and Loeb was infatuated with detective fiction, which often illuminates that borderland. That we would probably never know exactly what happened or why was not, however, the significant issue. For a historian the important question was not what happened and why. Rather, since the case has been repeatedly reframed, the question was how the story has been presented over time and what issues it propelled into public awareness.

The themes explored in the repeated reimaginings of the case were ones important to twentieth-century culture: childhood, sexuality, the nonrational self, and psychology as a way to understand these. And the implicit questions went deep—to the source of evil in modern life. It is my argument that in using those themes to explain a heinous crime, first the newspapers, through which the case initially exploded into the public arena, and then other cultural agencies participated in a public discourse that offered Americans the new terms *normality* and *abnormality* to understand transgressive behavior. Indeed, the judicial hearing that determined Leopold and Loeb's fate was guided, not by legal questions of responsibility, but by a psychiatrically driven defense that popularized those terms. That public discourse began in an uneasy way in the reportage of the 1920s and culminated in the 1950s in a coherent fiction. Perhaps because so much was at stake and the issues so tangled, the discourse consisted of stories told and retold. At its inception, the plot concocted by Nathan Leopold and Richard Loeb had been modeled on detective fiction, and its depiction always existed along the uncertain boundary between fact and fiction. Because the case and the protagonists were rapidly engulfed in the evolving public discourse and the stories were vivid, the public portrayals overwhelmed the identity of the individual characters. When Leopold eventually wrote his own memoirs, he had difficulty distinguishing the fact from the fiction of his identity, so completely had he and the story in which he had participated been enveloped and defined in the public spaces of the culture.

Publicity and Portrayal

From its first appearance in print, the story of Bobby Franks's kidnapping was unusual. On May 23, 1924, the day the newspapers reported that Bobby had been kidnapped, they also contained a detailed description of his dead body. The simultaneous public knowledge of the kidnapping and the murder set this story apart from earlier kidnapping stories, in which parents' willingness to accede to ransom demands might forestall harm to the abducted child. As the Franks story developed, sensational detail by sensational detail, the papers invested it with meaning and significance by linking it to widespread concerns about childhood and youth. When it finally left the front pages months later, the newspapers, which had started by sensationalizing an unusual kidnapping, had succeeded in normalizing a truly sensational case.

On the evening of May 21 the phone rang in the Hyde Park home of Jacob Franks, a wealthy Chicago businessman of Jewish origin who had embraced the Christian Science faith. The caller informed Flora Franks, Jacob's wife, that their youngest child and second son, Robert, aged fourteen, had been kidnapped but was alive and safe. Further information was promised for the next day. The next morning the Franks family received a carefully cast and neatly typed note that requested ten thousand dollars in ransom and enjoined Franks not to contact the police and to await further phone calls and instructions. Thus far the sequence of events and the ransom demand were very like those in other kidnappings, which, since the late nineteenth century, had become a staple of American life and police business.[1]

By the time the note was delivered, the naked body of an unidentified boy had been found under several feet of water in a culvert in a little-trafficked part of Chicago known as the Hegewisch swamp. This news was part of the normal police blotter of a metropolitan newspaper. The *Chicago Daily News* had meanwhile received an anonymous tip about the kidnapping of a wealthy boy. The coincidence led the *News* to assign one of its reporters, Alvin Goldstein, to probe a possible connection. At the importuning of this reporter, Jacob Franks sent his brother-in-law to look at the body, even though the description of the child and the fact that he was found with a pair of eyeglasses suggested that the corpse was not Bobby's. Shortly after Franks received his next call from the kidnappers, which directed him to a pharmacy to await further instructions about the delivery of the ransom money that he had already gathered from his bank, the brother-in-law identified Bobby's body at the funeral home where it had been taken. The newspaper had brought the two pieces of information together, ruining a self-consciously ingenious kidnap plot, saving Jacob Franks ten thousand dollars, and ending the last hope of his son's safe return.[2]

The newspapers would continue to play a strategic role in the unfolding story, providing their readers with continuous good copy of a sensational kidnap-murder and the prosecuting attorney with material assistance. When the pieces of the case came together, Nathan Leopold and Richard Loeb separately confessed to the crime they had jointly planned and committed. From the beginning the press participated in the creation of the Leopold and Loeb story, since its role in resolving the mystery of Bobby's murder made Leopold and Loeb public property.

The basic outlines of Leopold and Loeb's story is well and widely known, having been told and retold. Leopold—the brilliant and precocious son of one of America's most illustrious German Jewish families (a Chicago reporter wrote that "Nathan Leopold, Jr., is related to every branch of a little royalty of wealth which Chicago has long recognized"), a graduate at eighteen of the University of Chicago, qualified at nineteen to enter Harvard Law School, a published ornithographer who could speak eleven languages and was an amateur student of classic pornography—would eventually write his prison-based memoirs, *Life plus 99 Years*.[3] His partner was not so lucky. Not as brilliant, but equally precocious, Richard Loeb was the son of the vice-president of Sears, Roebuck and Company. The Loebs were even more prominent in German Jewish circles than the Leopolds, and Richard inhabited lavish homes in both Hyde Park and Charlevoix, Michigan. Handsome, debonair, and very collegiate in the 1920s manner, Loeb was extremely attractive to women, who flocked to his trial and reportedly showered him with letters when he went to jail. Having graduated at seventeen from the University of Michigan, he was the youngest graduate of the school. Loeb was distantly related to Bobby Franks and like him had attended the exclusive Harvard School in Chicago, from which he and Leopold had followed Bobby and abducted him. Loeb would die in prison, the victim of a slashing attack by a fellow inmate. All three families lived within walking distance of each other in the exclusive Hyde Park section of Chicago, within eyeshot of the University of Chicago, which both Leopold and Loeb attended at the time of the murder. Smart, accomplished, very rich, these boys of good family had committed, everyone agreed, "the crime of the century," an almost "perfect crime," baffling, fascinating, dangerous, and inscrutable.[4]

The discovery of Bobby Franks's identity presented the newspapers with a deep mystery, the motive for his death. Individual reporters (sometimes egged on by Loeb) became involved in solving the crime. When Leopold was called in to identify the eyeglasses, which had been traced to him as one of three possible owners, Goldstein and Mulroy tried to link the kidnap note (the only other distinct piece of evidence) to Leopold. When they tracked down his prelaw group study notes, whose imprint and characters matched that of the kidnap note, these provided key evidence that allowed the police to keep Leopold in custody and to bring Loeb in for questioning, since Loeb figured in Leopold's alibi for the day of the murder. When all parts of the case came together and the two began their long and detailed confessions, the press went to town. Newspapers published the confessions, interviewed the families and friends, and speculated about the nature of the "million-dollar defense" to be mounted by Clarence Darrow and his expensive psychiatric witnesses. They covered the criminal proceedings in minute detail, especially the testimony of the alienists and the extraordinary closing plea of Darrow, which became a classic of the genre.[5]

But coverage was only part of the press's job. Maintaining an almost constant presence on the front page, discussions of the crime and the case were mounted in a frenzy of competitive sensationalism. As one journalist noted in a book published in 1924, on the eve of the Leopold and Loeb explosion, "The problem of sensationalism resolves itself largely into a question of balance." Contemporary journals like the British *New Statesman* and American newspaper columnists observed and often criticized the extraordinary excesses of publicity about the case.[6] The sensationalism occurred, in part, because Leopold and Loeb were unlikely killers but also because rumors about the mutilation of the body and the body as the site of perverse practices started almost immediately after the discovery of the unclothed child, well before Leopold and Loeb were suspects. As early as May 24, Chief of Detectives Michael Hughes tried to squelch these rumors by noting that "after a hard day's work on the Franks mystery, I am convinced . . . that it was a plain case of kidnapping for ransom—not a case of a victim of perverts." The coroner's report found no evidence of sexual abuse, but these allegations lingered throughout the life of the case, and the judge had to continually remind the prosecutor that the rumors had been disproved. The rumors were subsequently inflamed by psychiatric reports and wide-ranging interviews that suggested boyish compacts and alluded to perversions (a code word for homosexuality) between Leopold and Loeb.[7]

The sexual undercurrents in a case of murder by two rich kids with no social responsibilities might seem tailor-made for sensationalism. But at a time when sex seemed suddenly everywhere, especially among the young, and religion still berated modernism in the daily press, the case of Leopold and Loeb was not simply a sexual curiosity, interesting only because of strange practices among strange boys.[8] Despite Leopold's and Loeb's wealth, brilliance, and alien religion, the newspapers insisted on manufacturing a story whose power lay in the explosive linkage of the two boys to others of their time and generation. Indeed, in its first significant incarnation, the Leopold and Loeb case became a cautionary story about the dangers of modern youth.

This did not happen at once. On the contrary, the initial portrayal of the killers, especially of Leopold, set them apart and represented them as larger than life. As one man on the street interviewed by the *Chicago Herald and Examiner* noted the day after they confessed, "I can't conceive of normal persons committing such a revolting deed."[9] As soon as Leopold stepped before the public eye, the press began to fashion a portrait of a Nietzsche-obsessed scientist who had destroyed his feelings in the interest of experimentation and cold ratiocination. Since there was no obvious motive and Bobby's identity was entirely incidental to the plot that Leopold and Loeb had concocted as a test and consummation of their friendship, making sense of the crime was no easy task.[10] In many ways, therefore, the portrayal of Leopold became a substitute for a motive.

Leopold's accomplishments, his brilliance, his precocity, his aloofness—all made him into a kind of strange bird. As the *Chicago Daily Tribune* noted in one of many similar observations: "Nathan is having an 'experience' that seems to bring him no 'regret,' no worry, no alarm. A marvelous opportunity to study his own reactions. And with a sense of detachment he watches—as a scientist might—his own curious lack of emotion." He was the "psychic adventurer de luxe," who, some speculated, might have left his glasses behind on purpose as a goad and an experiment to test the degree of his superiority to others. "The most brilliant boy of his age I've ever known," the prosecutor, Robert Crowe, reportedly called him.[11]

Certainly Leopold's extensive interests (only some of them scientific) and his awkward identification of himself and his friend with Nietzschean supermen gave some grounds to this portrayal, but the picture of him as the "mastermind" who had lured the naive Loeb into a horrible experiment on human life was extreme. "Is Loeb the Faun, Leopold the Svengali?" the *Chicago Herald and Examiner* asked on the front page. At the time of his confession, Leopold was quoted as saying that he "did it as easily as he would stick a pin through the back of a beetle." And the *Chicago Daily Tribune* commented that this was "an excellent analysis of his mental makeup."[12] The papers were full of pictures of the two, often dissected by lines and arrows, which pretended to physiological analysis. Leopold, with his dark, brooding Semitic looks, large nose, hooded eyes, and sensual lips, was especially vulnerable as the case became "the most cold-blooded and motiveless crime that has ever found mention in the pages of records of history." Loeb, the all-American boy and fraternity man, far less intellectual and more popular, who asked for his mother after his confession (and whose mother was not Jewish by birth), was initially let off the hook as "a suggestible type."[13]

The limning of Leopold as a monster with no conscience or emotions flew in the face of other statements in the same papers—that Leopold wished he could jump off a bridge, that he hoped his family would disown him, or, in courtroom psychiatric testimony, that he had become hysterical at the time of the crime. Initially, however, Leopold's sense of shame and humiliation had no part to play in the portrait of the cold-blooded fiend being constructed out of the science, philosophy, and learning (with whiffs of the Jew) that constituted Leopold's earliest newspaper persona. Initially, as a Chicago paper summarized it, the case was an exotic flower of evil.

> The diabolical spirit evinced in the planned kidnapping and murder; the wealth and prominence of the families whose sons are involved; the high mental attainments of the youths, the suggestions of perversions; the strange quirks indicated in the confession that the child was slain for a ransom, for experience, for the satisfaction of a desire for deep plotting; combined to *set the case in a class by itself.*[14]

The clear titillation this strange cocktail could provide put the newspapers in a bind. If Leopold was an alien fiend, and the case simply a quirk, it was difficult to justify its continuing prominence in the daily press. To make the case significant it had to become a reflection on modern life, an interpretation to which the papers were already committed before the identities of the killers were known, when poor Bobby's death had been used to illustrate "the Danger to the Children of Chicago." Indeed, as in all previous kidnappings, the Franks family was initially the focus of attention, as the press probed and pushed to get the most mileage from a mother in a state of collapse, pining for the son she fantasized would soon return, and a noble father (despite his pawnbroker roots) prepared to sacrifice his wealth and himself to do justice to his son. The use of the Franks family for sympathy and reader identification disappeared, as the newspapers refocused from the dead child to the live children. For the case was a sensation in part because, at nineteen and eighteen, Leopold and Loeb were children themselves, not much older than their victim.

Soon Leopold and Loeb were appropriated to a Fitzgeraldesque type of youth, suffering from ennui, overeducation, or overindulgence, and especially from intellectual precocity. Thus, Billy Sunday blamed the murder on "precocious brains, salacious books, infidel minds."[15]

Modern childhood remained the central theme, but as the newspapers attempted to understand the motiveless crime and its relation to the dangers of modern childhood, they turned readers' attention from children as victims to children as potential perpetrators of crime and immorality. Thus, according to the popular writer Elinor Glyn, the lesson of the case was to "awaken parents to the frightful responsibility of what thoughts they allow the subconscious minds of their children to absorb before they are twelve years old." A criminologist drew a generalizable lesson from the case: "There is a great responsibility to raise a baby to manhood. A child is like a clinging vine and clings to its environment." But it was Ben B. Lindsey, the Progressive juvenile judge from Denver and a well-known youth advocate in the 1920s, who most fully suggested the breadth of the case's significance:

> Let no parent flatter himself that the Leopold-Loeb case has no lesson for him. Let us all clearly understand that the crime was the fruit of the modern misdirection of youth. . . . It was more than the story of a murder. It was the story of modern youth, of modern parents, of modern economic and social conditions, and of modern education.[16]

The transition from senseless crime to moral lesson was made in two ways. First, the newspapers deflated the scientific imperturbability and distance that had set the case and especially Leopold apart from the multitudes. As the case evolved, and especially during the hearing, newspapers gave readers ample opportunity to reflect upon the often-conflicting views espoused by different spokesmen for the new science of psychiatry. The representation of psychiatry in the popular press reduced "science" from Olympian heights of objectivity to the awkward fumbling of vaudevillian figures. The press thus tamed the cold scientific monster of science (Leopold's first incarnation) into a clumsy, uncertain object of ridicule. Leopold, whom the defense psychiatrists insisted on calling by his nickname "Babe," lost his Svengali characteristics, becoming instead exposed, humbled, an object of demeaning testing and probing. The newspapers learned to control Leopold and the threat he posed by subjecting him to the science of psychiatry, without entirely accepting the new authority of psychiatry itself.

Second, the newspapers democratized Leopold and Loeb in ways that the two, Leopold especially, probably despised. They published the IQ puzzlers and tests to which Leopold was subjected and challenged readers to do them in the record time of Leopold, "the genius." IQ testing in the twenties was both an extremely popular new scientific instrument and a normalizing enterprise that reduced intellectual differences to variant notches on a single scale. (See Chapter 2.) This set readers on a continuum with Leopold and encouraged personal comparisons. They asked readers to vote in polls on many subjects, including whether the trial should be broadcast on the radio, something many readers supported because it would result in more democratic access to the trial. They showed "the boys" in prison garb, happily adapted to prison routine.[17] The papers tried every angle on this everyman theme, including a column by Winifred Black that asked each woman reader to consider how she would feel "If Your Son Were [the] Slayer?" "You who sit there at your breakfast table, so comfortable, so much at peace with all the world, this morning. . . . Would you stand for justice and for right, no matter if by taking such a stand you had to walk to the very foot of the gallows with your own son?" This process encouraged readers, if not to identify with the slayers, at least to be on a level with them; it thereby made Leopold and Loeb's ideas less alien and their crime less bizarre. It also made these extremely unusual children more "normal." As Maureen McKernan, a reporter for the *Herald and Examiner,* concluded:

> The attitude of the boys throughout the trial amazed everyone who watched them. Every day newspapers carried pictures of them smiling in the courtroom. When the crowd laughed, they laughed. . . . but those who watched them closely came to see . . . two frightened, foolish boys, who found themselves in a terrific mess with the eyes of the world upon them.[18]

In taming their monstrosity, the papers' portrayal of two "foolish boys" renegotiated the terms of the crime from the satanic to the domestic. The monsters who inhabited an alien world of learning, culture, and wealth, who had committed an incomprehensible crime, became just two boys, Babe and Dickie, who had tested certain limits of human behavior (sex and murder), but whose punishment lay within the realm of comprehensible retribution. In the process, the newspapers helped introduce Americans to the new psychology and to new concepts of the normal and the abnormal.

The Personal as Public

By the time the judicial phase of the Leopold and Loeb case began in judge John E. Caverly's courtroom on July 21, 1924 (the hearing was not broadcast on the radio), the issues of psychology and childhood identified with it had already been aired in the press. But the story was still erratic and sensational. In preparation for the hearings, the defense team began to provide the elements of a story of childhood written in the new language of modern psychology. Expert psychiatric testimony had been used long before the 1920s in court cases, most importantly in the famous trial of Charles Guiteau, President James A. Garfield's assassin in 1881. It had also played a part in the successful defense of Harry Thaw, Stanford White's killer, in 1906.[19] Indeed, by the time of the Leopold and Loeb case, one of the prosecution's alienists, W. I. Krohn, would earn Clarence Darrow's withering contempt as "a witness, a testifier" because he had abandoned all other professional duties to devote himself to giving expert court testimony. Psychiatric testimony was used throughout the twenties in new and probing ways. But the Leopold and Loeb case, because of its prominence, Darrow's innovative defense, and the role of the newspapers in promoting it as a pivotal modern event, gave the role of expert psychiatric testimony new visibility in popular culture.[20]

After Nathan Leopold had been held for more than a day on the evidence of his eyeglasses at the scene of the crime and the apparent similarity between the typewritten ransom note and his law group study notes, the Leopold family chauffeur provided the *coup de grace* by undermining an essential part of his alibi.[21] Loeb, who had been separately questioned for a shorter period, broke down and confessed, triggering Leopold's very similar description of the crime and his role. Their confessions contained essentially the same detailed descriptions. These were almost immediately corroborated as the police, with Leopold and Loeb's active cooperation, retraced the killers' steps, finding clue after clue and assembling the prosecution's elaborate evidence. All the pieces of the puzzle, which Leopold and Loeb prided themselves on constructing, fit together and provided irrefutable evidence of their shared guilt. The confessions differed only in some minor details (later straightened out) and one essential fact—each accused the other of administering the fateful blow.

Thus when, very belatedly, the boys were allowed to contact their parents to arrange for an attorney, Nathan and Richard not only had openly confessed but also had helped the police to amass the materials for what prosecutor Robert Crowe assumed would be an airtight case, which he repeatedly called "a hanging case." The pair's active participation in constructing their own scaffold confronted their attorneys with serious strategic problems. Since all three families were rich and very well connected in various circles, including legal ones (two of the defense attorneys, Benjamin Bachrach and Walter Bachrach, were Richard's cousins), no one was entirely surprised when Darrow was called in to lead the defense team in what soon was described in the press as the "million-dollar defense."[22] It was generally assumed by the prosecutor, the press, and others that Darrow's team would enlist medical specialists to assist in proving the two confessed slayers insane. Anticipating that the "crime of the century" would lead to the "battle of the alienists," the papers began to prepare the public with long and even learned discussions of the insanity defense and its history.[23]

After careful consideration, Darrow and the Bachrachs decided that their chances for an outright acquittal of the two extremely lucid and well-educated defendants was slim. Instead, and to the great surprise of most participants, they pleaded the pair guilty (rather than not guilty by reason of insanity) and introduced expert testimony to mitigate the *sentencing* of the defendants. In this way, the defense avoided a jury trial and the specific legal requirements of an insanity defense, which in addition often incurred much popular hostility. The sentences were left to the mercies of a judge, in a state in which juveniles had only rarely been executed.[24] As a result of the strategy, the issue in the case became not *insanity,* with its specific legal definitions, but mental *abnormality,* a much more flexible and fungible concept, and one open to modern winds of interpretation. Issues of legal insanity were bound by clear guidelines, the M'Naughton Rule, but abnormality (a psychological concept) had no legal definition and a chaotic boundary. As Darrow noted, "There are many persons who walk the streets who are subject to mental disease falling short of the legal definition of insanity." It was thus the defense's contention that while Leopold and Loeb knew what they were doing and certainly that it was wrong (the key to guilt in cases of insanity), their emotions were so disordered that they should not suffer the extreme sentence of death. As Walter Bachrach made clear to the court in defending the introduction of psychiatric evidence:

> We raise no issue as to the legal sanity of these defendants and make no contentions that by reason of the fact that they are suffering from a diseased mental condition, there should be any division or lessening of the responsibility to answer for the crime, the commission of which they have confessed. We do assert that they are suffering and were suffering at the time of the commission of the crime charged from a diseased mental condition, but we do not concern ourselves with the question of whether such

mental disease would constitute in the present case a defense to the charge of murder.

Crowe tried repeatedly to trip the defense into an insanity plea. But the defense team maintained that abnormality, according to a new psychological vision in which normal and abnormal were continuous and in which unconscious processes, rather than knowing intent, were paramount, differed from insanity. Darrow's defense, which was fully consistent with his own extremely dark and deterministic view of human behavior, used psychology in a maneuver that was new to the courts.[25]

The maneuver allowed for maximum attention in the press to the new psychiatric theories and stimulated the newspapers to ask ministers, professors, and doctors for their views on the legal, medical, and moral issues involved.[26] The defense strategy laid the groundwork for the media's active role in translating and interpreting the case for the public, and because so many issues in the case were related to the new psychology, the press became an active source of cultural news and information.

"Fifty Alienists to Fight for Slayers," announced the *Chicago Herald and Examiner* headline for June 14 in a typical burst of exaggeration. In fact, Darrow's experts were a much smaller team: First among the three star witnesses—invariably called "the Three Wise Men from the East" by the prosecutor and often by the press—was William Alanson White, chief of staff at St. Elizabeth's Hospital in Washington and professor of nervous and mental diseases at Georgetown University. As the head of St. Elizabeth's, White was one of the most important figures in American psychiatry. An early and very influential American interpreter of Sigmund Freud's ideas, he did much to bring European psychoanalytic theory into an American framework. The second star was William Healy, an expert on juvenile psychopathology and a pioneer in expert court testimony. Healy had been director of the psychopathic clinic in Chicago and was at the time of the trial the director of the Judge Baker Foundation in Boston, an organization devoted to issues of juvenile crime and justice. Healy had written extensively about the causes of juvenile crime. Dr. Bernard Glueck, the third witness, was former director of Sing Sing prison in New York, a member of the staff at the College of Physicians and Surgeons of Columbia University and the New York School of Social Research, the translator of several European works on psychoses, and an expert on the relationship between law and psychiatry who had in 1916 published *Studies in Forensic Psychiatry*. Less well known nationally was Ralph C. Hamill, a local and well-regarded neuropsychiatrist who helped prepare the written psychiatric evaluation on which the defense case was based.[27]

The defense team had also enlisted the aid of two other physicians, Harold S. Hulbert and Karl M. Bowman. They examined Leopold and Loeb for fourteen days, probing and measuring their body functions, mentality, intelligence, their family histories and fantasies, as well as the then-popular matter of the function of their endocrine glands to appraise the physical and mental basis for their behavior.[28] The result of their investigation was the notorious eighty-thousand-word Hulbert-Bowman report on Leopold and Loeb, which provided the basic text of the defense case, but not before its contents were stolen or leaked to the press and served up, alongside eggs and toast, as breakfast food for American newspaper consumers.

The Hulbert-Bowman report thus became famous even before it, became evidence. The most intimate facts of Loeb's and Leopold's lives, their fixations, and their "master-slave" relationship became a staple of Chicago diet as "perversions" were anchored in childhood fantasies and intellectual precocity absorbed into compensations for fears of physical inferiority. The report forced an entire revision of the assumed relationship between Leopold and Loeb; Loeb was now the "master" criminal and Leopold his willing slave and subordinate. This seemed initially to be the shocker: "Loeb is the king. It is he who has been the master-mind throughout. He is almost without emotions. . . . He has always been fond of crime stories." But any reader who went beyond the attention-grabbing summations would be presented with two very troubled boys. Much of this report, except for "the unprintable [sexual] matter," appeared in all the major Chicago newspapers, as well as in the book published very shortly after the trial by Maureen McKernan, who had been a reporter for the *Chicago Herald and Examiner.*[29]

The Hulbert-Bowman report did not explain away the death of the Franks child, but it substituted the troubled bodies and childhoods of the killers for the tragic loss of Bobby and the remainder of his childhood. One could hardly read Hulbert and Bowman's reports and not be affected by the fragile loneliness of Leopold's childhood, scarred by feelings of physical inferiority, the sexual abuse of a governess, and the loss of his mother when he was fourteen. "The patient states that there have been two experiences in his life which have completely altered his philosophy of life. His mother's death is one of these. . . . if his mother, who was such a good and exceptional person had to suffer so much in the world and that if God took her away from this world, then that God is a cruel and senseless God." In McKernan's very early account of Leopold's life, based on this report, the theme of the lonely, betrayed child rings clear: "A queer reserved chap, living to himself among his books, substituting his studies for the normal active interests of boys his own age." Similarly, it was difficult to deny the evil committed against a vulnerable Dickie Loeb by a well-meaning but pretentious and outrageously strict governess who took him over, denied him play time, and pushed him into extreme academic overachievement. The defense doctors, psychiatrists, and lawyers were very careful to avoid blaming the boys' families (specifically absolving them of genetic taint), and the governesses were clearly convenient substitutes for the parents. This defense stratagem appears to have succeeded: in letters and interviews ordinary citizens were divided on the question of parental guilt and responsibility and not strongly inclined to blame the parents. Nonetheless, whether parents or parent substitutes were at fault, the childhood of each boy had been distorted. As the psychiatric testimony continued, the warped childhoods of the two killers were embedded in the public awareness of the case. The prosecution derided White's image of Dickie nightly speaking his dreams and fantasies to his teddy bear, but the mental picture of the lonely child with his teddy lingered in the newspapers and throughout the hearing.[30]

Leopold and Loeb were not entirely tamed by the Hulbert-Bowman report or the psychiatric testimony, especially as the boys' sexual compact as master and slave became more firmly limned. But in the minds of readers who were willing to be informed and not just inflamed, the image of the bold, self-sufficient, criminal master-minds had been deeply shaken. The exposure of their privacy in the press was profoundly humiliating. The endless testing itself must have aggravated the humiliation, as the boys' every bodily and mental function became part of their "defense," and the subject of news and publicity. The newest scientific work was enlisted on their behalf. As the *Chicago Herald and Examiner* observed: "Physiology, psychology, biology, chemistry and a half dozen other sciences have been utilized in the research work." But this use of science also brought down their imperiousness and autonomy, as day after day the newspapers showed the pair hooked up to machines and discussed their test results. "Questions are hurled at them—staccato, urgent questions. They answer. More questions. . . . Then come the examinations—the hopping, the skipping, the jumping. First the one under examination stands on one foot, then on the other. Searching, prying fingers go over him. He winces and grins." In one particularly humiliating pair of photos, Leopold is shown first in his preconfession days, examining the bird that he had discovered, and then, birdlike, with a tube in his mouth, subjected to tests as an alienist used "all the resources of science to find evidences of some form of insanity." Leopold once railed against the testing: "Loeb and I are being trained like fleas to jump through hoops just to entertain the curious." As Leopold's and Loeb's genius and precocity were tested and demeaned, the fierceness of the crime was defused.[31]

In exposing Leopold and Loeb to prying scientific instruments and the prying public, the endless testing and the psychiatric evidence both democratized them and made them more controllable. The new psychology transformed them from arrogant Nietzschean criminals (the early representation of Leopold) into vulnerable boys (Loeb and his teddy bear) and linked them to the ordinary boys of America. The change made their crime less distant, but it may well have made it more broadly frightening. Dr. Carleton Simon, a criminologist and police deputy, took the occasion to instruct parents about the dangers of adolescence. "It is during the adolescent transition that so many youth turn toward a career of crime." And the newspaper that carried Simon's essay editorialized, "This is an article which every parent should read, an article which may result in saving many a youth from the wages of sin." By its use of an old-fashioned metaphor, the paper neatly transcended the difference between older religious authority and the scientific expertise offered by a criminologist. Given such lessons, it is hardly surprising that a minister observed that the crime "caused more heart searching on the part of parents than any crime within my memory of forty years in the ministry."[32]

Even before the sentencing hearing, Dr. Llewellys Barker, professor of clinical medicine at Johns Hopkins University, told a meeting of psychiatrists: "If the public could be accurately informed of the prevalence of *abnormal* thought, feeling, and behavior in the United States, such indifference as now exists regarding prevention would become inconceivable." During the hearing the public was thoroughly inducted into the term and the phenomenon. The defense psychiatrists' joint report repeated the terms *abnormal* and *normal* more often than any other set of concepts and added to them the special term of *supernormal* when referring to Leopold's intelligence. Although they drew on specialized categories to diagnose Leopold and Loeb's abnormality, the term *abnormal* was very loosely applied by the defense throughout the hearing, and this vaguer, more fungible concept was much more widely applicable. Among the "abnormal" childhood behaviors were too much private fantasizing, excessive reading of "exciting detective fiction," drinking at too early an age, and associating with those much older than oneself. Leopold "was not only precocious in his mental interests, but these interests assumed a degree of intensity and showed themselves in special directions which were in themselves indications of abnormality." Leopold's special brilliance and extraordinary interests became signs of an "abnormality" that had been much aggravated because "early recognition of his superior attainments by his teachers and by his mother made him feel unlike and apart from others and superior to them." In Loeb's case, "unscrupulousness, untruthfulness, unfairness, ingratitude and disloyalty assume a particularly abnormal nature when one views them in the light of the kind of home and social setting that he came from." In other words, traits usually condemned as dishonorable or possibly immoral were being redefined. They were abnormal because Loeb could not possibly have learned them in his home, one "noted for its high standards of virtue and culture." These were generous definitions of abnormality, indeed, and so broad and flexible as to be extremely frightening.[33]

Above all, according to the defense psychiatrists' report, Leopold and Loeb had indulged extreme fantasies.

> In contrast to the imaginative life of normal childhood which is always in touch more or less with the realities surrounding child life, Leopold's phantasies were from the beginning out of accord with the usual demands of social life, and never seem to have undergone the natural fate of phantasy life in being increasingly matched or assimilated into the facts of reality. Thus the normal child identifies himself with the persons in his immediate environment, he day-dreams himself being a motorman, an engineer, a policeman, showing thereby in his desires a normal response to the influences which surround him.

Probably neither Leopold nor Loeb daydreamed about being motormen or policemen (although Loeb's perfectly ordinary cowboy fantasies were damned as evidence of excessive aggression). But the psychiatrists' leveling, not to say banal, views of reality and realistic fantasies, which were even then criticized as substituting doctrine for insight, helped provide easy didactic lessons and fit well into the needs of newspapers to link the case to the bedrooms and nurseries of their readers.[34]

The newspapers wanted to have it two ways: to use psychiatric testimony for the information it provided and the authority it gave to simple domestic lessons but to knock psychiatrists off their scientific perch as so much inflated (and overpaid) ego. They had ample opportunity to demonstrate this confused attitude toward science and learning during the long week when Crowe subjected the "Three Wise Men from the East" to a withering populist cross-examination. The papers had a field day pitting Crowe as a David of common sense against the Goliath of psychiatric obscurantism and sissified intellect. And Crowe, rumored to be eager for higher elective office, played on this persona: "After noon, Mr. Crowe reminded the men and women of the country that he was just a layman, who didn't know much about fancy terms for psychoses. And he suggested that perhaps many of his comrades round about were just plain folks with plain terms for plain things." When Crowe scored a point, either confusing the alienists (White was his special target) or suggesting the limitations of their expertise, the papers registered it as a victory for the people against the hired evidence. On other days, the newspapers applauded the shrewd rejoinders of the defense or prosecution psychiatrists. The papers never reported that the alienists on both sides had offered to hold joint examinations and to submit common reports and that the prosecution had turned the offer down. Instead, the alienists were pitted against each other. The circus atmosphere surrounding the trial, at which three thousand people daily vied for a hundred seats, did not help, nor did the newspapers' competitive grandstanding. The papers were using the psychiatrists in some grand public demonstration of modernism and its discontents, and indeed, William Randolph Hearst had tried to hire Sigmund Freud to testify at the trial.[35]

The carnival atmosphere almost obscures the important but subtle way the papers democratized the trial by bringing Leopold and Loeb and the assorted bigwig doctors and lawyers down to a common level, transforming the event from the distant and bizarre to the vaguely familiar and socially consequential. The killers became anything but the Nietzschean supermen whom they claimed to be and whose self-sufficiency initially alarmed the public. Instead they became children, precocious and wounded certainly, but children who could provide lessons about how to normalize childhood. "There is not an act in all this horrible tragedy," Darrow said, "that was not the act of a child." As the psychiatrists persisted in describing the pair as Dickie and Babe, Crowe became understandably irate at the testimony's tendency to make them into ordinary boys. And at one point, Crowe, who wanted to make them "normal" and therefore responsible for their actions but monstrous, burst out in his cross-examination of William Healy, "You don't get in your courts many college graduates whose fathers are millionaires."[36] He thus suggested that Healy's experience with ordinary juvenile delinquents did not cover this case. Of course Healy's very presence on the defense team suggested that the case was being absorbed into this larger category (and specialty) of juvenile delinquency, much expanded in this trial to include the children of the privileged as well as of the deprived. The Leopold and Loeb case thus problematized childhood (and not, as previous concerns about juvenile delinquency had, only the children of the poor) and made it the site of significant preventive knowledge. The case had attached categories of normality and abnormality to definitions of childhood, and the association was more significant than the often slippery distinctions that were made between them. At a time when child-rearing advice was avidly sought by parents and increasingly dispensed by a variety of experts, the Leopold and Loeb case stimulated psychological explorations of childhood development and experience.

The verbal pushing and shoving in court as the prosecutor tried to show that these pampered "fiends" (Crowe never gave up suggesting that Bobby had been mutilated) were perfectly sane and normal and the defense team tried to make them just kids, very human but mentally abnormal, made the concepts of normal and abnormal, in all their rich confusion, daily staples of newspaper copy. In the written psychiatric report, the defense team emphasized the killers' "abnormal mental life. This has made a situation so unique that it probably will never repeat itself. There is justification for stressing the uniqueness of this case if for no other reason than that it has created wide-spread panic among parents of young people."[37] The psychiatric report implied that the newspaper coverage had succeeded in alarming parents, but the report left unclear whether parents panicked because their children might be victims or, as became increasingly likely in view of the lessons offered by Leopold and Loeb, perpetrators of horrible crimes.

While Leopold and Loeb did not hang, that victory did not necessarily validate the defense claim that the case was unique or that it should be decided on the basis of new visions of psychological abnormality (Caverly based his ruling on their age) or on the alienists' conclusions. (Indeed, subsequent cases in the decade in which young men were accused of heinous crimes against children, like those of William Hickman and Harrison Noel, may have suffered from the connection with Leopold and Loeb.) Rather, the press presented and the public heard the alienists' views in tandem with Crowe's challenges. In the end what ruled the day was, as Mr. Dooley put it, the perception that "th' throupe if thrained alyenists at ivry murdher thrile is always a riot. This is prob'bly th'highest price vowdyville act on th' big cirket."[38] Science took it in the knees in the public press, while the Leopold and Loeb case familiarized Americans with a wide range of terms, concepts, and values drawn from psychiatry. Nevertheless, psychiatrists had defused the crime, not because it was unique, but because they lodged its causes in the childhoods of the young men who had killed, not for an intentional "thrill" as first reported, but for deeply psychological reasons. They had made psychology a form of explanation far more comprehensible (and far less disturbing) than the initial Nietzschean portrait that the papers had exploited. If Leopold and Loeb were not quite like any other two boys, they were declawed, and their crime became a moral lesson that Americans could ponder as they put their own children into their cradles and cribs at night.

The Crime Grows Up

The orgy of publicity surrounding the crime, confessions, trial, judge Caverly's sentencing, and Leopold and Loeb's imprisonment would have made the case notable even if Leopold and Loeb had thereafter disappeared from the public record, tightly shut up from freedom and from view at Joliet and Stateville prisons. As the *New Statesman* told its English readers, "No crime that the modern world knows of can be set beside the killing of the boy Robert Franks by Nathan Leopold and Richard Loeb. . . . The affair has dominated the American newspapers for four months in a fashion that no short description could make real to English readers." After their confession, "there began the exploitation of Leopold and Loeb on a scale and with a recklessness going beyond anything hitherto known." That exploitation, as we have seen, both tamed the criminals and gave the public cause for concern about the inclinations and rearing of "normal" children. The case also had effects in professional circles. S. Sheldon Glueck, an expert on forensic psychiatry and juvenile delinquency, noted in 1925, "In Illinois and throughout America, the much journalized and discussed Leopold-Loeb hearing is even now bearing fruit in the shape of numerous articles, on different angles of the problem of mental disorder and the criminal law, published in scientific periodicals and professional journals."[39]

But the two convicts did not disappear. Similar crimes later in the decade inevitably brought newspaper recollections and comparisons, and sometimes other criminals suggested that they had imitated the famous pair.[40] Such crimes, the way the killers had been represented to the public, and Leopold and Loeb's experiences in prison kept the case alive.

Despite the reputation of the 1920s as an era of sexual revolt, the sexuality in the Leopold and Loeb case was not fully explored then. Instead, the public discussion of sexuality was marginalized or shortcircuited and largely restricted to rumor and innuendo. Perhaps this was because the story that became central in the press was about childhood, and because the boys' story was normalized at a time when heterosexuality dominated public discussions of youthful misbehavior. Indeed, the newspapers frequently emphasized Richard Loeb's special attraction for women and his many girlfriends. In 1924 the public was largely guarded from specific knowledge about the details of Leopold and Loeb's homosexual relationship. The newspapers did not print the sexual sections of the psychiatric reports; McKernan's important collection excised what she called "the unprintable matter." Even professional journals such as the *Journal of the American Institute of Criminal Law and Criminology* excluded "the murderers' sexual history" when it printed large excerpts and case summaries.

Judge Caverly had asked the attorneys to approach the bench when these matters were discussed in court. He ordered women, even female reporters, out of the courtroom. That the two had been sexual partners of some kind was nevertheless commonly assumed to be part of their "folie à deux," if not indeed at the root of their crime. Even though the press eschewed vivid or graphic descriptions, the rumors, innuendos, and use of such terms as perversions and fiend fed popular imaginings.[41]

It was this cloud of sex stuff that erupted when Richard Loeb was brutally and horribly murdered in the Illinois Penitentiary at Stateville in 1936. Loeb had been literally "slashed to ribbons" in the shower by James Day, a fellow inmate. "The killing of Loeb rivaled in brutality the killing of the Franks boy," the *New York Times* announced in its front-page coverage. It seemed that twelve years after his own heinous act, Loeb had gotten his and, appropriately, as a result of a sexual goad. Day immediately played on the sexual in his own story and defense. Day often changed the details of his story, but he stood by the accusation of sexual assault. In the *Chicago Tribune* he was quoted as saying, "I can't talk about Loeb or why I dislike him while there's a lady present," but he must have assumed that ladies did not read the *Los Angeles Times*, for in an interview for that paper, he contended that "ever since I have been a prisoner here . . . Loeb has been hounding me with improper advances." Since both Loeb and Day were undressed at the time of the murder, the accusation seemed plausible.[42]

In his memoir, Leopold claimed that Loeb would not have instigated a sexual rendezvous with Day.[43] State's Attorney William R. McCabe, called in to investigate the case, believed Loeb had been set up as a result of "a plot among fellow convicts. . . . I disbelieve Day's story almost in its entirety. . . . What he says of Loeb's morality is directly opposed to all that was known of Loeb." Rather than being interpreted as a sexual story, "the slaying of Loeb was regarded by many public officials as the crowning episode in the inefficiency and violence that have characterized the history of the state prisons under Governor Homer." Some speculated that Loeb, because of his wealth and ability to buy special privileges from corrupt prison officials, was murdered by resentful prisoners, as equally resentful guards looked the other way. But, as journalist-historian Hal Higdon observed, "Undoubtedly, many people accepted the story that Loeb did make homosexual advances as true because they wanted it to be true. They considered the Franks murder an act of perversion—which was never proved—so it seemed fitting that Loeb die while attempting another perverted act."[44]

It is significant that what was remembered about Loeb's death had nothing to do with inequalities in prison or lack of discipline and enforcement of rules. Loeb's death was remembered by journalists and the public as a tale of sexual perversion, not of state corruption. Beginning in the 1930s, especially with the publicity surrounding Loeb's death, the sexual materials that had been largely inhibited in the original case spilled forth in explicit public representations. Less than a week after Loeb's death, *Time* magazine, for example, described the event in its "Crime" department by remembering Leopold and Loeb as "two perverted Chicago youths" who had "violated" Bobby Franks before they killed him. "Prison," *Time* declared, had "only exaggerated Loeb's unnatural appetites."[45]

Subsequently, Loeb's horrible end became the subject of even more titillating imaginings. One had an especially pungent twist. In *The Madhouse on Madison Street,* his memoirs as a newspaperman, George Murray described "Dickie Loeb" as "in love, desperately and insanely. He lusted for the body of the Negro boy he coveted and he was driven mad by jealousy when he saw the boy so much as talk to another prisoner." He *quotes* the "Negro boy" as saying, "White boy, keep your hands to yourself. Quit writing me love letters. I need a woman bad but I sure don't need the kind of satisfaction you keep offering." Murray finishes his recollection by quoting the story lead from fellow journalist Edwin A. Lahey of the *Chicago Daily News:* "Richard Loeb, who graduated with honors from college at the age of fifteen and who was a master of the English language, today ended his sentence with a proposition." Murray not only misrepresented Day as black (his pictures in the newspapers clearly showed a white man) but also misquoted from a colleague who in his clever haste had loaded his news copy with double entendres. Murray thereby made Loeb even more precocious than he was (he graduated at seventeen).[46] The full engagement with Leopold and Loeb's homosexuality occurred in the 1980s and 1990s, when the pair became part of the self-conscious history of homoerotic love. But the sexuality implicit in the story would not wait that long.

After the 1930s, with Leopold older and in prison and Loeb dead, the case was no longer about childhood. Sexuality and psychology began to dominate the public memories and representations. Removed from public view and therefore from newsprint, it now moved to other forms and toward the boundaries between fact and fiction. If the facts in Loeb's death could be fictionalized, it was no great surprise that fictional representations could deliver a huge payoff of exact details and entire pages lifted from the historical record. In *Compulsion,* a 1956 novel based on the case, Meyer Levin obscured the boundary between fact and fiction by including the text of Darrow's famous summation, an exact replica of the criminal investigation, the confessions, and the sequence of court evidence. Moreover, by endowing Judah (Judd) Steiner with almost all of Leopold's interests and borrowing aspects of the personalities of the historical characters for his fictional ones (Artie Straus was Dickie Loeb), he made it very difficult, in fact impossible, to know where facts leave off and fictions begin. Levin made no secret of his exploitation of the case.

> If I have followed an actual case, are these, then, actual persons? Here I would avoid the modern novelist's conventional disclaimer, which no one fully believes in any case. I follow known events. . . . I suppose *Compulsion* may be called a contemporary historical novel or a documentary novel, as distinct from a roman à clef.[47]

Anyone deeply familiar with the case, as I have become, would be caught short trying to find the boundary between what she knows from the evidence and what Levin has interpolated or re-created in his book, with two exceptions. *Compulsion* is full of a psychologizing much more sophisticated than that presented in the trial, and the shutters have been taken off the sexual materials. From the beginning, as we have seen, psychology and sexuality clung to the case, but in the atmosphere of the twenties the public discussions were choked off. Psychiatry was made very public in the Leopold and Loeb case, but it was humiliated and short-circuited, confused with public morality. Levin makes his psychological explanation of the story fully Freudian, accenting symbolism in the murder and drawing out aspects of the relationship between the boys that neither William Alanson White nor anyone else had publicly discussed in the twenties. The sexuality of the two had been whispered about in the twenties, but women had been sheltered from the facts and the subject never seriously engaged in public. Levin proposes sexual drive as the motive force for Leopold's involvement, making the homosexual dimension of the boys' relationship just one facet of a more complex sexual energy that propels Leopold. He even interpolates a heterosexual rape scene that seems to spill forth from Leopold's imagination, engorged on World War I propaganda. (In his summation, Darrow had drawn attention to the violent consequences of the war and wartime propaganda for the culture as a whole, not just the defendants, and the defense psychiatrists had mentioned in their report Leopold's *fantasies* of German soldiers raping captives.) Indeed, in Levin's novel the two boys are always looking for "gash" and parading their sexual prowess. Their girlfriends anxiously consider experiencing sex a necessary part of being modern and up-to-date. By the 1950s such overt sexuality, although sometimes criticized as vulgar in reviews of the book, had become a necessary ingredient of realistic fiction.[48] Levin thus took the two most powerful latent themes of the case, psychiatry and sexuality, and built his novel around them, making it thereafter impossible to imagine that the story of Leopold and Loeb had earlier been about anything else. Full of fifties themes, but built on twenties events, the novel became a best-seller and eventually sold more than one million copies in its Pocketbook paperback edition. In the fifties—after another, even more brutal war—sex, violence, and psychoanalysis seemed the right mix of clues to penetrate the terrible conundrum at the base of the century's understanding of evil, a mystery that the Leopold and Loeb case, with its pointed questions about childhood danger, had from the beginning promised to expose. In the fifties, the explanatory power of psychology, a fixation on the omnipotence of sex, and an obsession with normality came together in Levin's re-creation, contributing to its broad popularity.

The fifties was not just the decade when Freudian psychology and sexually explicit novels arrived. In the fifties, Nathan Leopold, having survived over thirty years in prison, was beginning to dream of the possibility of parole. Levin believed that *Compulsion,* which carried forward the psychological humanizing that the alienists had begun in 1924, assisted Leopold in his parole efforts, and Levin even testified, unbidden, on Leopold's behalf at the latter's 1957 executive clemency hearing. According to Levin, "Some of the members of the Board told me they read the book and it changed their thinking about Leopold."[49] If Levin is to be believed, his fictionalized re-creation positively affected the image of Leopold. But Leopold, who had already been deeply exposed and humiliated in the 1920s by the press and psychiatrists, felt otherwise. He believed that the book infringed on his private property, that is, his person, identity, and personality; it made up incidents and took liberties with the truth, all the while parading as a fiction that everyone assumed to be fact. On October 2, 1959, shortly after his release on parole, he and his lawyer, Elmer Gertz, filed suit against Levin, his publisher, Simon and Schuster, and Darryl F. Zanuck Productions, Inc., which had just released a movie based on the book. Levin, who had also written a play based on his book, wrote the screenplay. Like the novel, the movie altered cases and renamed characters, but it was extensively advertised as based on the Leopold and Loeb case.[50]

After long delays, on April 15, 1964, Leopold won the right to sue for $1,405,000 in the Circuit Court of Cook County, Illinois. In the decision, Judge Thomas E. Kluczynski observed:

defendants claim the protection of the First Amendment. . . . Freedom of speech and of the press does not encompass freedom to exploit commercially or "make merchandise" of one's name or likeness in an advertisement. . . . Although plaintiff is "disguised" by the use of pseudonym in the book, plaintiff's name is prominently displayed on the coverjacket. . . . Similarly the plaintiff was used to sell the motion picture. . . . The unauthorized publication of plaintiff's name and likeness to advertise both the book and the movie constitutes a classic instance of an invasion of the right of privacy, for which the courts have allowed redress.

Leopold appeared to have won back from the public arena the right to his identity.[51] The case did not end there, however. Although the Illinois Supreme Court first upheld Kluczynski's ruling in the Leopold suit, "which was in the nature of a suit alleging violation of the right of privacy," the decision was overturned, on an appeal by Levin, by the same court on May 27, 1970.[52] The final judgment delivered by Justice Daniel P. Ward noted that "public interest in the crime and its principals did not wane with the passage of time." As a result:

> We hold here that *the plaintiff did not have a legally protected right of privacy*. Considerations which in our judgment require this conclusion include: the liberty of expression constitutionally assured in a matter of public interest, as the one here; the enduring public attention to the plaintiff's crime and prosecution, which remain an American cause célèbre; and the plaintiff's consequent and continuing status as a public figure.

Justice Ward dismissed Leopold's fury at the explicit sexuality the book contained and his contention that the book's fictionalizations were an "outrage to the community's notion of decency," by noting that "we consider that the fictionalized aspects of the book and motion picture were reasonably comparable to, or conceivable from facts of record from which they were drawn, or minor in offensiveness when viewed in the light of such facts." The indelicate materials that in 1924 had prompted Judge Caverly to order women out of the courtroom were now judged reasonable and could be made publicly available not only as facts but as extrapolations from known facts. Leopold had participated in a public event that was part of the "historical record. That conduct was without benefit of privacy."[53]

In effect, the final judgment in the *Compulsion* case removed the boundary between fact and fiction. Once an event or an individual became public and part of the historical record, "reasonable" fictionalizations of all sorts were permissible. Indeed, those fictionalizations could entirely recast the meanings of the initial record. Ironically, the very historicity of an event made it vulnerable to fictionalization. In many ways, Justice Ward merely confirmed what had long ago happened to Leopold and Loeb. "The story," one of Leopold's parole board members had noted, "is already a legend."[54]

The process of changing representation—which had first proposed that Nathan Leopold was a Nietzschean monster, had then used him and his partner to expose the dangers lurking in modern childhood and to explore the insights offered by psychology, and had ended in Levin's book with Leopold romping unclothed with Loeb in his fraternity room and raping his own girlfriend—was more than a public appropriation of private events. For Leopold, awaiting parole, it was a matter of personal self-awareness and of painful dependence on public opinion. Leopold's interest in Levin's book was profoundly "personal." At stake was his self-representation as he attempted to prove to the parole board, the governor, and the public that he merited release from prison because he was a "new man."

The first stage of this self re-creation required that Leopold sharply distance himself from his partner in crime, the boy he had loved, even revered, and heroized as a superman. ("I admired Richard Loeb extravagantly, beyond all bounds. I literally lived and died on his approval or disapproval.") That process began at a parole hearing on June 7, 1957, where Abel Brown, Leopold's former University of Chicago classmate, observed:

> There has been a great misconception about Leopold and Loeb in the minds of the public. In the minds of a good many people they have been thought of as one individual. That is not true. They were totally different as youngsters. Their life patterns have been totally different. Loeb was a leader, aggressive, crafty, smart. Leopold was definitely a follower. Loeb induced Leopold to make the tragic mistake of his life.

With Loeb dead and unable to speak for himself, Leopold and those who spoke for him began the final process of self-confession. Loeb was now made into the "master criminal" he had craved to become in his boyhood fantasies and the one who had been responsible for the deathblow. In the original court testimony, two defense psychiatrists had reported that Loeb admitted striking the blow, but that had hardly figured in the original case in which the boys and their two families had stood together and Leopold and Loeb had been tried as jointly responsible. Now, especially in view of Loeb's violent death, it became essential to make the distinction. Loeb became the villain, who had lured an innocent Leopold, *a quiet, studious, serious, very gentle boy,* to commit murder. And Gertz, Leopold's attorney, argued that Judge Caverly had confided in a nun who nursed him in his final illness "his impression that Leopold was completely under the domination of Loeb and would do whatever Loeb wanted." This was, of course, a complete inversion of the first public representations of Leopold.[55]

Having put the bloody chisel in Loeb's hand and the crime in his partner's mind, Leopold now began the difficult process of persuading the world that whatever he was as a child, innocent and gulled, as Brown portrayed him, or not, his older self had been rehabilitated. "Gentlemen," his lawyer argued in 1958,

> let me say this openly and without equivocation, Nathan Leopold is not now, and has not been since his imprisonment, a sexual deviate, or indeed, a sexual problem in any respect. The prison records will bear out, and the public should know it, that there is not the slightest evidence of any sexual impropriety on his part. Whatever his pre-prison infatuation for Loeb was, he completely outgrew it, and there was not the slightest tinge of homosexuality from the moment he entered prison to this very moment.[56]

With the sexual shroud lifted by his lawyer, Leopold then represented himself to the parole board. Prison had given him time to "regret bitterly, to repent fervently . . . the horrible crime of which Richard Loeb and I were guilty." "At nineteen my growth and developments were *unnatural* . . . my emotions were at least five years behind my thinking." Where the young Leopold had once preferred prison to being judged insane, he now freely accepted that he had once been "unnatural." Since then he had grown, matured, and learned that the only thing that helped him forget his crime was "to try to be useful to others." "I never had the philosophy of Nietzsche," he argued, and now he claimed, "I am a practicing, believing Jew." Leopold's parole representation thus reviewed the three issues that had been embedded in the case from its beginning—precocious childhood behavior, psychological abnormality, and sexuality. After thirty-three years in prison, Leopold, eager for parole, actively accepted the framework of definition that by the 1950s securely anchored the case. The three issues were packaged together and safely placed in the past. Leopold had "outgrown" his "infatuation" for Loeb and admitted that he had been an "unnatural" youth because his emotions were "five years behind his thinking." Leopold thus fully accepted the accusation of precocity, which had been important in the initial newspaper coverage of the case. Since he was now almost an old man, this admission was hardly explosive or, in the context of the late 1950s, threatening. In the fifties, teenagers seemed less intellectually precocious than immature and rowdy, and reading comic books, not Nietzsche, was the prevailing social bogeyman. In re-presenting himself, Leopold had renounced his sexual partner and his sexual past, outgrown the precocious child, and converted from abnormality to Judaism (a mainstream religion by the 1950s).[57]

Finally, and perhaps above all, Leopold now wanted completely to shun the limelight and to "find some quiet spot with some organization where I can live quietly and modestly in an attempt to atone for my crime, by service to others." "I want to get *lost,* want to get away from notoriety." In the attempt to re-create himself, Leopold knew that he somehow had to become purely personal again. His lawyer told Leopold that Carl Sandburg, who had testified at the hearing, said, "You were a struggler from the darkness into light. . . . You were transfigured." Leopold had taken himself from the other world of crime to the inner sanctum of social approval.[58]

Leopold had not only taken this new self before the parole board but had also labored for several years on a book, *Life plus 99 Years* (the title was based on the terms of his sentence), that described in detail his life in prison and how that new self had been created. In it Leopold lambasted Levin's book as 60 percent fiction and hurtful: "Mr. Levin accuses Judd Steiner of felonies I never dreamed of committing. He puts into Judd's mouth and very brain words and thoughts that were never in mine. Some make me blush; some make me want to weep." The book, he said, made him "physically sick." But in distancing himself from his own past, Leopold also made an interesting elision: "I hope—I know—that I am in no sense today the same person as that horrible, vicious, conceited, 'supersmart'—and pathetically stupid—Judd Steiner in the book. There's only one trouble. I share a memory with the monster; a memory, that is, covering those things that actually did happen." Having re-created himself in the present, he was forced to collapse his former self into Levin's fictionalized creation. In putting his past behind him and outside him, Leopold could not entirely distinguish it from the other selves that had been created around his crime.[59]

Leopold's book was mostly about his life in prison, where he had started and run an extremely successful correspondence school and participated in World War II malaria testing. The book started after the "crime of the century" was committed: "I am back on the evening of May 21, 1924. It is a little after nine o'clock. 'Well,' I said to myself, 'it's over. There's no turning back now. How on earth could I have got involved in this thing? It was horrible—more horrible even than I figured it was going to be. But that's behind me now.'" This bland beginning, lacking both insight and verisimilitude, was all Leopold wished to say, perhaps all he could say, about the crime and the earlier self that his prison experience, which fills most of the remaining 350 pages, had transformed. At the end of the memoir, Leopold portrays himself invoking "God's help in prayer. I shall pray for guidance and for strength. I shall pray for mercy and compassion. I shall pray for the wisdom and moral strength to justify by my conduct the rightness of the Board's decision, if it is favorable." Leopold had become a man who, publicly at least, accepted society's judgment of himself and his crime. As soon as the book appeared, it was sent to the parole board.[60]

Leopold claimed that "publicity has been my worst enemy for thirty-three years." Now, ironically, he needed just that publicity to lay his past to rest and to redeem himself from the public. Even before the publication of *Life plus 99 Years*, he had allowed John Bartlow Martin to write a series of articles about him for the *Saturday Evening Post* in which he was portrayed as a new man, a model prisoner, and a potentially valuable citizen. Before their publication as a book, his memoirs were serialized in the *Chicago Daily News*. He chose Erle Stanley Gardner (author of the Perry Mason mysteries) to write a preface.[61] By choosing Gardner for this task, Leopold completed, consciously or unconsciously (it is always difficult to tell with Leopold), a cycle of fact and fiction that had begun before the crime itself. For Richard Loeb, an avid reader of detective fiction, had constructed, over the course of more than six months in 1923–1924 and with the active cooperation of his friend, Nathan Leopold, a "perfect crime" on the basis of his reading of the crime genre.[62]

While "life itself" might be "a rotten writer of detective stories," as Leopold learned after thirty-three years in prison, real-life crimes and mysteries have been an irresistible source for writers of all kinds. Drawn to the unexplainable murder of a fourteen-year-old by two other teenagers (perhaps the crime was as banal as Leopold's remembrance), writers and directors such as Levin and Richard Fleischer in *Compulsion*, Alfred Hitchcock in *Rope*, and, most recently, Tom Kalin in *Swoon* have drawn and redrawn the figures and the story to suit their times, their needs, and their imaginations. Kalin, whose 1992 version of the case centers on the homosexual bond between the protagonists, observed, "The idea was to reframe the historical materials for a more modern reading of the case." As this history of "readings" of the case indicates, it has been repeatedly reframed, thereby becoming the vehicle for the merging of fact and fiction that Modris Eksteins identifies as the core of twentieth-century sensibility and the modernist aesthetic.[63]

"I am interested in the whole subject of juvenile delinquency, particularly as it relates to murder and crimes of violence," Erle Stanley Gardner observed in his introduction to Leopold's memoir. He thus suggested why the case of Leopold and Loeb was always more than just another 1920s murder case—an example of frenzied publicity and commonly packaged titillations. Almost from the beginning, the case had been read as an instance of the relationship between youth, crime, and sex and the new means, psychology, to understand and contain them. That combination, with juvenile delinquency as its specialized node, has kept the case alive throughout the twentieth century as the popular imagination participated in the new knowledge of the times.[64] Decisions made by the defense team stimulated that knowledge, but it was the newspapers that exploited it in a frantic combination of titillation and information. The initial spotlight provided by publicity locked the pair into the public world and, as we have seen, into a larger cultural discourse. Still quite fresh in the 1920s, even crude, explanations that were "scientific" had to compete with (and were sometimes conflated with) older moralizing standards. Spokesmen for the new scientific expertise were still suspect and derided even as they began to be paraded as public authorities. But just as the case of Leopold and Loeb was not left behind in the mere glare of twenties sensationalism, the insights it offered were not remaindered amid the rough beginnings of twenties discourse. Instead, the case and the themes it offered have continued to evolve throughout the twentieth century and to give meaning to human behavior. In providing new explanations and in feeding many forms of imagination, the case offered itself as a subject for twentieth-century popular culture. Over time, the themes of childhood, psychology, and sexuality gathered strength sufficient to make us (almost) forget that in 1924 Leopold and Loeb were two rich kids who tried to get away with murder.[65]

NOTES

This article was published in the *Journal of American History,* vol. 80, no. 3, December 1993, 919–951 and is reprinted here with permission.

1. See Hank Messick and Burt Goldblatt, *Kidnapping: The Illustrated History* (New York, 1974); Edward Dean Sullivan, *The Snatch Racket* (New York, 1932); and Paula S. Fass, *Kidnapped: Child Abduction in America* (New York: Oxford University Press, 1997), chapter 1.

2. This story is told compactly in Hal Higdon, *The Crime of the Century: The Leopold and Loeb Case* (New York, 1975), 34–38; and Maureen McKernan, *The Amazing Crime and Trial of Leopold and Loeb* (Chicago, 1924), 7–12. See also *Chicago Daily Tribune,* May 23, 1924, sec. 1, p. 2.

3. McKernan, *Amazing Crime and Trial of Leopold and Loeb,* 54; Nathan Leopold, *Life plus 99 Years* (Garden City, 1958). At his death, Nathan Leopold was credited with knowing twenty-seven languages; see *Chicago Daily Tribune,* Aug. 30, 1971, sec. 1, p. 7. For Leopold's famous bird piece, in which he describes the habits of a bird until then believed to be extinct, the Kirkland warbler, see *Chicago Herald and Examiner,* June 5, 1924, p. 3; ibid, June 7, 1924, p. 4; ibid., June 8, 1924, p. 2.

4. On women's interest in Richard Loeb, see *Chicago Daily Tribune,* June 4, sec. 1, p. 2. The perfect crime idea dogged Leopold until his death; see his obituary, *New York Times,* Aug. 31, 1971, p. 36.

5. For Alvin Goldstein and James Mulroy's role as described by the prosecution, see Alvin V. Sellers, *The Loeb–Leopold Case, with Excerpts from the Evidence of the Alienists and Including the Arguments to the Court by Counsel for the People and the Defense* (Brunswick, Ga., 1926), 81.

6. On sensational crimes and murders in the decade, see John R. Brazil, "Murder Trials, Murder, and Twenties America," *American Quarterly,* 33 (Summer 1981), 163–84; John D. Stevens, *Sensationalism and the Press* (New York, 1991), 103–54; and Charles Merz, "Bigger and Better Murders," *Harper's Monthly Magazine,* 155 (Aug. 1927), 338–43. Nelson Antrim Crawford, *The Ethics of Journalism* (New York, 1924), 110; "Leopold and Loeb," *New Statesman,* Sept. 20, 1924, p. 670; *Chicago Herald and Examiner,* Aug. 12, 1924, p. 3.

7. *Chicago Daily Tribune,* May 24, 1924, sec. 1, p. 1. Throughout the proceedings the prosecution continued to suggest that perversion was one aim of the killing. See Sellers, *Loeb–Leopold Case,* 247. For Judge John Caverly's warning to Robert Crowe, the chief prosecutor, see *Chicago Herald and Examiner,* Aug. 27, 1924, p. 1. See "Whispers 'Incredible Pact' between Boys," ibid., Aug. 5, 1924, p. 3.

8. See Paula S. Fass, *The Damned and the Beautiful: American Youth in the 1920s* (New York, 1977), 13–52. For contemporary comments, see *Chicago Herald and Examiner,* June 1, 1924, part 1, p. 4; Judge Ben B. Lindsey and Wainright Evans, *The Revolt of Modern Youth* (Garden City, N.Y., 1925).

9. *Chicago Herald and Examiner,* June 1, 1924, part 1, p. 3.

10. The centrality of the compact was William Healy's most important contribution to the trial. On his testimony, see ibid., Aug. 5, 1924, pp. 1–3; ibid., Aug. 6, 1924, pp. 1, 2.

11. *Chicago Daily Tribune,* May 31, 1924, sec. 1, p. 3; ibid., June 1, 1924, sec. 1, p. 1; ibid., May 31, 1924, sec. 1, p. 2.

12. For an account that accepts the superman ideal as the essential significance of the case, see Frederick Hoffman, *The Twenties: American Writing in the Postwar Decade* (New York, 1962), 362–63. Alfred Hitchcock similarly portrays the boys as eager to put their amoral philosophy and sense of superiority into practice. *Rope,* dir. Alfred Hitchcock (Warner Brothers, 1948). *Chicago Herald and Examiner,* June 12, 1924, p. 1; *Chicago Daily Tribune,* June 16, 1924, sec. 1, p. 9. Leopold later claimed that he was talking about the way he was questioned by the press; Leopold, *Life plus 99 Years,* 48–49.

13. *Chicago Herald and Examiner* June 1, 1924, p. 1. Crowe called the crime "the most atrocious, cruel, brutal, cowardly, dastardly murder in the history of American jurisprudence." See ibid., July 24, 1924, p. 3. For examples of physiological analysis, see ibid., June 4, 1924, p. 2; and ibid., June 7, 1924, p. 2. For the claim that the prosecution would heavily base its case on such photographic analysis, see ibid., July 21, 1924, p. 3. Ibid., June 1, 1924, p. 2. For the patently false statement that Loeb and Leopold had agreed that the latter had killed Bobby, although this issue remained very much in dispute between the two, see ibid., May 31, 1924, part 3, p. 2.

14. Leopold's responses are hard to assess because the papers reported such different things, including his supposed suicide in prison during the hearing. Ibid., Aug. 18, 1924, p. 1. Leopold claimed years later that he wanted to be hanged because it would be easier for the defendants and would release the families from the "humiliation and shame." Leopold, *Life plus 99 Years,* 78. *Chicago Sunday Tribune,* June 1, 1924, sec. 1, p. 1, emphasis added.

15. *Chicago Herald and Examiner,* May 28, 1924, p. 8; ibid., June 5, 1924, p. 3. On ennui, see ibid., June 1, 1924, p. 1; ibid., June 10, 1924, p. 2; ibid., Aug. 28, 1924, p. 8. In the twenties, modernism was often contrasted to morality and religious training. Thus, Chicago pastors used the Leopold and Loeb case to preach religion. See ibid., June 8, 1924, p. 4. It was probably because so much was made of their modern atheism that Leopold and Loeb's Jewishness was not stressed in the press. For changing perspectives on precocity in America between 1830 and 1930 and on how it was connected with social and personal disease, see Joseph F. Kett, "Curing the Disease of Precocity," in *Turning Points: Historical and Sociological Essays on the Family,* ed. John Demos and Sarane Spence Boocock (Chicago, 1978), 183–211. For Billy Sunday's remark, see *Chicago Herald and Examiner,* June 5, 1924, p. 3. In another place, the paper noted that "the end results of precocity are often perversion." Ibid. June 1, 1924, part 1, p. 3.

16. *Chicago Herald and Examiner,* July 30, 1924, p. 2; ibid., June 11, 1924, p. 6; Lindsey and Evans, *Revolt of Modern Youth,* 104. See also Ben Lindsey's comments in the *Chicago Daily Times,* June 8, 1924, sec. 1, p. 2.

17. On IQ testing in the 1920s, see Paula S. Fass, *Outside In: Minorities and the Transformation of American Education* (New York, 1989), 44–54, and above Chapter 2. For the radio poll, see *Chicago Daily Tribune,* July 17, 1924, sec. 1, p. 1; ibid., July 18, 1924, sec. 1, pp. 1, 2, 3; ibid., July 19, 1924, sec. 1, p. 3. See the questioning of men and women on the street by Arthur Brisbane on whether Leopold and Loeb should hang, *Chicago Herald and Examiner,* July 31, 1924, p. 1. For one of the IQ tests Leopold took, see ibid., Aug. 2, 1924, p. 2. For opinions on the verdict, see *Chicago Daily Tribune,* Sept. 11, 1924, sec. 1, pp. 3, 4.

18. *Chicago Herald and Examiner,* June 9, 1924, p. 2; McKernan, *Amazing Crime and Trial of Leopold and Loeb,* 72–73. On the phenomenon of newspapers seeking to help their readers identify with criminals, see Brazil, "Murder Trials." For contemporary analyses of the newspapers' role in crime, see Frances Fenton, "The Influence of Newspaper Presentations upon the Growth of Crime and Other Anti-Social Activity," *American Journal of Sociology,* 16 (Nov. 1910), 342–71; Frances Fenton, "The Influence of Newspaper Presentations upon the Growth of Crime and Other Anti-Social Activity (Continued)," ibid. (Jan. 1911), 538–76; Joseph L. Holmes, "Crime and the Press," *Journal of the American Institute of Criminal Law and Criminology,* 20 (May 1929), 6–59; Joseph L. Holmes, "Crime and the Press [Concluded from the Last Number]," ibid. (Aug. 1929), 246–93; Robert D. Highfill, "The Effect of News of Crime and Scandal upon Public Opinion," ibid., 17 (May 1926), 41–103. For a contemporary popular commentary, see Merz, "Bigger and Better Murders," 338–43.

19. Charles E. Rosenberg, *The Trial of the Assassin Guiteau: Psychiatry and Law in the Gilded Age* (Chicago, 1968). The case of Harry Thaw was sensationally covered in the press, but one newspaper critic noted, "No newspaper or magazine . . . published a sound, understandable explanation of the sexual psychopathy with which Thaw was and is afflicted, or discussed the means of guarding against the menace of this condition in human life." Crawford, *Ethics of Journalism,* 116. For the use of a psychological defense in the second trial, see John Holland Cassity, *The Quality of Murder: A Psychiatric and Legal Evaluation of Motives and Responsibilities Involved in the Plea of Insanity as Revealed in Outstanding Murder Cases of This Century* (New York, 1958), 34–36.

20. Sellers, *Loeb–Leopold Case,* 191; Richard Cantillon, *In Defense of the Fox: The Trial of William Edward Hickman* (Atlanta, 1972). For a discussion of the Hickman case, see Fass, *Kidnapped: Child Abduction in America,* 71–72. The Leopold and Loeb case occasioned wide discussion of the role of medical expertise in the law. For professional discussions, see William A. White, "The Need for Cooperation between the Legal Profession and the Psychiatrist in Dealing with the Crime Problem," *American Journal of Psychiatry,* 7 (Nov. 1927), 493–505; V. C. Branham, "The Reconciliation of the Legal and Psychiatric Viewpoints of Delinquency," *Journal of the American Institute of Criminal Law and Criminology,* 17 (Aug. 1926), 173–82; S. Sheldon Glueck, "Some Implications of the Leopold and Loeb Hearing in Mitigation," *Mental Hygiene,* 9 (July 1925), 449–68; "The Crime and Trial of Loeb and Leopold," editorial, *Journal of Abnormal Psychology and Social Psychology,* 19 (Oct. Dec. 1924), 221–29; and editorials and comments in *Journal of the American Institute of Criminal Law and Criminology,* 15 (Nov. 1924). For popular comments, see James J. Walsh, "Criminal Responsibility and the Medical Experts," *America,* Oct. 4, 1924, pp. 586–88; "Crime and the Expert," *Outlook,* Aug. 27, 1924, p. 626; George W. Kirchwey, "Old Law and New Understanding," *Survey,* Oct. 1, 1924, pp. 7–8, 64.

21. *Chicago Daily Tribune,* May 31, 1924, sec. 1, p. 1.

22. The newspapers repeatedly estimated the combined wealth of the three families involved. Initially one paper put it at around $25 million. *Chicago Herald and Examiner,* June 2, 1924, p. 2. Because of the fear that wealth would undermine justice, the fathers of the defendants issued a joint statement, promising, "In no event will the families of the accused boys use money in any attempt to defeat justice." Ibid., June 7, 1924, p. 1. This remained a loaded issue throughout the trial and after the sentencing. See the brief news reports from across the country in *Chicago Daily Tribune,* Sept. 11, 1924, sec. 1, p. 4; and "Rich and Poor Murderers," *Literary Digest,* Sept. 27, 1924, pp. 10–11.

23. *Chicago Herald and Examiner,* June 3, 1924, p. 2. Even before Leopold and Loeb were known to be the slayers, Jacob Franks noted that the slayers of his son had to have been insane. *Chicago Sunday Tribune,* June 1, 1924, part 1, p. 4. See also the huge headlines, "Slayers' Parents First Statement Bases All Hope on Insanity Plea," *Chicago Herald and Examiner,* June 7, 1924, p. 1. For discussions of the insanity defense, see ibid., June 4, 1924, p. 3; ibid, June 6, 1924, p. 2; ibid., June 7, 1924, p. 3; ibid, June 8, 1924, p. 2; ibid., June 9, 1924, p. 3.

24. The defense lawyers described their reasons for choosing this strategy in Clarence Darrow and Walter Bachrach, "Introduction," in McKernan, *Amazing Crime and Trial of Leopold and Loeb,* 3–5. For hostility to pleas of insanity, see, for example, *Chicago Herald and Examiner,* June 6, 1924, p. 2. This seems still to be the case; see Richard Moran, "Preface," *Annals of the American Academy of Political and Social Science,* 477 (Jan. 1985), 9–11.

25. Richard Moran, "The Modern Foundations for the Insanity Defense," *Annals of the American Academy of Political and Social Science,* 477 (Jan. 1985), 31–42; A. Moresby White, "Legal Insanity in Criminal Cases: Past, Present, Future," *Journal of the American Institute of Criminal Law and Criminology,* 18 (Aug. 1927), 165–74; Winfred Overholzer, "The Role of Psychiatry in the Administration of Criminal Justice," *Journal of the American Medical Association,* 93 (Sept. 14, 1929), 830–34. William Alanson White called responsibility, which underlies the idea of insanity, a "legal fiction," in his courtroom testimony. *Chicago Herald and Examiner,* Aug. 3, 1924, p. 2. For Clarence Darrow's remark and the defense statement, see Sellers, *Loeb–Leopold Case,* 93, 90–91. See Clarence Darrow, *Crime: Its Causes and Treatment* (New York, 1922). For the critiques of this view, see "Editorial Comment," *Catholic World,* 119 (July 1924), 546–51; and C. O. Weber, "Pseudo-Science and the Problem of Criminal Responsibility," *Journal of the American Institute of Criminal Law and Criminology,* 19 (Aug. 1928), 181–95.

26. For interviews with Chicago ministers, many of whom saw the case as a warning to parents and advocated more Bible study, see *Chicago Herald and Examiner,* June 9, 1924, p. 4. For an alienist who blamed "egoism," see ibid., June 10, 1924, p. 3. For professors' views, see ibid., June 9, 1924, p. 4; and ibid., June 10, 1924, p. 3. For psychiatrists' see ibid., June 11, 1924, p. 6.

27. Ibid., June 14, 1924, p. 1. For works by the defense experts, see, for example, William Healy, *The Practical Value of Scientific Study of Juvenile Delinquents* (Washington, 1922); William Healy with Augusta F. Bronner, *Delinquents and Criminals: Their Making and Unmaking* (New York, 1926); and Bernard Glueck, *Studies in Forensic Psychiatry* (Boston, 1916).

28. "All is referred back to the glands. They are the Alpha and Omega of personality." *Chicago Herald and Examiner,* June 18, 1924, p. 3.

29. *Chicago Daily Tribune,* July 28, 1924, sec. 1, p. 1. (There were separate reports on Leopold and on Loeb jointly written by Harold S. Hulbert and Karl M. Bowman and a psychiatrists' report to which they contributed. The two reports they wrote jointly were called the Hulbert-Bowman report.) For the report, see this issue generally. It was Maureen McKernan who used the term "unprintable." McKernan, *Amazing Crime and Trial of Leopold and Loeb,* 82.

30. *Chicago Daily Tribune,* July 28, 1924, sec. 1, p. 2; McKernan, *Amazing Crime and Trial of Leopold and Loeb,* 56, 108, 140. On references to "guiltless parents" and their "horrible suffering," in letters received by Judge Caverly, see *Chicago Herald and Examiner,* July 30, 1924, p. 2. For a contrasting view, see the interviews with a man in the street, ibid., July 31, 1924, p. 1. For a sympathetic portrait of Leopold's father, see ibid., Aug. 12, 1924, p. 3. On the fear of parent substitutes and the tendency to blame parents for relying on them, see Arthur Calhoun, *Social History of the American Family,* vol. III (Cleveland, 1919), 134–36. On Loeb and the teddy bear, see, for example, *Chicago Herald and Examiner,* Aug. 2, 1924, p. 2; and ibid, Aug. 4, 1924, p. 3, with picture.

31. *Chicago Herald and Examiner,* June 19, 1924, p. 9; ibid., June 15, 1924, part 1, p. 3; ibid., June 16, 1924, p. 4; ibid., June 16, 1924, p. 1. This same newspaper also announced that the doctors were measuring the pair's "vanity." Ibid., June 17, 1924, p. 1.

32. Ibid., Aug. 4, 1924, p. 3; ibid., June 9, 1924, p. 4.

33. *Chicago Daily Tribune,* June 5, 1924, sec. 1, p. 3; emphasis added. See "Psychiatrists' Report for the Defense (Joint Summary)," *Journal of the American Institute of Criminal Law and Criminology,* 15 (Nov. 1924), 370. Sellers, *Loeb–Leopold Case,* 157, 117; "Psychiatrists' Report for the Defense," 361, 362, 374.

34. "Psychiatrists' Report for the Defense," 366. For the cowboy fantasy, see ibid., 374. See also the photograph in *Chicago Herald and Examiner,* Aug. 6, 1924, p. 3. For contemporary criticism, see the editorial, "Crime and Trial of Loeb and Leopold," 223–29; and the response, Glueck, "Some Implications of the Leopold-Loeb Hearing," 448–68. For lessons drawn by psychiatric experts, see, for example, *Chicago Herald and Examiner,* June 3, 1924, p. 3; ibid., June 5, 1924, p. 2; ibid., July 25, 1924, p. 3.

35. *Chicago Daily Tribune,* Aug. 2, 1924, sec. 1, p. 1. Of Crowe's performance, the *New Statesman* concluded, "Of Mr. Crowe, the State's Attorney, perhaps the most charitable thing to say is that he provided the psychiatrists with a subject of study not much less interesting than Leopold and Loeb." "Leopold and Loeb," 670. "Crime and Trial," 226. Hearst offered to pay Sigmund Freud's one-half million dollars and his transatlantic transportation costs. Freud refused because, he said, he was too ill to travel. See *Chicago Herald and Examiner,* June 18, 1924, p. 3.

36. Sellers, *Loeb–Leopold Case,* 173; *Chicago Daily Tribune,* Aug. 6, 1924, sec. 1, p. 2.

37. McKernan, *Amazing Crime and Trial of Leopold and Loeb,* 142.

38. See Thomas W Salmon, "The Psychiatrist's Day in Court," *Survey,* Oct. 15, 1925, pp. 74–75; Branham, "Reconciliation of the Legal and Psychiatric Viewpoints," 173–82; and Clara Cushman, "Do Alienists Disagree?" *Mental Hygiene,* 13 (July 1929), 449–61. *Chicago Sunday Tribune,* magazine section, Aug. 17, 1924, part 5, p. 1.

39. "Leopold and Loeb," 669; S. Sheldon Glueck, *Mental Disorder and the Criminal Law: A Study in Medico-Sociological Jurisprudence* (Boston, 1925), xiii.

40. See, for example, *New York World,* Sept. 18, 1925, p. 3S.

41. For the growing normalization of heterosexuality in the early twentieth century, see Carroll Smith-Rosenberg, *Disorderly Conduct: Visions of Gender in Victorian America* (New York, 1985), 245–96. At Caverly's order, the women, including reporters, left. *Chicago Herald and Examiner,* Aug. 27, 1924, p. 2. For a reference to *folie à deux* by a defense psychiatrist, Bernard Glueck, see ibid., Aug. 4, 1924, p. 1. In his prison memoir, Leopold noted that when the "newspapers reported the proceedings, they did so in terms that misled a large part of the public: 'At this point the testimony became of such a nature as will not be reported in this paper,' and this would be followed by a whole row of asterisks. What a lot of sordid imaginings laid behind those asterisks." Leopold, *Life plus 99 Years,* 266–79.

42. *New York Times,* Jan. 29, 1936, p. 1; *Chicago Tribune,* Jan. 29, 1936, sec. 1, p. 2; *Los Angeles Times,* Jan. 29, 1936, p. 1. Day subsequently told other stories, including one in *True Detective Magazine* about a prison-break plot organized by Loeb. See Higdon, *Crime of the Century,* 291–303.

43. Leopold's motives in this denial are open to question since his amour propre might have been wounded or his sense of decorum offended by his heroized Loeb having any physical relationship with the insignificant Day. For Leopold's story of the death, see Leopold, *Life plus 99 Years,* 266–79.

44. *Chicago Tribune,* Jan. 31, 1936, sec. 1, p. 1; ibid., Feb. 1, 1936, p. 4. This paper also discusses a plot involving high levels of secret explosives. See ibid., Feb. 2, 1936, sec. 1, p. 7; ibid, Feb. 3, 1936, sec. 1, p. 4. *New York Times,* Jan. 29, 1936, p. 1; Higdon, *Crime of the Century,* 298.

45. "Last of Loeb," *Time,* Feb. 10, 1936, p. 15.

46. George Murray, *The Madhouse on Madison Street* (Chicago, 1965), 343, 344. The *Chicago Daily News* article did not even give Loeb's age at graduation, which was evidently made up by Murray. *Chicago Daily News,* June 29, 1936.

47. Meyer Levin, *Compulsion* (New York, 1955), ix.

48. See, for example, Genevieve Forbes Herrick, "Novel Based on Loeb–Leopold Case," *Chicago Sunday Tribune Magazine of Books,* Oct. 28, 1956, part 4, p. 2.

49. See the book by Leopold's parole counsel, Elmer Gertz, *A Handful of Clients* (Chicago, 1965), 6–110. Gertz also includes the best summary of Leopold's character dur-

ing those thirty-plus years: "Leopold was wise in the ways of prison." Ibid., 11. To get a sense of this wisdom, see John Bartlow Martin, "Murder on His Conscience, Part One," *Saturday Evening Post,* April 2, 1955, pp. 17–18, 86–88, 90; John Bartlow Martin, "Murder on His Conscience, Part Two," ibid., April 9, 1955, pp. 32–33, 65–66, 71–72; John Bartlow Martin, "Murder on His Conscience, Part Three," ibid., April 16, 1955, pp. 36, 198, 201–2; John Bartlow Martin, "Murder on His Conscience, Part Four"; ibid., April 23, 1955, pp. 28, 135–38. Gertz, *Handful of Clients,* 163. Carl Sandburg, several journalists, and other literary figures, including Erle Stanley Gardner, had appeared for Leopold or submitted statements on his behalf.

50. On the case, Leopold v. Levin, see Gertz, *Handful of Clients,* 150–92.

51. Gertz, *Handful of Clients,* 189–90. See *Chicago Tribune,* April 16, 1964, sec. 1A, p. 18.

52. Paul Birgiel, "Leopold v. Levin: Privacy 1970," *John Marshall Journal of Practice and Procedure,* 4 (Winter 1970), 143.

53. Leopold v. Levin, 45 Ill. 2d 434, 259 N.E. 2d 250, 252, 254, 255–56, emphasis added.

54. Gertz, *Handful of Clients,* 156.

55. On Leopold's admiration of Loeb, see Gertz, *Handful of Clients,* 98. Cf. Leopold, *Life plus 99 Years,* 270. For Abel Brown's statement, see Gertz, *Handful of Clients,* 16–17, esp. 17, emphasis added. Ibid. 56.

56. Gertz, *Handful of Clients,* 62–63.

57. *Chicago Herald and Examiner,* June 16, 1924, pp. 1, 2; Gertz, *Handful of Clients,* 98, 99, 100, 102; James Gilbert, *A Cycle of Outrage: America's Reaction to the Juvenile Delinquent in the 1950's* (New York, 1986).

58. Gertz, *Handful of Clients,* 101, 108.

59. Leopold, *Life plus 99 Years,* 370.

60. Ibid., 23, 381.

61. Gertz, *Handful of Clients,* 104; Martin, "Murder on His Conscience." Leopold had considered asking Levin to collaborate on his memoirs, before *Compulsion* was published. See Meyer Levin, *The Obsession* (New York, 1973), 106–13; Leopold, *Life plus 99 Years,* 367–68.

62. When the discovery of Bobby's body was reported in the press, in the first notice of the case, the *Chicago Daily Tribune* reported that the kidnap note resembled a similar note in a recent *Detective Story* magazine. *Chicago Daily Tribune,* May 24, 1924, sec. 1, p. 2.

63. *Compulsion,* dir. Richard Fleischer (Twentieth-Century Fox, 1959); *Rope; Swoon,* dir. Tom Kalin (Fine Line Features, 1992). For an interview with Tom Kalin, see *Boston Globe,* Oct. 25, 1992, sec. B, p. 2. Modris Eksteins, *Rites of Spring: The Great War and the Birth of the Modern Age* (New York, 1989), 4.

64. Erle Stanley Gardner, "Preface," in Leopold, *Life plus 99 Years,* 15. Production of the vast literature on juvenile delinquency began just before the 1920s. During the twenties, it was decidedly psychological. See, for example, Healy, *Practical Value of Scientific Study of Juvenile Delinquents;* Healy and Bronner, *Delinquents and Criminals;* Cyril Burt, *The Young Delinquent* (New York, 1925); John Slawson, *The Delinquent Boy: A Socio-Psychological Study* (Boston, 1926); William Healy and Augusta F. Bronner, *New Light on Delinquency and Its Treatment* (New Haven, 1936); Henry W. Thurston, *Concerning Juvenile Delinquency* (New York, 1942). In the 1920s, Healy was the most widely recognized authority on juvenile delinquency. Later Sheldon Glueck, who often collaborated with Eleanor Glueck, became the best-known authority. See, for example, Sheldon Glueck and Eleanor Glueck, *Delinquents in the Making: Paths to Prevention* (New York, 1952). Sheldon was Bernard Glueck's brother. Thus, two leading twentieth-century authorities on delinquency had a relation to the Leopold and Loeb case.

65. This paper was prepared during a year in residence as a fellow at the Center for Advanced Study in the Behavioral Sciences in 1991–1992. For financial support during that year, I am very grateful to the National Endowment for the Humanities (#RA-20017-88), the Andrew W. Mellon Foundation, and the University of California at Berkeley Humanities Research Committee. Several of my colleagues at the center offered valuable suggestions: Daniel Rodgers and Gert Brieger, who kindly read an early draft; Peter Novick,

Sissela Bok, and Ming Tsuang, with whom I had extremely important conversations; and Carol Baxter, who both read it with care and helped me set it up on the computer. I would also like to thank my Berkeley colleagues and students, especially Robin Einhorn, Jack Lesch, and Oz Frankel for their inspired readings; Eric Weisbard for extraordinary work as my research assistant. A. Russell Maylone at Library Special Collections, Northwestern University, provided valuable assistance. My thanks also to David Thelen, Susan Armeny, and Meg Meneghel (at the *Journal of American History*), who made it better in important ways.

5

A Sign of Family Disorder?

Changing Representations of Parental Kidnapping

In the summer of 1873, "a gentleman of high social position" in Williamstown, New York, hired a "fast livery team" and carried off both his children. He presumably fled with them to Europe, since as "a man of means," he would "spare no money to cover up the trail." Although the courts had given this man, a Mr. Neil, custody of one his daughters in the "decree of separation on the ground of incompatibility of temperament," the other daughter, whom he also took with him, had been awarded to his wife, who now suffered "fearfully over the theft."[1] Recorded in the *New York Times* 128 years ago, Mr. Neil's abduction of his daughter was an example of what is known today as parental kidnapping. That episode and others like it, while unusual and newsworthy, were hardly unknown more than a century ago because then, as today, husbands and wives fought over the custody of their children. And children were even then pawns in an uncertain legal struggle among the mother, the father, and the state.[2]

An especially vivid glimpse of the parental tug-of-war over a child took place in New York in 1879 when Henry Coolidge and his former wife Belthiede were found quarreling on West Sixteenth Street in Manhattan over possession of their daughter. "The woman had the child by one arm and the man by the other arm and they were pulling the little girl hither and thither." Pending the outcome of the divorce instituted by Henry, the judge had ordered one of their daughters to be placed in the custody of the maternal grandmother and the other with a friend of the family. Henry had taken the older girl from the grandmother's house, "ostensibly for a walk," but he had not returned her. The mother, with the assistance of her own father had retaken the girl and had just met Coolidge on the street where he attempted once again to take the child. This was the background for the little drama that was enacted on the street in New York.

When brought before the local magistrate, Coolidge did not deny his wife's story, but noted that he was rescuing his daughter from being subjected to "immoral influences," a charge strenuously denied by Mrs. Coolidge and her mother. The judge ordered the child returned in accordance with the original determination of temporary custody.[3]

For the Coolidges and for many divorcing couples in the nineteenth century, the court had rendered a judgment that at least one of the contending parties found painful, harmful, or unjust, and it led to personal attempts to correct the situation. As with the Coolidges too, many cases involved extended kin who became actively involved in the dispute over the children. Then as now, the cost of these disputes was often best expressed in the striking visual image of "pulling the little girl hither and thither."

These two episodes from the 1870s are an important reminder that the kidnapping of children by their parents or other family members is not a new social experience. Indeed, few of the essential *human* elements have changed very much in the more than 100 years since the Coolidges struggled over their daughter on a New York street. Certain issues have changed however. Two are of primary significance: In sheer numbers, these abductions have increased together with the enormous rise in divorce. And they have been given a dramatic new public prominence and visibility as the public lamentations over the state of the family and its trustworthiness as a source of child welfare has grown. These two issues are obviously related to each other, but that relationship is not simple. On the contrary, in this chapter I will suggest that parental kidnapping, as the most extreme instance of individual family disorder and one of its most hostile expressions has, over the last twenty-five years, been portrayed as an ominous social problem because of its symbolic power as a sign of the erosion of contemporary family life. Indeed, in the past twenty-five years the horror that has been associated with child kidnapping has become an effective means to dramatize the extreme disintegration which is presumed now to characterize much of family life in the United States, and increasingly elsewhere in the Western world. During the decade of the 1990s, parental kidnapping has also been used seriously to question the intrusive and insensitive role of the state in regulating family relationships. Thus parental kidnapping is both a real experience and a form of cultural representation which gives us a revealing glimpse of how divorce, custody, and child abuse issues have come together in the vivid portrayal of the "new" crime of parental kidnapping. As the following pages will show, parental kidnapping has literally come to haunt a culture caught in a paralyzing vision of family disintegration, gender conflict, and judicial incompetence.

In 1993, a federal appeals court in Richmond, Virginia, ruled that a natural mother was exempt from federal kidnap law (the Lindbergh Act). In this case, a woman, with the aid of two friends had tied, gagged, roughed up, and robbed her children's foster parents, and then abducted the children from their new home in Missouri. In excluding the mother alone (the others had already been sentenced to prison), the justices noted that the Lindbergh Act exempted parents from the crime of kidnapping. The ruling further asserted that the state court could "not alter the identity of a biological parent," even though it could end a parents' right to custody. The case suggests some of the legal complications implicit in the very concept of parental kidnapping.[4]

The Lindbergh Act was the first federal kidnapping legislation in the United States, but its predecessors both in England and the American states had also excluded parents either entirely or from the full force of kidnapping penalties. In England, the first legislation, "An Act for the More Effectual Prevention of Child Stealing," enacted in 1814 specifically *excluded* "any Person who shall have claimed to be the Father of an illegitimate Child," effectively excluding all natural or legal fathers from kidnapping. Since the law declared that the child was being stolen to "deprive its Parent or Parents . . . of the Possession of such Child," it presumed that fathers of legitimate children could not possibly be violators since a father could not steal what was already his. The updated Act of 1892 excluded all those "claiming in good faith a right to the possession of the child," thus bringing mothers under the protective umbrella, commensurate with their newly gained status as potential custodians. The law effectively remained the same until the 1980s, when the Child Abduction Act of 1984 made it an offense for a parent or guardian given custody to remove a child from Great Britain without appropriate legal consent, or for a person not having custody or guardianship to take such a child or "to keep him out of lawful control of any person entitled to his control." This updated vision of custody, as we shall see, corresponded to a growing recognition in the West of the explosive possibilities of child custody cum kidnapping offenses. The English Custody Act of 1985 brought English law into compliance with new protocols in international custody disputes.[5]

In the United States, through most of the nineteenth century, case law had evolved erratically concerning parental kidnapping by drawing upon the English common law definition of kidnapping—the forcible carrying of a child to another location (initially out of the country) without consent. In a Massachusetts case of 1862, the court ruled that "A child of the age of nine years is incapable of giving a valid assent to a forcible transfer of him by a stranger from the legal custody of his father to the custody of his mother, who had no right thereto; and evidence of such assent is incompetent in defense to an indictment of an assault and battery upon him in making such transfer." In another case, the theft of a four-year-old by his father was defined as "unlawfully and forcibly carrying the child out of the state," in accordance with the kidnapping definition. But in Georgia, in 1894, the court ruled that "A father cannot be charged with kidnapping his minor child, where he has not parted with his parental right to its custody." And in Kansas in 1889, the court ruled that even a third party "who assists a mother in leaving her husband and taking away the infant child of herself and husband is *not guilty* of kidnapping, since she is as much entitled to the custody of the child as its father." In these last cases, both parents were absolved of guilt in child stealing. But these rulings, like their enforcement in the nineteenth century, were vague, erratic, and changeable.[6]

Starting in the early twentieth century, as more and more state legislatures began to institute or beef up laws against kidnapping, they often found it necessary specifically to distinguish abductions perpetrated by strangers from those by parents. In so doing, they sometimes also instituted punishments for parental kidnappings. When in 1911 New York specifically exempted parents from the newly harsh penalties called for in kidnap legislation (though they were not entirely excluded from all penalty), one legislator noted that it was "pretty generally recognized that there are extenuating circumstances where, through affection and love, a parent tries to get possession of his child." This view reflected the dominant contemporary perspective on children as priceless emotional assets rather than possessions or investments, and assumed that parental action was ultimately based on affection. And for a long time, both social attitudes and criminal justice proceedings reflected this belief. Just as nineteenth-century English law assumed that no father could steal what was already his, most American courts and police throughout most of the twentieth assumed that parental kidnapping bespoke an act of love, which could hardly be a serious crime.[7]

The distinction between kidnapping by strangers and parents begun in state laws at the beginning of the century and subsequently enshrined (by excluding parents) in the federal statutes of the 1930s remained in place until the 1970s and 1980s when, as we shall see, the astronomical increase in divorce and the resulting custody and jurisdictional disputes projected parental kidnapping into the center of a much larger public discourse over family breakdown. That discourse eroded the sharp boundaries between parental and stranger kidnapping earlier put in place. The strong move to criminalize parental kidnapping in the 1980s marked a new public posture toward family life. Until then, while the courts could intrude in extreme detail in the relations between parents and children as families exposed themselves to state supervision through breakup, parental kidnapping remained largely a social rather than a legal issue.

Parental Kidnapping in the First Half of the Twentieth Century

In the first decades of the twentieth century, the divorce rate had already begun the rise that would accelerate rapidly with the unfolding century. And that rise naturally increased the momentum for aggrieved parents to attempt to resolve custody disputes and unhappiness over custody decrees through child snatching. Besides the sharp rise in divorce, perhaps the most notable social change to influence parental kidnapping was the introduction of the automobile. Just as the automobile put the lives of young children, especially in the cities, at risk generally, it increased the risk to children of feuding, separated, or divorced parents to abduction. Starting in the early twentieth century children were whisked away, sometimes within sight of their other parent, in an automobile. "Boy Spirited Away by Five Men in Auto," read one headline that recounted a parental abduction; "Boy Kidnapped by Woman in Auto," read another.[8]

Despite the potential for suffering by parents and children involved in these events, newspapers adopted a tone of amusement when they described parental kidnappings. Thus, when nine-year-old Dean McLaughlin was abducted in an automobile, the New York Times observed that "The boy has been kidnapped so many times by his father and his mother that he appears to be enjoying the experience." This attitude prevailed even though the abductions were deadly serious for the parents and sometimes involved physical force or the use of threatening weapons. In abducting Beverly Lorraine Whitgreave, eighteen months of age and great-granddaughter of a local Chicago hero, the mother was reported by the Chicago Tribune to have announced: "I've come for my baby. . . . I've got a revolver and I'll kill you if you don't give her up." This was the fourth time that the baby had been kidnapped. "The first time she was taken by her father, the second time by her mother, and the last time by her father." Even this phrasing in the New York Times turned the experience into a game or contest.[9]

The view of parental snatchings as somehow part of the droll battle between the sexes of a drawing room comedy was exaggerated in the 1920s and 1930s by the fact that most of the news stories involved custody disputes among the socially prominent. In the late nineteenth century, and to some extent even in the early twentieth, the domestic disputes of poorer folks also made news, and children were reported as abducted even in the absence of divorce decrees, a situation that prevailed among the poor. After the First World War, the press largely restricted its coverage of these issues to the rich. Through the peephole of parental abduction, the public could enter into the unsavory domestic affairs of the socially prominent who were thereby shown to be in no way morally superior. As a result of this selective coverage parental kidnapping was portrayed as unusual rather than ordinary, and appeared to be mostly confined to those whose lives were in all ways exceptional and morally suspect. The public representations of the problem of parental abductions thus gave the impression that parental kidnapping was hardly a general social problem. When, in the 1970s and 1980s, the media shifted its vision to dramatically report on the prevalence of parental abductions among all classes and in escalating numbers fed by increased divorce, the phenomenon seemed new and unprecedented. In fact, parental abductions have been firmly a feature of twentieth-century domestic relations among all classes, with deep roots in the nineteenth-century.

The San Francisco press riveted the attention of its readers in the mid-1920s with the exploits of the fantastically beautiful socialite, Milo Abercrombie Swenson, whom Charles Dana Gibson had called "one of the most beautiful girls in America." The dissolution of Milo's second marriage to Navy Lieutenant Lyman Knute Swenson in 1925 led to a tangled and extended controversy over the visitation rights Swenson had to his two children and eventually to Milo losing custody of the children. In 1929, rather than surrender custody, Milo disappeared with her children. Similarly, in 1924 newspapers in the Midwest were full of the abduction by oil and real-estate magnate Charles Bliss of his son from the Chicago hotel room of his beautiful opera star wife, Beryl Brown Bliss. In these headline-grabbing cases certain features of the controversy stood out. Above all, parents who kidnapped their children often accused the other parent of gross misconduct, especially sexual impropriety. In the Swenson case, Milo accused her husband of sexually molesting her four-year-old daughter Cecelia, while Charles Bliss accused his wife of being too "modern" and caring more for her career than for a settled family life. When Josephine Sullivan Kieffer snatched her daughter from her husband, a prominent New York attorney with a Harvard and Rhodes-scholar pedigree, she not only accused him of infidelity, but noted that he "neglected and has at times slapped, beaten and otherwise abused the said child." The Swensons, Blisses, and Kieffers had each found just the right lever to push in their contentious quarrels over custody. The kidnapping of their children was an extension of those quarrels.[10]

Impugning the reputation of the opposing party was only one of the means used in custody battles that could serve to legitimate kidnappings and attempts to reverse custody decisions. The other tactic was to use the power that came from divergent jurisdictions. When Charles Bliss kidnapped his son from his wife's hotel room in Chicago, he took him back to Tulsa, Oklahoma. Bliss's possession of the child in Tulsa helped him to obtain temporary custody of his son. The judge allowed him to keep Charles, Jr., in "the jurisdiction of the Tulsa county court until after a settlement of the divorce case." Having the child within the jurisdiction of one of the contending parties often resulted in at least temporary orders acknowledging that parent's right. In this context, it was not uncommon for the other parents to attempt to rekidnap a child and thereby achieve a legal victory in another jurisdiction. Because custody came within the exclusive jurisdiction of each state, the courts were quite impotent beyond their own borders, and conflicting orders were often in place.[11]

A New Perspective and New Laws

Fifty years later, the domestic issues in parental kidnapping had changed very little, but the public problem and its representation had been utterly transformed. The source of society sensations had become the democratic "Agony of the 80s," in the words of USA Today, and parental kidnapping was often described as an epidemic—a rapidly spreading and terrifying illness of the society. Newspapers, women's magazines, and news journals, as well as novels and personal memoirs focused on the problem and gave it extensive popular exposure. Parents who had lost their children testified in the press and at congressional hearings and told their stories on television talk shows. Americans still occasionally learned about the snatches of the rich and famous, but these had receded in the enormous waves of the perceived problem. Starting in the 1970s the media portrayed the painful experiences of middle Americans, and purveyed statistics which defined parental kidnapping as a problem for thousands, even hundreds of thousands of families. The new profile of the kidnapping family was composed not of the society swells and their beautiful but unconventional wives, but of ordinary people whose lives were seared when their spouses or former spouses kidnapped their children. Precisely because it was so ordinary, parental kidnapping suggested that even families that seemed normal might hide some deep pathology.[12]

Certainly, the dimensions of the phenomenon had changed. Although we have no figures for parental abductions in the nineteenth century (or for most of the twentieth century either), the breathtaking increase in divorce, and especially of divorce where children were involved after 1960, created a vastly larger potential for abductions. And just as the automobile had changed abductions in the early twentieth century, the democratization of plane travel in the period after the 1960s made escape to other states and even to foreign countries accessible to more than the rich.

Initially, indeed, it was this new mobility and its potential for jurisdictional disputes in custody that rang the alarm bells and called for action. Snatching seemed to be a by-product of jurisdictional shopping, as a disaffected parent, unhappy with the custody ruling in one state, took the child to another where he was granted custody in the absence of the other parent. With an appropriate court order, the parent could feel himself or herself comfortably in compliance with the law. Although the child had been snatched, the custody decree in a new jurisdiction seemed to legitimize the action. And if shopping for custody was the problem, the remedy seemed simple—a stricter enforcement of the initial decree and compliance by sister states. In fact, rationalizing custody procedures was not simple, since the Supreme Court imposed the full faith and credit clause of the United States Constitution only to a limited degree to custody cases, and because state courts, according to an expert observer, "believed strongly that flexibility was necessary to best protect children's interests."[13]

Throughout the 1970s, much attention and energy, both in the popular media and among legal experts, was directed to enforcing custody decrees across state lines, and most discussion took as its objective the enactment by the fifty states of the model laws proposed in the Uniform Child Custody Jurisdiction Act (UCCJA), which was not a law but a voluntary agreement to which states could subscribe. Initially approved by the National Conference of Commissions on Uniform State Laws in 1968, by the mid-1980s almost all the states had subscribed to the agreement.[14]

It soon became apparent that the UCCJA was not the solution many had foreseen. Although reliable statistics about the problem were still not available, the publicity surrounding parental kidnapping remained clamorous and the problem seemed far from solved. In part because many parents abducted their children before any custody order was in place (as they always had); in part because communications and enforcement between states was slipshod; in part because police were not eager to be bothered by what they saw as "domestic disputes," the new state agreements on mutual enforcement seemed to have only a marginal impact on the perceived incidence of the problem or the sense of social malfunction caused by that perception.

In 1980, in response to growing media attention, the federal government finally took note of the problem, and with much fanfare and publicity, Congress passed, and President Jimmy Carter signed, the Parental Kidnapping

Prevention Act (PKPA). The PKPA did not reverse the protection offered to parents by the Lindbergh Act, and did not make parental kidnapping a federal offense. The new law was intended to enhance the UCCJA, by requiring states to give full faith and credit to custody decrees of other states, and made the Federal Parent Locator Service available to parents trying to find their children. It also facilitated the work of state and local agencies in enforcing their own parental kidnapping laws. Throughout the period of the 1970s and 1980s, states were enacting legislation that made parental kidnapping a criminal offense. Although these laws differed among themselves, with some states defining parental abductions as felonies and others merely as misdemeanors, by 1991, every state and the District of Columbia had a criminal statute prohibiting parental kidnapping.[15]

In 1982 and 1984, the federal government increased its role in parental kidnapping cases (and other forms of child disappearance) by passing the Missing Children's Act and the Missing Children's Assistance Act. Both provided informational and material assistance to parents and local governments in their attempts to locate children. These acts also, for the first time, made the FBI available as a resource of information. By 1984, the federal government had authorized the establishment of a national clearinghouse for information about missing children and a toll free hot line for reporting abductions. The United States had also been instrumental in negotiating the Hague Convention on the Civil Aspects of International Child Abduction, and became in 1988 one of only a handful of signatories who voluntarily agreed to surrender children brought into their jurisdiction in international custody disputes. Throughout the 1980s, therefore, the federal government had taken note of and responded to the growing sense of alarm about parental kidnapping.[16]

In good part, federal action was a response to an already flourishing grassroots movement of private self-help agencies, like Child Find and Children's Rights, Inc., which offered information and tools to help parents locate children lost to all kinds of abductions and mischance. Hardly an article, pamphlet, or book published on the subject in the last twenty-five years failed to give parents advice on how to respond in the event that they had a child snatched or how to prevent such a snatching. Parents were often urged to seek assistance from these private organizations. A substantial part of the federal response was also the result of the fact that these organizations had mobilized public opinion and congressional action by conflating the problem of parental kidnapping with that of stranger abduction as they dedicated themselves to finding abducted children of all kinds. In so doing they had increased the sense of alarm and fear associated with parental snatching by blending it with the even more frightening forms of stranger abductions. The federal government had now added another layer to a burgeoning industry based in a deeply rooted network of information and alarm. In addition to the work of these organizations and their spokespeople and in part as a result of the attention they drew to the problem, throughout the 1970s and '80s popular news journals, as well as women's and parents' magazines were full of haunting pictures of children stolen from and presumably forever lost to their parents, together with searing stories of their parents' anguish. Altogether, private organizations, federal and state laws, and the media had turned parental kidnapping into a major public problem.[17]

Parental Kidnapping and the Social Agendas of the 1970s, '80s, and '90s

As parental kidnapping became widely denominated as a serious social problem it became part of other contemporary agendas, especially the feminist critique of the family and its patriarchal social supports. The question of child custody had always been deeply a woman's issue. Since the last half of the nineteenth century, unless they were judged unfit or they were incapable of caring for them, women were considered the proper custodians of their children. By the 1980s, however, the widespread commitment to granting mothers custody of their children except when unfit had faded with older stereotypes of women as most states replaced earlier presumptions in favor of maternal custody with a gender-neutral standard. By then, thirty-seven states had adopted rules which facilitated the adoption of joint custody in child dispositions. Even though the original feminist agenda helped to underwrite changes in custodial determinations that stressed greater paternal involvement, women increasingly saw the difficulties for themselves and the conflicts for their children that resulted from the need to continue negotiating with former spouses in matters concerning their children. Less immediately apparent, but just as significant for parental kidnapping, was the fact that joint custody often rendered new laws concerning parental abduction inoperative. As a 1989 Justice Department pamphlet to parents observed, "Ironically the increased use of joint or shared custody—often pursuant to newer State statutes establishing a legislative preference for joint custody arrangement—has had the unintended side effect of hindering successful prosecution of some parental kidnapping cases. . . . in several cases . . . defendants have successfully argued that an accused parent cannot, by virtue of his or her joint custodial rights, be guilty of criminal custodial interference."[18]

Because it was portrayed as the most dramatic manifestation of the destabilization of the American family and as an index of family disorder, parental kidnapping rapidly became laced into almost every conceivable issue related to the contemporary family, from child custody to wife battering and sexual abuse. And it became a kind of talisman of contemporary anxiety about the family. By the 1980s, what had been in the 1920s and 1930s a window on other people's misbehavior and figured in a psychology of *schadenfreude,* became an index of social pathology and a reflection of the state of the family itself.

The issue which even as recently as the 1970s seemed a simple matter of getting states to comply with the custody decrees of other states became ever less simple and clear. What had once had a straightforward objective—returning the child to its custodial parent—became in the 1990s deeply contested. Indeed, as the state became an object of suspicion, public sympathy often turned to parents who kidnapped their children in order to rescue them from conditions where they were exposed to sexual abuse or physical neglect, situations in which the state had placed them when it granted custody or visitation rights to the other parent. That basis for snatching was not new. As we have seen, earlier in the century Milo Abercrombie and Josephine Sullivan Kieffer abducted children from situations they believed to be abusive. By the 1990s, however, these abductions were supported by an underground network which thrived on images of widespread family dysfunction. By then, too, the government's role, initially sought after, became much murkier and problematic especially as the federal government became more visibly involved. A bureaucratic and rule-driven government which seemed once to provide solutions to a problem of national dimensions seemed ever more distant and impersonal. As a government pamphlet noted, "Parental kidnapping is not the right answer; but it is an answer to which many parents resort in desperation. To the degree that judges and law enforcement officials can pay closer attention to parents with serious and apparently well-grounded fears for the physical, mental, and emotional well being of their children, one important part of the overall parental kidnapping problem may be eliminated at its source." The issue had come full circle as the officials became not the saviors but suspects in the problem.[19]

In the 1990s, as the state and government at all levels came in for increasingly harsh scrutiny, the state's role as an arbiter of family feelings and relationships became ever more suspect. Thus, ironically, just at the time when the family was viewed as unstable and pathological, the state, too, was increasingly seen as incompetent to come to the rescue of children.

Personal Kidnap Narratives:
The Heroic Mode in a Democratic Society

Parental kidnapping in the last twenty-five years has been defined and articulated as a social pathology through a huge and variegated literature and media presentations. These include news reports, expert social science analyses, and conference reports; novels and television programs based on true stories and fictions; and personal snatch narratives. Together, these forms of popular and expert testimony have defined parental abduction as a massive problem and as a measure of family change and dysfunction.[20]

Probably the most socially revealing of these forms are the snatch narratives. These are witness to the unique combination of the common and the extraordinary which has come to define the public representation of parental kidnapping as a contemporary experience. The narratives testify to the stunning, even heroic, experiences of ordinary people as their lives are transformed by the loss of a child and propelled into articulation. The experience of child loss creates the need to share with other victims and potential victims the understanding, techniques, and personal wisdom gained from this experience.

The narratives are based on the assumption that the problem is widespread because family breakup is a familiar part of the social landscape. Where parental kidnap narratives end with the child successfully recaptured, they usually close with the healing provided by a new family created out of the painful death of the old. Thus, the typical parental kidnapping narrative is the memoir not only of wrenching loss and victimization, but of family disenchantment and a new dependence on alternative family forms, usually involving extended kin and often a new mate. Parental kidnapping narratives thus testify to the decline of the conventional family and propose that the family changes of the 1970s and 1980s are healthful and therapeutic.

The personal narrative is a variation and extension of the human interest stories developed in many magazines in the 1970s and 1980s to publicize the phenomenon of parental kidnapping. "It was a cool evening in March 1977 when Robin Reiss, her parents and two-and-a-half-year-old son, Kevin, walked away from a friendly diner in Brooklyn, N.Y.," one such article in the *Ladies Home Journal* began. "The boy was giggling when Robin felt her grip on his hand suddenly tighten. It was at that moment that a horrible, ongoing nightmare began. From across the street, six burly thugs were sprinting toward her family. . . . Kevin screamed 'Mama,' and Robin saw the toddler reaching his arms toward her before she was blinded and silenced by a faceful of burning mace." Here the violent abduction on the father's behalf plays on, and the article specifically alludes to, fears about stranger abductions as it attempts to create an emotional equivalence between the two. The authors, Sally Abrahms and Joseph Bell, go on to tell several similar stories, and later expanded their efforts in a book. This article, like many others, escalates the level of terribleness with each successive segment, selectively choosing the most harrowing details and combining them into a tale of horror.[21]

Individual narratives like that of Eileen Crowley in *Good Housekeeping* usually began much less dramatically than that of Abrahms and Bell. The problems began for Crowley two years after her divorce, when her daughter, Robyn, did not return after an ordinary visit with her father. Crowley recounts her problems with the authorities who did not want to get involved in "a domestic matter." She hires lawyers and detectives, the usual devises of stunned parents. None of these legal means work. Neither do *habeas corpus* writs and court orders. Friends and family provide support, assistance, and comfort. The child, as in most such narratives, is eventually found through a happy coincidence, almost never through the work of law enforcement agencies. In Crowley's case, "on Friday, June 4, 1982 [seven years after the abduction], I received a letter from an old friend on Long Island. 'Yesterday I heard a girl yell out 'Robyn,' . . . I turned around and saw a miniature you as I remember you from our childhood together." Crowley and her new husband immediately make plans to retrieve the girl, now almost twelve years old. Crowley, her husband and their son, together with Robyn now form a new kind of family. There are brief problems of adjustment, but the story ends happily: "Mommy, I love you."[22]

Crowley's story reflects the general pattern of such accounts—loss, a desperate search, the help of kin and friends, the impotence and incompetence of authorities, a new family, and then an almost miraculous reunion. But while Crowley obviously blames her former husband for the loss of her child, she does not characterize him as anything more than a snatcher. Other narratives develop the evil and vindictive possibilities of the snatching husband in great detail.[23]

As the alarum over parental kidnapping increased in the late 1970s and early 1980s, this theme of parental selfishness came to the fore. Traditionally, the legal distinction between stranger abductions and parental kidnapping hinged on the belief that parents stole their children out of love. As part of the effort to paint parental kidnapping as a real crime, many of the arguments used by participants and activists in the evolving public discourse and in the personal narratives began to paint a very different picture, not of a loving parent, but of a vindictive husband who kidnapped his children in order to punish his former wife. Since this was the period in which the women's movement peaked, this portrayal dovetailed with feminist pictures of family dynamics. In a *Ms* magazine article, abducting mothers were almost completely ignored as Lindsy Van Gelder concluded that "many of the abducting fathers are newly spurned husbands, reacting to the news that their wives want a divorce." Van Gelder used parental kidnapping to attack "the myth that the cornerstone of American life and law is 'the sanctity of the family,'" arguing instead that the family was balanced on women's pain and that the law was not available to women. "In the course of researching this article I found one case in which the law *voluntarily* went after a child-snatcher: here the offender was a *woman*." Similarly, Adrienne Rich's introduction to Anna Demeter's *Legal Kidnapping* turns the story into a feminist exposé. "The mother-child relationship can be seen as the first relationship violated by patriarchy. Mother and child, as objects of possession by the fathers, are reduced to pieces of property and to relationships in which men can feel in control, powerful, wherever else they feel impotent." Rich argues that "legally, economically, and through unwritten sanctions, including the unlegislated male-bonding network documented in this book, the mother and child live under male control although males assume a minimal direct responsibility for children." Thus, the snatch narratives that gave a dramatic face to the most extreme kinds of family disintegration in this period, incorporated many of that period's most challenging issues.[24]

Whether the tales have a feminist twist or not, most of the snatch narratives describe the snatcher as emotionally unstable and depict children as painfully exposed to the brutality that results from parental selfishness. *Child Snatched: The Danny Strickland Story* by Margaret Strickland provides a homey account of one family's experiences which poignantly exposes the pathological possibilities. David Strickland and Joan O'Brien were a couple of kids when they were married in 1971 in Cocoa Beach, Florida. She was a high school drop-out; he a student in a local community college. Joan was already pregnant. Not long after the child's birth, Joan left David for one of David's coworkers, and took Danny with her.[25]

David Strickland and his parents soon became concerned over Danny's welfare. Joan puts her own interests above the needs of the child, leaving him in parked cars until late at night while she cavorts with men or visits bars. She leaves him in the care of irresponsible sitters who are often drunk. She is a forger, a shoplifter, and is somehow involved in drugs. Joan is obviously an irresponsible mother and the court eventually gives permanent custody to David Strickland and visitation rights of one week every month to Joan. The visits with the mother are not successful and Danny begins to bring home tales of his other "daddy," whose many sexual antics he has observed. Danny draws indecent pictures of sex acts and takes his clothes off whimsically. "During his short, one week stay with Joan, Danny had undergone a complete change in personality. He was no longer the normal, spirited boy one knew so well." Worse is to follow. His body has a series of scabs ("Mama Joan did it with a knife"); he has a large head wound. Finally, he pleads not to have to "go with Mama Joan again," and he warns them "they're going to keep me."[26]

Joan had become the daughter-in-law from hell—irresponsible, abusive, foul mouthed, erratic, untrustworthy, sexually permissive—even before the day that two cars with several burly men and their barely concealed weapons accompany Joan when she collects her son for his usual noncustodial visit. Although the Stricklands do not want to believe it at first, it soon becomes plain that Danny is not coming back.[27]

The Stricklands follow all the rules: they get contempt motions, writs of attachment, and orders terminating visitation. They deliver these to the state attorney general's office, which ignores them. They can't even get the sheriff to file a missing person's report. "If this child is with a relative, now mind you, I did not say *mother*, I can't help you." They appeal to the governor of Florida who replies, "Depend on your local law enforcement agency." Margaret's response is, "What a joke!" They run up massive legal expenses, requiring the sale of valued property. They hire a detective. To pay him Margaret keeps his children for the summer at no cost while his wife attends nursing school. The Stricklands have a down-home attitude and values. They learn to do what they do best—draw upon their own resources and their friends for aid and comfort. The courts, the state, the local police, are a "joke."[28]

In the end they are lucky. Following through on an FBI lead on the most recent man with whom Joan was living and the fact that Joan is pregnant, a wild set of coincidences puts Margaret Strickland's good friend, Kathryn Case, in the same Colorado Springs maternity waiting room with little Danny Strickland. "Only God," Case notes, "could have produced and arranged such a logical sequence of events, such happiness."[29]

The Stricklands' happiness was not complete and was to be severely tried by the challenge mounted by the O'Briens (Joan's family) in the courts and in the press. "After Danny's return, we were on a legal merry-go-round that never stopped. Seldom did Danny go two consecutive days without court ordered activities." Their lives and the life of the child are not normal. In Strickland's narrative, the state, the police, and the courts only seem to make matters worse. In the end, this narrative and the final decree, which kept Danny in his father's custody, were their vindication.[30]

The divorce, the abduction, the pursuit, the reunion, and the acrimonious court battles were not the only costs of the experience. Little Danny

Strickland, only six years old when he is finally returned to the Strick-lands, had been the object of it all, and he became its real victim. He was, according to David Strickland, "an innocent child caught in the web of legal jargon." He suffers emotional wounds. Even the final custody order provides no real closure. The child is quoted as saying "he did not like himself—would like to kill himself." Confused and unable to keep up at school, Danny was assigned a court counselor but he "had precious little peace of mind."[31]

This narrative, despite its down-to-earth tone, is shot through with a vision of personal pathology and child endangerment, court interference in tandem with official incompetence. It all culminates in the need for psychological intervention and anticipates the most recent perspectives on parental kidnapping. Danny's story had in fact helped to change the laws as the publicity about the case finally forces Florida (long a holdout) to subscribe to the UCCJA. In an addendum to her story, Margaret discusses how this lightened the burden for others who followed. But the passage of the new laws also shifted the center of gravity of the problem. With its emphasis on emotional disorder and its innuendos of sexual abuse, the Strickland story highlighted family pathology rather than legislation as the central issue in parental kidnapping cases.

Measuring the Problem

In 1990, in fulfillment of the requirements of the 1984 Missing Children's Act, the Justice Department published the first ever statistical analysis of the missing children's problem. The study was a response to the general furor over missing children that had been created in the 1970s and 1980s of which parental kidnapping was one significant part. In the attempt to criminalize parental kidnapping, advocates and the media had associated it with the searing anxieties about stranger abduction and they had conflated the statistics of the two, at once making stranger abductions seem more common and parental abductions more frightening. As a result, wild figures for the prevalence of stranger abductions were floated in newspapers and congressional hearings. These statistics eventually resulted in a series of jaundiced-eye examinations which attempted to deflate the balloon. Many of these cast serious doubt on the scope of the problem and raised important methodological questions about the manner in which different kinds of phenomena had been juxtaposed to inflame popular feelings. One of these examinations, a series in the *Denver Post,* garnered headlines and approval when it won the Pulitzer Prize.[32]

The Justice Department study first of all refined definitions, treating different categories of missing children as distinct and separate issues, and then gave two kinds of numbers within each category. For a long time, advocates of government intervention had inflated numbers by downplaying distinctions, and by counting every possible incident or attempted occurrence, as part of the phenomenon. In first distinguishing among five different kinds of child loss, and then differentiating what it called "broad scope" problems which included all incidents (even very minor ones) from more serious ones, the study provided a more realistic profile of the problem. The second set of numbers was usually from one-half to one-fifteenth the size of the broad scope numbers.[33]

The Justice Department study made clear that most kidnapped children were abducted by their parents. Using only the narrower definitions, family abductions accounted for the most numerous group of missing children in 1988. The 163,200 cases suggested a very significant problem. By the more flexible definition, which included every instance when a child was taken "in violation of a custody agreement or decree, or a child was not returned on time from an agreed upon overnight visit," there were 354,100 cases, a number even greater than proposed by most vocal advocates of federal action. But this kind of violation of agreements hardly met the image of parental kidnapping created in the media—an abrupt rupture in parent-child relations, and a long-term disappearance where one parent did not know the child's whereabouts. The broad focus abductions were usually only defined as abductions at all because they conformed to a strictly "legal conception."

The 163,200 cases that met the more stringent definition were large enough, however. These cases met the criteria of "intentional concealment" and included cases where attempts were made to prevent contact with the child; or the child was transported out of the state; or "there was evidence that the abductor had the intent to keep the child indefinitely or to permanently alter custodial privileges." Statistically, at least, parental kidnapping was a real and substantial social problem, larger than most had imagined.[34]

The Justice Department study created a careful, focused picture of the parental kidnapping phenomenon. The most common times for abductions were January and August during periods of extended visitations. They were rarely long term: "Most of the episodes lasted two days to a week, with very few, 10 percent, a month or more. In only a tiny fraction, 1 percent or less, was the child still being held by the abductor."[35] In other words, most parental kidnapping were resolved in fairly short order. While the numbers seemed to substantiate the furor over parental kidnapping that began in the early 1970s, many of the specific facts did not.

Most articles in the 1970s and 1980s had claimed that only about 10 percent of all children abducted by parents would ever be returned. In the personal narratives where children were recovered, the period of loss ranged from many months to many years. Danny Strickland had been gone for three years; Robyn Crowley for seven. The Justice Department study made it clear that only 10 percent of all children were gone even a month or more and that very few were never returned. In only one-half of all the cases did the caretaking parent not know *at all times* the child's whereabouts. The media representations of parental kidnapping were hardly representative.

It is always important not to confuse numbers with significance. Each of the abductions was a serious loss and a wrenching and painful experience no matter its duration. Parents were victimized when their children did not come home, even for a few days, or a few hours. In some cases, the children may have been at risk for some physical harm, though in many others they had merely overstayed an otherwise normal visit with one parent. But it is also important not to read the statistics without the specific qualifications to which they were attached, or to confuse them with the picture of children lost all over America with parents responsible for their lasting disappearance which had circulated in stories since the 1970s.

To those who had attached themselves to the missing children's phenomenon these official numbers became a kind of holy grail. Indeed, the agency most directly affected, the National Center for Missing and Exploited Children (NCMEC), which had been assigned the information-clearinghouse functions required by the federal law in 1984, began to redefine its own agenda after 1990, shifting from an emphasis on stranger abduction to dedicate itself to parental abductions (increasingly called family abductions), in the light of these statistics. Its director, Ernie Allen, now identified parental kidnapping as monumental and still growing at "an alarming rate." Allen and the NCMEC used the much larger, broad-focus figures in their public statements and analyses. In its pamphlet, "The Kid Is with a Parent. How Bad Can it Be?" the NCMEC called the situation "a crisis" and boldly pronounced that it was very bad indeed, when 4 percent of all these children experienced serious physical harm, 4 percent physical abuse, 1 percent sexual abuse, and 16 percent mental abuse. In absolute numbers the children affected in this way were greater than those who suffered from measles or Lyme disease. In calculating the number of children presumably at risk for harm, the pamphlet assumed that the number of children who suffered from each type of abuse could be added, rather than that many of these abuses were experienced by the same children.[36] The Justice Department numbers were now available for those who had all along been committed to using parental kidnapping as a window on contemporary family abuse and dysfunction, or for those who had a stake in portraying the problem of abduction (of any variety) as rampant.

Parental Kidnapping in a New Global Perspective

All through the discussions of the 1970s and 1980s, wildly fluctuating statistics had been accompanied in the public portrait of parental kidnapping by personal stories of emotional distress and family disorder. As the statistics were stabilized and made "official," the center of discussion shifted to an examination of the psychological dimensions of the kidnap experience. While the newspapers earlier in the century had portrayed the problem of parental kidnapping as a game in which the children participated, by the late twentieth century, social science and psychology transformed the experience into childhood trauma. At the turn of the millennium this psychological perspective on the welfare of children has become the basis for outrage and action. Initially, these conclusions were conjecture or based on very small samples of individuals who came to the attention of therapists in clinical practice.[37]

In 1993, however, the first comprehensive profile of abducted children and their families was published, based on interviews with people discovered through an innovative sampling technique that captured a far larger and more diverse group. The authors, Geoffrey Greif and Rebecca Hegar, worked hard to diffuse the sensationalism that had come to mark most of the publicity surrounding parental kidnapping; they accepted few of the common stereotypes and their conclusions are temperate and evenhanded. Not all abducted children are abused, or traumatized, or unhappy. Unlike earlier feminist accounts, Greif and Hegar showed that both mothers and fathers kidnap their children; parents who kidnap are often loving and caring as well as vindictive and abusive. The authors shrewdly understand that many of the charges and countercharges about abuse come from escalated conflicts in custody disputes. Nevertheless, as clinicians oriented to issues of pathology, Greif and Hegar's varied stories are similar in the commonness of the overall family pathology that they detail. There are an enormous number of drug or drink addicted parents, a startling amount of violence between parents, and many of the homes from which abducted children come can only be described as chaotic. And, they implicitly raise questions about how children can be rescued from abuse, the issue which has come to define the problem, and increasingly also to legitimate parental kidnapping since the 1990s.[38]

One of Greif and Hegar's most compelling findings is that a significant disproportion of *serious* family kidnappings are international or intercultural. This conclusion correlates with mounting evidence that the UCCJA could hardly help many parents whose children had been abducted, because they had been taken overseas and beyond the jurisdiction of American courts. Many of the most intransigent (and long term) cases of parental kidnapping are of this type. While any abducted child might be transported abroad (as even Mr. Neil's daughters were presumably transported in 1873), in fact many of these children are abducted by parents who were nationals of other countries and who now shed American citizenship and return to earlier cultural identities. As the issues accruing to globalization have become prominent, so too has this global dimension of parental abduction.[39] Indeed, the matter has been injected into the highest levels at international meetings. In the absence of cooperation from the country to which a child has been abducted, his or her retrieval is beyond the *legal* means available to parents. Some countries, like Portugal and nations in the Balkans and Middle East, simply do not recognize a mother's right to her child, and since they are not affiliated with the Hague Convention, fathers who abduct their children to these locations are usually home free. But even among the almost fifty countries which are now signatories to the Hague Convention, there have been snags and often serious impediments to the return of children, as Lady Catherine Meyer, the wife of the British ambassador to the United States, discovered and described in her own wrenching story. So serious is the problem of international abductions that the State Department published a self-help pamphlet advising parents of their rights and options. In October 1996, the Departments of State and Justice announced that the U.S. government would help defray the expenses of needy parents who traveled abroad to recover children abducted by spouses. In May 2000, the U.S. Senate and House unanimously passed a resolution calling for the enforcement of the Hague Convention on child abduction, while President Bill Clinton raised the matter in his meeting with German chancellor Gerhard Schröder a month later.[40] Most press and media attention in the last several years has focused on these cases.

The newspapers and other media have also been highlighting the vigilante groups that have developed in response. Trained as a Delta Force Commando, Don Feeney and others in the North Carolina group he organized, "Corporate Training Unlimited," have had several spectacular successes "rescuing" children from Iraq, Bangladesh, Jordan, Tunisia, and elsewhere. Their successful adventure in reabducting a girl from Jordan even became the subject of an NBC television movie. The members of the group are portrayed as both American freedom fighters and dedicated to parental justice. Don Feeney and his wife, Judy, who works with him, have become modern-day frontier gunslingers, fighting along the boundary between law and justice. Operating along this erratic line, they rekidnap children and break the laws of other countries.[41]

In this way, the public image of parental kidnapping has taken a new turn. In addition to its new global theater, the response to parental kidnapping emphasizes individual righteousness operating outside the law. What had begun in the 1970s as a drive to bring the laws into line with changing social conditions, twenty years later centers on desperate acts in opposition to law. Just as the Feeney commandos operate outside of American law to kidnap children from foreign countries and break the laws of those countries, recent stories about domestic parental kidnapping often focus on parents who become heroes by kidnapping their own children in the United States. When Dr. Elizabeth Morgan, with the assistance of her parents, kidnapped her daughter to New Zealand, in order to prevent her dentist husband from exercising his visitation rights, she accused him of child molestation. She went to jail for her defiance of the court, only to emerge a media star and the subject of a very sympathetic 1992 television movie. In Marin County, California, Paula Oldham repeated the Morgan saga and became a local heroine in 1994. When popular columnist Anna Quindlen featured her in one of Quindlen's last *New York Times* articles, Oldham became a national figure and a new feminist champion. Quindlen accepts her story as fact, and not only justifies the abduction but condemns the courts and the law which put Oldham in jail and then sent "the child . . . to live with the man Paula believed was a pedophile: her daughter's father, who denies the allegation." Oldham's husband not only denied the charge, but refused to be identified in the media, knowing the fate of those who are even vaguely associated with such behavior. He has strong allies among law enforcement authorities. According to Marin County deputy district attorney Al Dair, "Oldham simply made up the allegation to punish and deny custody rights to her former husband, whom he has labeled the victim in the case."[42]

In the past, it was usually a mother's access to her children that was threatened by aspersions about immoral sexual behavior, and this was the basis upon which she could be judged "unfit." Today, a father's visitation rights, or custody, can most effectively be threatened by accusations of sexual abuse of the child. The charges are not new. Milo Abercrombie had used them against Lyman Swenson in 1925. But the contemporary reverberations are more extensive. Now linked up with spreading allegations about the prevalence of incest and questions about how common child sexual abuse is even in the most "respectable" families, and how often repressed memories of this abuse are recalled later in life under therapeutic conditions, parental kidnapping has become attached to radiating circles linked to a general discourse of family pathology and an increasing focus on the family as the source of many modern social ills.

And just as the Feeney commandos have become famous for rescuing children from the clutches of foreign countries to which they were abducted by their parents, an underground woman's network most visibly represented by Faye Yager has emerged to save women and their children from male violence and the American legal system. Yager, and the Children's Underground Network which she founded, is part of a growing self-help movement aimed at rescuing women and their children from abusive and sexually depraved husbands and fathers. Yager, whose own daughter was raped by Yager's first husband, has become a female Rambo, meting out justice where law has misfired. Described as having "nothing but contempt for the judiciary; and . . . comfortable in the role of avenger. . . . she is obsessive in pressing her case that America has given up its children not merely to individual deviates but to a conspiracy of satanists—preachers and politicians and mafiosi and Masons—bent on stealing souls." In painting her as a Bible Belt paranoid, *Life* magazines' hostile portrait of Yager shows her to be relentless. "If she believes that you have sexually molested your own brood, she will accuse you loudly and fearlessly, on TV and in print, oblivious to lawsuits for libel and slander, pointing a finger until she has divested you not only of your children but also of what remains of your reputation." Yager is a sharp thorn in the side of officials. But she has a devoted following who help her to relocate women and their children by providing them with safe houses and new identities. Accused by police of hiding and browbeating children into making accusations against their fathers, she was herself tried and acquitted on kidnapping charges in Atlanta in 1990, an event that served loosely as the basis of a television *Law and Order* episode. Speaking "with the passion of an abolitionist," Yager reports that she has helped "about half of the 2,000 families she has counseled to go into hiding."[43]

Yager has come to represent the unmet needs of America's abused children and the failures of American courts. At her trial, the defense, "was able to discuss child abuse in general and . . . turned the trial into an emotional, at times horrifying, evocation of children betrayed by abuse and perversion." One juror told Mrs. Yager afterward that she'd made her want to start a "safe house for such children." As the *New York Times* concluded, Yager's trial "and those attending it provide a glimpse into the *darkest edges of domestic disorder,* in which truth can be exceedingly difficult to ascertain."[44]

Today, this tangle of sexual innuendo and its justification for law breaking is often at the heart of parental kidnapping as a public issue.

Even the National Center for Missing and Exploited Children has been forced to take a public position. Noting that "less than 1 per cent," of all parental abductions involve "allegations of child sexual assault," the center insists that "the key is to work within the legal system . . . **not to advocate that parents take the law in their own hands and flee.**" But the legal system has increasingly come to be seen as a serious part of the problem. No longer an infraction that results from inadequate laws, parental kidnapping has become a recourse *against family pathology* that is assumed by many to be the essence of contemporary family life and a struggle against the corrupt laws that support it.[45]

Conclusions

I have examined parental kidnapping historically to show that while it is not a new problem, contemporary concerns about family breakdown and pathology have transformed domestic child stealing into a powerful sign and symptom of family distress. We simply do not know how prevalent parental kidnappings were in the past. Unquestionably, the incidence has increased over the course of the twentieth century and especially in the last twenty-five years as divorce has increased dramatically. But, defining the exact nature of the problem, let alone solving it, is not simple since its public portrayal and elevation into a compelling social issue is a form of social commentary and has become a means to lament the conditions of contemporary family life. Parental kidnapping is not new, as many modern commentators seem to believe, but it has become laden with new meanings. Even in the recent past, those meanings have changed: from defining the inadequacy of national standards and laws protecting custody determinations to providing a means to question the legitimacy and sensitivity of custody decrees and the safety provided within the family. Increasingly, the depiction of parental kidnapping has helped to portray the family as a pathological environment in which children are hostage to parental selfishness. As a means for Americans to comment on other family problems, parental kidnapping is a vehicle for expressing wider anxieties and concerns about the family. This does not mean that parental kidnapping is not a serious issue, especially in light of the large number of abductions that take place each year. It does mean that we must understand how family abduction is embedded in a wide web of representation and advocacy, perception, and portrayal.

As a result, designing effective social policies in relation to parental kidnapping is tricky. Historians, even more than other social analysts, are aware of the multiple and ambiguous consequences of change, including purposive policy changes. With parental kidnapping, especially, the problem itself exists as a by-product of other social policy decisions, in areas of divorce and custody above all, and it is possible to argue that parental kidnapping (since the passage of the laws in the 1980s) requires no direct action itself. As we have seen, even laws meant to protect the rights of custodial parents have not entirely quelled the issue since custodial parents may themselves kidnap their children in order to protect them from what they believe or imagine to be abuse during noncustodial visits.

Nevertheless, a two-pronged response as a minimum policy seems clearly desirable. The first is to clarify and enforce the existing laws, including domestic laws and the Hague Convention (difficult as this might be in view of the multiple legal systems involved). The second is to have the courts be prepared to more quickly abrogate visitation by some parents. They might also be asked to pay more careful attention to serious clues to potentials for abuse by either parent and alert to possible mental imbalance. This may infringe on the rights of noncustodial parents, but is in line with commitment to putting the interests and needs of the child first. More broadly, parental kidnapping may force us to reevaluate imposed joint custody, because this disposition may actually increase the level of parental conflict and lead one parent to try to put the other out of the picture either by kidnapping or by child abuse accusations. Neither of these will entirely ensure that every problem will be effectively addressed, but some cases, at least, will be eliminated simply through clarification and enforcement.

As we have seen, however, the courts have hardly been equal to the many challenges that surround the issues of divorce today, and they (as well as other officials) have been often suspect among families who resort to kidnapping. It is not especially realistic to believe that the courts will be able to prevent (or rectify) the more than 163,000 serious parental kidnappings that occur annually. We should also be aware that a court-ordered abrogation of the rights of a noncustodial parent may lead to more parental kidnapping as a last and heroic attempt is made to continue contact with the child or for other motives. Kidnapping could also increase as parents disapprove of new and unfamiliar relationships and arrangements established by former spouses. And the most terrifying and legally irremediable forms of abduction, those to foreign countries outside the aegis of the Hague protocols, may increase as a natural by-product of our increasingly multicultural society.

In a larger historical sense, however, policy may be the least significant implication of this essay, since I have focused more on a history of perceptions and public portrayals than on behavior. What parental kidnapping means has changed over time as the public's vision of who the problem families are has changed. In other words, the public issue underlying parental kidnapping concerns not primarily the theft of children, but our modern visions of the family. As a crime against its own children, family kidnapping is, in some sense, a contradiction, and we have been legally struggling with this contradiction for the greater part of the twentieth century. As long as children were understood to belong to the family, to both mother and father since the late nineteenth century, how could they be stolen by either parent? How could parents who loved their children harm them? King Solomon, after all, depended on the fact that a "real" mother would protect her child from harm even at the cost of losing that child. As soon however, as the family ceased to be viewed as a stable and dependable unit of social space (first among the rich and then much more generally), and more recently as the family was no longer assumed to be a safe haven, parental kidnapping became a possible offense. It has indeed become a symbolic crime, a product of selfish feuding parents who prey on each other and on their own children. It is not surprising, therefore, that at a time when all bets are off, when we find it difficult even to say what the family is, let alone how it is constituted or when it is a better or worse instrument of child rearing, our public imagination fills with pictures of parents stealing their own children. Parental kidnapping is certainly an extreme expression of contemporary life, but maybe it is also an uncanny symbol of our ambiguous perspectives on family life today.

NOTES

This essay originally appeared in *All Our Families: New Policies for a New Century*, edited by Mary Ann Mason, Arlene Skolnick, and Stephen D. Sugarman, first published in 1998, (revised second edition, New York: Oxford University Press, 2003), 170–195.

1. *New York Times*, August 13, 1873, p. 2.
2. Mary Ann Mason, *From Father's Property to Children's Rights* (New York: Columbia University Press, 1994), 59.
3. *New York Times*, December 10, 1879, p. 3.
4. *New York Times*, April 2, 1993, p. 11.
5. E. G. Ewaschuk, "Abduction of Children by Parents," *Criminal Law Quarterly*, 21 (1978–79), 176–77; Margaret R. De Haas, *Domestic Injunctions* (London: Seet and Maxwell, 1987), 52–53.
6. Commonwealth v. Nickerson, 87 Mass. 5 (Allen) 518; State v. Farrar, 41 N. H. 53; Hunt v. Hunt, 94 Ga 257, 21 S.E. 515; State v. Angel, 42 Kan. 216 21 Pac. 1075. The cases are summarized in *Century Edition of the American Digest*, vol. 31(St. Paul, 1902) (my emphasis).
7. *New York Times*, July 9, 1911, p. 4; April 14, 1911, p. 10; June 28, 1910, p. 7.
8. *New York Times*, June 11, 1927, p. 24; June 28, 1910, p. 7. For the dangers to children from automobiles, see Viviana A. Zelizer, *Pricing the Priceless Child: The Changing Social Value of Children* (New York: Basic Books, 1985).
9. *New York Times*, November 11, 1910, p. 9; *Chicago Tribune*, August 28, 1916, p. 1; *New York Times*, August 28, 1916, p. 9.

10. *San Francisco Chronicle,* July 18, 1966, p. 24; July 10, 1935, p. 15. *New York Times,* July 12, 1921, p. 17; July 11, 1921, p. 1.

11. *Chicago Tribune,* September 14, 1924, p. 1; September 17, 1924, p. 2.

12. *USA Today,* July 15, 1983, p. 4d. For the language of epidemic, see, for example, *U.S. News and World Report,* 87 (September 3, 1979), 57; Bruce W. Most, "The Child Stealing Epidemic," *Nation,* 224 (May 7, 1977), 559.

13. Sanford N. Katz, *Child Snatching: The Legal Response to the Abduction of Children,* Section of Family Law, American Bar Association (American Bar Association Press, 1981), 3, 11–12.

14. Katz, *Child Snatching,* 15.

15. David Finkelhor, Gerald Hotaling, and Andrea Sedlak, *Missing, Abducted, Runaway, and Thrownaway Children in America: First Report: Numbers and Characteristics. National Incidence Studies,* Executive Summary, May 1990, U.S. Department of Justice, Office of Juvenile Justice and Delinquency Prevention, 40; Katz, *Child Snatching,* 123.

16. United States Department of State, Bureau of Consular Affairs, *International Parental Abduction,* 3rd edition, 1989, p. 21. See also, *National Law Journal,* 12 (October 9, 1989), 3, 34.

17. *The Denver Post* featured a scathing analysis of the numbers and the hype; see Louis Kitzer and Diana Griego, "The Truth about Missing Kids," *Sunday Denver Post,* May 12, 1985, pp. 1A, 13A; the follow-up *Denver Post,* May 13, 1985, p. 1A, 10A; and the editorial, May 19, 1985, p. 6H. Probably the most influential social science critique is Joel Best, *Threatened Children: Rhetoric and Concern abut Child-Victims* (Chicago: University of Chicago Press, 1990). For an excellent discussion of how issues of this kind are created and disseminated, see Cynthia Gentry, "The Social Construction of Abducted Children as a Social Problem," *Sociological Inquiry,* 58 (1988), 413–25.

18. Mason, *From Father's Property to Children's Rights,* 130; U.S. Department of Justice, Office of Juvenile Justice and Delinquency Prevention, U.S. Attorney General's Advisory Board on Missing Children, 1988, *Missing and Exploited Children: The Challenge Continues* (Washington, D.C., 1988), 42.

19. *Missing and Exploited Children: The Challenge Continues,* 49.

20. One mother was able to locate her child when her abducting husband appeared on the "Donahue" show on child snatching. When Donahue refused to disclose vital information about her husband, she sued and won a 5.9 million dollar court settlement; see *Newsweek,* 101 (May 30, 1983), 101.

21. Sally Abrahms and Joseph N. Bell, "Have You Seen These Children? Child Snatching: The Cruelest Crime, " *Ladies Home Journal,* 98 (April 1981), 77; Abrahms and Bell, *Children in the Crossfire: The Tragedy of Parental Kidnapping* (New York: Atheneum, 1983).

22. Eileen Crowley, as told to Karen Freifeld, "I Found My Kidnapped Daughter," *Good Housekeeping,* 197 (August 1983), 117, 180, 182.

23. Among other narratives, see Bonnie Black, *Somewhere Child* (New York: Viking, 1981); Anna Demeter, *Legal Kidnapping: What Happens to a Family When the Father Kidnaps Two Children* (Boston: Beacon, 1977); Thomas Froncek, *Take Away One* (New York: St. Martin's, 1985); and the novel by Joy Fielding, *Kiss Mommy Goodbye* (New York: New American Library, 1981), which closely parallels the personal narrative form.

24. Lindsy Van Gelder, "Beyond Custody: When Parents Steal Their Own Children," *Ms.,* 5 (May 1978), 52, 94 (emphasis in original); Adrienne Rich, Introduction, Demeter, *Legal Kidnapping,* xiv–xv.

25. Margaret Strickland, "Child Snatched: The Danny Strickland Case," in *How to Deal with a Parental Kidnapping,* compiled by Margaret Strickland (Moorehaven, Fla.: Rainbow Books, 1983, originally published 1979).

26. Strickland, *Child Snatched,* 193, 194–195, 202–203, 204, 207

27. Strickland, *Child Snatched,* 210.

28. Strickland, *Child Snatched,* 212 (emphasis in original).

29. Strickland, *Child Snatched,* 232–33, 234.

30. Strickland, *Child Snatched,* 237, 248.

31. Strickland, *Child Snatched,* 187, 250, 248.

32. *Denver Sunday Post,* May 13, 1985, A1. For other studies which question the statis-

tics and the exaggerated alarm, see Best, *Threatened Children;* Martin L. Forst and Martha-Elin Blomquist, *Missing Children: Rhetoric and Reality* (New York: Lexington Books, 1991).

33. Finkelhor, Hotaling, and Sedlak, *Missing, Abducted, Runaway, and Thrownaway Children in America,* Executive Summary, 5.

34. Finkelhor, Hotaling, Sedlak, *Missing, Abducted, Runaway, and Thrownaway Children in America: First Report,* 45. Finkelhor, Hotaling and Sedlak, *Missing, Abducted, Runaway, and Thrownaway Children in America,* Executive Summary, 6.

35. Finkelhor, Hotaling, Sedlak, *Missing, Abducted, Runaway, and Thrownaway Children in America,* Executive Summary, 6.

36. Ernie Allen, "The Crisis of Family Abductions in America," *FBI Law Enforcement Bulletin,* 61 (August 1992), 18–19; Allen, "The Kid Is with a Parent, How Bad Can it Be?" National Center for Missing and Exploited Children, Washington, D.C., no date, 2–3.

37. For clinical studies, Diane H. Sehetky and Lee H. Haller, "Child Psychiatry and Law: Parental Kidnapping," *Journal of the American Academy of Child Psychiatry,* 22 (1983), 279–285; Neil Senior, Toba Gladstone, and Barry Nurcombe, "Child Snatching: A Case Report, "*Journal of the American Academy of Child Psychiatry,* 21 (1982), 578–83. Finkelhor, Hoteling, Sedlak, *Missing, Abducted, Runaway, and Thrownaway Children in America, First Report,* 60.

38. Geoffrey L. Greif and Rebecca L. Hegar, *When Parents Kidnap: The Families behind the Headlines* (New York: Free Press, 1993), vii, 34, 32, and *passim.*

39. Greif and Hegar, *When Parents Kidnap,* 179–195. This was, in fact, the plot at the center of Thomas Francek's parental kidnapping narrative, *Take One Away,* as well as Bonnie Black's wrenching *Somewhere Child.*

40. United States Department of State, Bureau of Consular Affairs, *International Parental Abduction,* 3rd edition, 1989, and "Child Custody Unit Helps Parents Keep Track," *U.S. Department of State Dispatch,* 2 (January 21, 1991), 49. *San Francisco Chronicle,* October 11, 1996, p. 11. Lady Meyer has become a notable activist in this area. See Catherine Meyer, *They Are My Children Too: A Mother's Struggle for Her Sons* (New York: Public Affairs, 1999).

41. *New York Times,* September 5, 1994, p. 1; *Los Angeles Times,* November 13, 1994, p. A1. For the Feeneys, see *Newsweek,* 118 (July 8, 1993), 31; *New York Times,* September 5, 1994, p. 1; *Los Angeles Times,* November 13, 1994, pp. A1, A30; "The Search for Lauren," *Readers' Digest,* 135 (August, 1987), 77–84. The movie, "Desperate Rescue: The Cathy Mahone Story," was first broadcast on NBC on January 28, 1993, and starred Mariel Hemingway.

42. "The Elizabeth Morgan Story" was aired on ABC, November 29, 1992. For Paula Oldham, *New York Times,* December 10, 1994, p. 15; *SF Weekly,* June 22, 1994, p. 7. For a very sympathetic portrayal of Oldham, see the appropriately titled, "Kidnap or Rescue?" *SF Weekly,* April 6, 1994, pp. 11–14.

43. Tom Junod, "The Last Angry Woman," *Life,* 14 (April 1991), 65. *New York Times,* April 27, 1992, p. A1; *New York Times,* May 16, 1992, p. A6; *Atlanta Constitution,* May 16, 1992, p. B5; *New York Times,* April 27, 1992, pp. A1, B10 (my emphasis). The *Law and Order* segment was aired on NBC, January 6, 1993.

44. *New York Times,* May 16, 1992, p. A6; April 27, 1992, p. B10. *Atlanta Constitution,* May 16, 1992, p. B5.

45. "Position Statement of the National Center for Missing and Exploited Children on the 'Underground Railroad,'" no date (boldface in original).

6

Bringing It Home

Children, Technology, and Family in the Post–World War II World

The end of the Second World War came with twinned explosions. The nuclear bomb that destroyed Nagasaki, Japan, ended the costliest foreign war in American history. The baby boom that began at the same time ended one hundred years of steadily declining birth rates. Both of these events would have long-lasting consequences, but unlike the searing fireball that mushroomed in the skies over Japan on August 9, 1945, the explosion in fertility in the United States caused neither havoc nor fear. Instead, it seemed to herald new hope and expectations about a much brighter future. Like its twin, however, it would become intimately linked to the brilliant emergence of American technological and economic superiority. The babies born at the time of the bomb could hardly have known it, but the childhoods that they were about to begin and the lives of the children who would follow them until the end of the century would be defined by this fact. Some of the sources of their experience had begun earlier, of course, some of it half a century before. But, it was not until the second half of the twentieth century, after America had become a truly international power, that the dimensions and meanings of these changes became clear.

To name a few of the technological changes that these children were about to inherit and create is to gain some sense of the changed dimensions of the world in which they would grow up: atomic and hydrogen bombs, and automatic weapons; television, VCRs, and CDs; jet travel, satellites, moon walks, and manned space stations; wireless telephones, silicon chips, personal computers, the Internet; contact lenses and artificial organs; birth control pills, IUDs, in vitro fertilization, egg donations and stem cells; freeze-dried foods and microwaves; antibiotics and the polio vaccine; LSD, methamphetamines, Prozac, and Ritalin. Never in the history of the world would a mere two and one-half historical generations experience so many fundamental technological breakthroughs. These technologies would affect how they were conceived and born, and how (and when) they discovered the thrills of sex; what they ate and when; how they spent their time in work and in play; what they studied in school. It also affected what was considered a proper childhood.

Some of these changes came so abruptly that each succeeding group of young people seemed altogether different from its predecessor, so much so that journalists began to denominate them separately (though without proper names), calling them generation X or Y. No child in the 1950s could have anticipated childhood in the 1980s, and looking backward a child in 1995 would have thought that the childhood of his mother in the early 1960s was quaint. Nevertheless, in looking back over a half century, some continuous trends are visible. The first is a growing sense of alarm that childhood, as it had been understood for a century, was being endangered by all the changes taking place. By the end of the century, more and more Americans worried that childhood, as it had been understood for at least a century, was disappearing. The second can best be described as an inexorable move toward the social detachment from issues regarding children and toward the absorption of children into increasingly private places. These two trends, as we will see, were related to each other, and both resulted from a disassembling of the role that the family had played as a mediating social institution. As public supports for childhood and family life declined, parents increasingly came to view their children as a form of personal expression, an extension of the self, rather than as their contribution to a socially approved and highly valued common enterprise. Although many of these trends had begun earlier, indeed could be traced all the way back to the beginning of the twentieth century and before, the consequences for the relations between parents and children and the effects on the society became marked only in the last part of the twentieth century.

Let the Good Times Roll

Three and four (even five). These were the strange numbers that demographers began to see as they charted the unusual patterns that graphs of family size revealed by the mid-1950s. Since the turn of the twentieth century, the middle classes had been steadying their sights on the number two, while the working classes, immigrants, and rural populations had wider fluctuations and tended toward larger size. In the 1930s, even these groups had sharply limited the number of children they bore, some settling for very late marriage as a means, or determining to have no children at all in response to the economic hard times. Even immigrants and farmers who had once clung to large families as a mark of pride or God's gift (and an intergenerational form of old-age insurance) had submitted to the new trend. As a result, the birthrate in 1933 stood at an astonishingly low 76.3 percent. Then starting just before the war ended, and accelerating to the middle of the 1950s, the patterns swung conspicuously and unexpectedly, among all groups everywhere in the country, far in the other direction. More children, and children born (quite intentionally) closer together early in the marriage became a sign of the new times. Young Americans married earlier and had their children sooner afterward than at any time in the twentieth century. By 1957, the birthrate stood at 122.9 percent, an enormous increase in just twenty-four years.[1] Children seemed to be a sign of the good times people expected to realize after the war, a sign of the conveniences offered by new kitchen appliances and steadier work, a response to rapidly assembled single-family homes in new suburban tracts (financed by the GI Bill of veterans' benefits after the war). Perhaps above all, it seemed to be the product of a commitment to motherhood and fatherhood as goods in themselves.

Since early in the century, the fine art of parenting had been placed on the American public agenda as an aspiration, and clothed in the rubrics of science. And the middle classes had responded with enthusiasm to child-rearing manuals, pediatric advice, psychological and cognitive measures and standards. By the Second World War, much of this attention had already been subjected to modern vicissitudes of fads in psychology and health. First, behaviorism and then variants of Freudian psychology had infused beliefs about children's proper development, while new nutritional guidelines about calories, concerns about balancing vitamins, injunctions to sterilize newly standardized infant formulas made parents aware of how strategically they could influence the well-being of their offspring. This desire to raise the physically healthy, psychologically well-adjusted, effectively socialized child had initially developed in the context of a shrinking household and declining childhood mortality, obvious by the 1920s. In this context maternal attention could be effectively concentrated and expectantly rewarded.

After the war, the craving to raise perfect children had a much larger terrain for expression. Not only had traditional middle-class families grown in size, but the attention to these matters grew in ever wider circles that expanded what it meant to be middle class. The middle class grew and its boundaries expanded as defined by standards of domestic stability, steady work made possible by union membership, the security provided by old-age insurance, and the widespread secondary education of older children. The middle class had also grown through an acculturated second generation of immigrants, and rural migrants recently come into the cities during the boom in war industries. Through newspapers, magazines, school guidance clinics, and hospital births, as well as pamphlets and books, more and more children began to be raised according to expert advice. In this atmosphere, the child-rearing advisor had the potential to become something of a public oracle. Very quickly after the war, this role was appropriated by Dr. Benjamin Spock, a pediatrician with an ear for psychological nuance and a nose for public anxiety.

Benjamin Spock dominated the raising of the first postwar generation of children like no other single individual—more than any president, more even than any rock 'n' roll star. His advice came neatly bound between the covers of Baby and Child Care, first published in 1946, and then repeatedly reissued, revised, expanded, and updated for the next several decades. Baby and Child Care had a reserved seat on the best-seller list and was on the shelves of more homes in America than any book other than the Bible, and it was far more likely to be read and followed. One historian has wittily described Dr. Spock as a confidence man, summarizing both the advice he dispensed and the likely role he played in the home (while hinting at the neat trick he was pulling off).[2] He was trusted by tens of millions of parents as he confidently told them how to distinguish between measles and chicken pox, the difference between serious developmental delays and ordinary willfulness, and when to call the doctor. Knowing that over the course of the century, mothers had grown increasingly anxious about their inadequacies (under the tutelage of other child-care experts), he advised them, above all, to relax and enjoy their babies. Avuncular and assured, but also relaxed and user friendly, Spock's book was just what the culture needed as Americans set themselves the task of raising the largest, best fed, and best housed generation in American history. Spock could speak with new authority to a generation of mothers who could expect to be protected from childbirth infections by sulfa drugs and whose children's doctors administered antibiotics to protect them from the complications of a variety of childhood ailments. Fueled by the war, American prosperity and technology had provided both the wherewithal and the know-how to overcome the many social deficits that FDR had made a matter of public concern and policy during the depression. Now Dr. Benjamin Spock was going to show the country how to bring it home where it counted.

While Spock's advice would change over time, and each household adapted it to its own inclinations, children raised under Spock's aegis could expect to receive little, if any, physical correction and parents were not to bully them emotionally. Instead, a child would be raised to participate in a democratically organized household in which his or her views mattered. Children were encouraged to verbalize their emotions and to understand their misbehavior. A Spock-raised child was likely to have had some role in his or her own toilet training. Spock was also sympathetic to the libidinal theories of the Freudians and to their concern that children's instincts not be repressed. By the 1960s, Dr. Spock would be accused of encouraging a "permissive" form of child rearing, one that put the children in control, and he certainly could be read as someone alert to the dangers of raising children on disciplinary techniques that relied on authoritarian methods. But Spock was eager for children's behavior to be directed and corrected, and for parents to teach them to manage their own emotions, rather than to encourage self-indulgence. However far Spock might be read as leading parents toward a child-centered expressiveness, he certainly never allowed parents much room for their own self-indulgence, though he technically encouraged their enjoyment. And historians have not tired of pointing out that it was almost always the mother, as homebody (homemaker was the preferred 1950s word), and would-be apprentice-child-rearing expert, now surrounded by a growing clutch of children closely spaced together, who bore the brunt of reading, interpreting, and applying Spock's advice.

The techniques of child rearing were but one of the growing number of technologies that invaded the home after the war. Communications technologies had begun to nest there earlier in the century in the form of the telephone and radio, which allowed voice connections to and from the neighborhood and beyond. Now, after the war, pictures arrived as well. Where formerly, cinematic entertainments required a trip down the street, downtown or into a neighboring town, the television set delivered entertainment into the private home on several channels, and all times of the day. When the first finely cabineted sets began to arrive in the homes of the technologically daring in the late 1940s, no one could have foreseen the television's potential as a ubiquitous part of daily life, nor its constant companionship for children growing up. Even in the 1950s, when a majority of Americans became familiar with its blinking features (and frequent malfunctions), it still stood squarely in the middle of the living room—an embodiment of family entertainment. Early morning children's television programs, like *Ding-Dong School,* were still carefully monitored and educational, and after-school programming like the *Howdy Doody Show* bore the imprint of adult supervision.

It was only in later decades, when the television was released from its furnishings and became portable, that the TV as a personal companion found its way into the private bedroom, of children as well as adults. Then it rapidly fell into the embrace of marketers who targeted its programming to individual audiences, honed by age, and advertisers keen to prey on the sweet teeth of children and their fascination with gadgety toys. In the 1950s, still dominated by Western heroes like the Lone Ranger, Gene Autry, and Roy Rogers, variety shows like Ed Sullivan, movie reruns and slapstick sitcoms, television was already widely used as a means to entertain. It already helped to create fads, like the Davy Crockett "Coonskin Cap," but it was hardly yet an all-purpose entertainment medium, full of sports and action dramas, news magazines and reality programs, and no one dreamed that it might become the locale for music videos, or VCR-imported pornography. But the children of the 1950s were the first to grow up with the possibility of being amused at almost any time of day in a way which required little active participation or effort. Here technology seemed to provide them with a free ticket to ride.

Far less free, it soon became clear, were the demands that technology was about to make on their schooling. Since at least the 1920s, one of the marks of American democracy and economic prosperity had been the vast extension of schooling upward into the teen years, years in which previous generations had been forced to work and help their families provide. Where in 1900, a little over 50 percent of white children, ages 5–19, and just over 13 percent of nonwhite children of this age were enrolled in school, by 1960, almost 90 percent of white children and just a few nonwhites were enrolled. By the later date, over 90 percent of all 14–17 year olds were in school, registering the extraordinary growth in high school attendance during the first half of the twentieth century.[3] This extension had initially been accompanied by very moderate intellectual demands. Instead, the newly comprehensive high schools and junior highs had evolved multiple programs to meet the needs and aspirations of their increasingly diverse populations. Commercial and vocational programs became as familiar across America as the traditional classical and scientific curricula. And now that everyone could be expected to attend (if not to graduate), more effort was expended to satisfy their needs for citizenship and other kinds of energetic engagements. Sports, musicals, dramatics, debate, school government, and school dances as well as many other diversions began to fill the school day and year. (See Chapter 3 in this volume.)

Since the early twentieth century, progressive educators had guided this development, urging that the needs of the "whole child" be considered in his education. Nowhere was this more true than for adolescents who might otherwise leave school and drift off into delinquencies. As a result, by the late 1940s and early 1950s, American children could all expect to go to school and to proceed to high school without being asked to do too much that was intellectually taxing. Schooling was as much about directing their behavior away from the streets as it was a way of disciplining their minds. By the mid-fifties this extended development had come to be defined as a necessary part of growing up when psychologist Erik Erikson called for a "moratorium" during adolescence that would facilitate ego integration and strength.[4] America's relaxed attitude toward schooled intellect was in sharp contrast to most of the rest of the world, Europe in particular, where entry into the lycée or gymnasium was highly competitive and selective and adolescent education was seen to serve the purpose of professional preparation, state advancement, and class prerogative. In contrast, American education encouraged the development of youth as a form of temporary leisure class, democratically extended to all. That democratic extension had also assured a good measure of assimilation to the children of the enormous group of European newcomers to the United States who arrived in the early twentieth century. For some members of this immigrant second generation, it provided real opportunities for social mobility and professional prominence.

After the war, however, American technological know-how and its new position on the world stage was poised to make invigorated demands on this vast, though unintegrated, and locally controlled form of schooling. The end of the war had left the United State the one and only nuclear power. But not for long. The technological superiority embodied in that briefly held position soon created challenges of all kinds. The most daunting was that created by the rapid technological advancement of the Soviet Union with whom the United States by the late 1940s was engaged in a Cold War, with potential hot spots all over the world. A war of ideologies and nerves, the friction of that conflict was usually expressed in competitive machinery—more atomic, and then, hydrogen bombs, more and better missiles for long-range delivery, more warships and nuclear submarines, more bases around the world. Finally, the conflict and race was carried out in space. When in 1956 the Soviet Union successfully orbited a satellite in space (known as Sputnik) and followed this with orbiting space satellites that contained first animals and then humans, Americans were put on notice that their educational apparatus could be much more effectively utilized. In the late 1960s the United States would catch up and exceed the Soviet success as it landed a man on the moon, but in the 1950s, its earliest space-directed efforts were more likely to result in collapsed booster rockets than successful space orbits.

The federal government had never been more than marginally involved in American public education, although it had helped to establish the great state universities through land grants in the nineteenth century, and experimented with a variety of school-based welfare programs during the New Deal. But by the late 1950s, the threat of Soviet technological and scientific advantage forced the federal government to seek out means to enlist the public schools in a quest to better educate national manpower and womanpower. Government and industry scouted various means to find scientific talent and to encourage greater academic competence. The general tone and sense of a national emergency was one means; the other was talent selection. All schools began more regularly to test children's aptitudes, and the junior high schools and high schools added enriched science and math curricula as well as a host of new foreign languages to their programs. Industry and private foundations began talent searches and science fairs. The states spent more money on schooling in general and scientific schooling in particular, and the colleges and universities especially became places in which the federal expenditures could be used to leverage success in the lower schools.

Going to college became a much more widely shared goal in the 1950s and 1960s. In part this resulted from the new exposure to college of war veterans who took advantage of provisions of the G.I. Bill of Rights. As college going became much more widespread and natural, it also became an increasingly desirable objective. One result of the new importance of higher education was a significant expansion in community and junior colleges, which allowed students to further develop their skills, and which helped to democratize college attendance. But, for many parents and students, true access to higher learning could only be achieved through the more vigorous traditional college curriculum. And those especially keen to succeed through education placed new pressure on the best and most elite schools, which began to feel the new competitive strain by the early 1960s. The *New York Times* registered the alarm of those eager to go to the best schools. In 1961, Fred Hechinger, the *Times* education reporter, noted the new gloom about competitive application, and the tightening of admissions requirements at the Ivy League and other prominent schools. Hechinger also observed the irony of the greater stringency at selective institutions at a time when places in higher education generally were opening up. "Space may be Plentiful, but Not at the Preferred Colleges," was one headline. The article noted that it was that time of year when "high school seniors in hundreds of thousands of families are again waiting for the mailman to bring the crucial letter from the colleges of their choice."[5] Although it did not implicate all American youth yet, this trend meant that for those with the highest ambitions, as going to college became more competitive, high school became a more meaningful testing ground for the expression of excellence and academic exertion.

Colleges and universities, which by the 1920s were dominated by research agendas and increasingly devoted to innovation, had been central to American success during the war. By the late 1950s and 1960s, the federal government looked to them as strategic places to fund specialized (and often secret) research necessary to American security during the Cold War. Here federal dollars could be spent with the expectation of effective return. The Departments of Defense and State, the various armed services, the Atomic Energy Commission, as well as the National Science Foundation supported a variety of researches in widely dispersed fields. These dollars also expanded available facilities and made colleges more and more central to the success aspirations of American youth.

Going to college became a mark of middle-class standing for the family and a route to future success for the child. The sifting process that would create a competent citizenry and an educated elite that Thomas Jefferson had early in the history of the republic defined as necessary to democratic success was now put at the direct disposal of the state whose concerns about national security made it eager to find and to train talent. As the schools became more directly linked to this goal, and even the less competitive colleges and universities imposed higher admissions standards, students eager for success worked harder and competed with each other in new ways. And the members of the biggest birth cohort in the twentieth century, who had recently acquired the name "baby boom generation," once carefully socialized to express themselves, faced each other in a stiffer competition to get to the more desirable college degrees.

The new college-going aspirations also had other unexpected consequences. Unlike other aspects of American education, higher education was never free, although state-funded colleges were certainly much lower in cost than the private colleges and universities whose many varieties were spread all over the American landscape. But students who went to college had to be supported into ever older ages in ways that incurred a variety of costs beyond tuition. In striving now for new ways to facilitate their children's desire for successful self-definition, many women went to work once their children were out of their dependent childhood years. This was what women had always done to help their families through unexpected expenses or hard times. Now, however, married women's work invaded the precincts of the middle class, not just the poor or widowed or deserted wife. New aspirations, rather than need and dire poverty, were beginning to accustom families to dual-earner households, though certainly not when the children were young.

College aspirations in the 1960s were still overwhelmingly white ambitions. Few African American or Latino children were either trained to competition at school or inspired toward the goal at home that now became common for children of native white groups, and also among newer immigrants such as Italians, Greeks, and Armenians among others. The man who would become Malcolm X and the leader of a militant generation of African American youth learned this early in his life and never forgot it. But the very expansion of higher education, its newly articulated social role as a site for youth development, and its increasing centrality to mobility aspirations meant that soon this white domination would be challenged as colleges and universities began to figure in national policies. Even in the 1960s, some colleges and universities began to practice early forms of affirmative action policies as talented African American youth especially were encouraged to attend elite colleges.[6] It was not until the end of the decade that many schools started to debate and to adopt curricular innovations in response to the new constituencies that federal policies began to require colleges actively to recruit.

The Times They Are A-Changin'

Colleges and universities had adjusted throughout the twentieth century to changing student populations and new cultural cues, and college life was always defined as much by the young as by those who were technically in charge and officially *in loco parentis*. By the mid-1960s, these had profoundly changed the ancient institution. When Linda LeClair was found to be living off campus with her boyfriend in 1968 the scandal made the front pages of newspapers across the country and the national news on television. An undergraduate at Barnard College in New York City, one of the esteemed Seven Sister schools that had pioneered in women's higher education a century earlier, LeClair was well aware of the byzantine parietal rules that were supposed to guide the social lives of college students everywhere. And she had knowingly broken them. These rules were meant to protect a woman's reputation (which largely meant sexual honor and its associated behaviors) as colleges guarded their charges' social lives as well as their intellectual adventures through college.[7]

By 1968, however, the peer-mediated rules that governed undergraduate life were being dismantled and reassembled. The beer binges and risqué panty raids of the late 1950s and early 1960s in which men stood eagerly outside girls' dorm windows pleading for a favor of underwear, and which had mildly challenged the earlier rules, had been overshadowed. The new student reality was associated with protests against the Vietnam War and by new habits, including sexual initiations for women as well as men, and various experiments with drugs such as marijuana and LSD. A new youth culture was visible on colleges across the country, a culture recognizable in dress and music tastes, sexual habits and intoxicants, philosophical explorations and political ideas. Certainly, not all college students either identified with or participated in this culture, but it was a national phenomenon and had become prominent in the media and the public mind. That culture markedly separated young people (and their older admirers) from most adults on campus as well as from their parents at home. Its manifestations would haunt and challenge the rest of the century.

The relationship between youth and their elders had been uneasy throughout the twentieth century, as the generations increasingly viewed each other across a hostile divide of taste and behavior. And throughout the century, such accoutrements of identity as music and clothes had become commonplace forms of separation. By the late 1960s, these divides had become sharper and more piercing. The culture of the young in general was permeated by music, whether they were part of the visible youth culture of the time or more mainstream, and increasingly helped to define and guide their sensibility. Music, which had begun for many of these young people as a form of entertainment on television's *American Bandstand* and on rock 'n' roll dominated radio stations in the 1950s, and usually was an accompaniment to sock hops, proms, and Sweet Sixteens, became by the late 1960s a measure of mood rather than a form of dance. The sexuality that alarmed 1950s parents in Elvis Presley's voice and moves (and those of his many imitators) became much more subversive as it embraced disenchantment and drugs in the Rolling Stones, the Doors, and Bob Dylan. The Beatles invasion of the United States in 1964 had been a first taste of what was to come—their boyish charm always tinged with riotous neglect of convention in dress, hairstyles, and speech. And an anticonventional mood was just what exploded around and through the music of the later 1960s.

Like other historical manifestations of the spirit of revivalism that was peer inspired, staged in outdoor spaces, and wedged in generational irritations, the radical version of 1960s youth culture partook of deep antagonisms to authority and drew heavily on perceptions about the hypocrisy and empty forms of powerful elders. In the 1960s, the growing threat of the draft for all young people was fueling resentments against an increasingly unpopular war, still publicly defended in the language of a canting liberalism. The war and its defenders were confronted with a generation which was increasingly following Emerson's injunctions to follow their own genius by "doing their own thing" and saying it "like it is." And Americans since Emerson's time had certainly looked to youth for revitalization and spiritual innovation. By the 1960s, this spiritual investment bore political fruit. For a sizable portion of the young, the Vietnam War draft (encroaching by the end of the 1960s even on college graduates), government-funded secret research on campus, and the Civil Rights struggle which had reignited the language of American idealism and brotherhood, came together to fuel generational (and class) antagonism and to embolden youth's sense that they knew so much more about what was really important than their convention-driven elders. Some of that knowledge came from books written by some of those very elders who became contemporary gurus, such as Paul Goodman, Herbert Marcuse, and Norman O. Brown. These attacked the structure of capitalism or the sexual repressions of the middle class. Some came from the more direct inspiration of pot smoking or from ingesting the new synthetic drug LSD hyped by Harvard psychologist Timothy Leary.

Almost all of it rejected the technological civilization and the science that had made much of it possible. Yearning for new communion with nature, the youth culture of the 1960s condemned the technological civilization that had come to define their lives after the Second World War. Young people belittled the all-electric kitchens that eased their mothers' lives, excoriated the bomb (and the sham of bomb shelters) that had made their nation powerful, and raged against the government research that allowed napalm to be dropped on Vietnamese villagers. They hated the guardians of that civilization whether they were college professors, presidential advisors, or street cops. And they did so in language that overthrew the many etiquettes carefully developed over the course of the century as their parents and grandparents had sought respectability. Even if they did not speak for all youth (and they did not even speak for all youth at college), they were certainly extremely vocal and, like most inspired minorities, dominated the public vision of the time.

Most of them attacked the very institutions—the schools—that had made their moratorium possible, and their presence both visible and powerful. Few of them thought much about how the sexuality so fundamental to their new sense of the power of nature had been carefully nurtured by the very technologies they now abhorred.

Birth control was nothing new in the 1960s. But 99 percent effective birth control available for the asking was very new. Since the early twentieth century, first middle-class wives and then gradually others besides the middle class could have birth control prescribed by doctors while condoms had become commonplace for men since the First World War. But American pharmaceutical research in the 1950s had developed two powerful new contraceptives, the intrauterine device and the birth control pill (invented by Carl Djerassi in 1960), that transformed sexual behavior in the United States and eventually elsewhere in the world as well. Though still somewhat crude, both means now radically separated sex from conception. The insertion of the IUD by a doctor or the daily morning habit of pill taking meant that women could now be ready to have sex at any time without expecting any consequences. Unlike the diaphragm, which had a substantial failure rate (it was estimated that this resulted in an often unplanned forth or fifth child in the 1950s) and which required synchronized insertion, both the pill and the IUD were at once much more effective and required no thought at all. And unlike the condom, these means were wholly within a woman's control. As a result, sex and conception for women were separated effectively for the first time in human history in ways that could make even a respectable undergraduate happy and secure while she challenged her mother's hypocrisies.

The sexual revolution of the 1960s was thus powerfully built on new technological knowledge and, unlike previous revolutions, powerfully affected unmarried as well as married women (because the risks were so much lower). And it brought in its wake other revolutions as well, although, of course, it could not fully account for or fully explain these. First, modern feminism, which spun rapidly out of the antiauthoritarian and anticonventional mood of the 1960s, began seriously to challenge all gendered differences because the most prominent bio-social difference (childbearing) could now be discounted. Then, gay liberation which took the sexual pleasures articulated by a liberated 1960s to their logical conclusion by proclaiming sexual pleasure as a good in itself regardless of the preferred partner (no longer naturally limited by an implicit goal of conception). These two powerful cultural revolutions necessarily required the effective and permanent divide that opened in the 1960s between sex and conception, sex and child bearing, sex and parenthood, between older generation and newer.

The destruction of those links would alter the nature of family life and the patterns of childhood in ways that no one, standing at the threshold of the 1950s, could ever have imagined. Instead of parenthood as a central human condition and a proud emblem of American success, the young people who left colleges, universities, and high schools in the 1960s and 1970s opened up the possibility of a new kind of childless future.

Bust Follows Boom

During the first two decades after the war, having a child was a desirable social goal and parenting had a secure place within the culture. This meant that those who could not conceive often sought to adopt children that they would raise as their own. Taking care of children was an honorable social act, and in adopting a child the personal desire for parenthood meshed with the needs of children for care. Those adoptions were monitored by social service agencies who were usually sectarian and tried to select among applicants those whose marriages were stable, incomes secure, and future home life promising. This did not mean that all children were perfectly placed, but the placements existed within a context that presumed this to be a social activity and that the adoption was for the good of the child and useful to the society which had taken over its care.

Since the early twentieth century, family placements, rather than institutions, were the preferred choice for children who were unwanted at birth or whose parents could not care for them properly. The family was invested with social purpose and emotional function as the primary caretaker of children, whatever other function it had shed in the process of industrialization. Adoption—the legal incorporation of a child from the family of birth into a family of desire—was one route; the other was family foster care, which grew throughout the century as an alternative to orphanages for children who needed to be placed on a temporary basis, or who were unlikely to be adopted. Orphanages were never entirely eclipsed, although they were distinctly viewed as less desirable. In both adoptions and foster care, the community through various welfare agencies oversaw the proper disposition of the children and took an interest in their welfare, even after their placement.

In the 1950s and 1960s, almost all adoptions were both supervised and secret, meaning that the records were sealed and unavailable to all parties concerned. Neither the natural mother (or parents) nor the adoptive parents and child could know the identities of the others, in perpetuity. This corresponded with the presumed desire for privacy of all the parties: the natural mother, usually unmarried, did not want her identity made known since what society described as her "moral" failure was probably why she surrendered the child in the first place; the adoptive parents wanted to behave like all the spontaneous families around them, unchallenged in their identity as parents. Thus the childhood of the adoptee should blend into the childhoods around her. The child would eventually be told she was adopted because she was loved and wanted by her adoptive parents, but nothing more. This was the bargain struck at the height of the baby boom. All children were wanted; all children should have families; everyone participated in a social compact which protected the identity of the unmarried woman and protected children from being less than fully cared for by "complete" families. There was considerable hypocrisy in all this and, of course, there were always children who were not wanted and not placed. These tended to come from groups whose futures could not be easily blended into the hegemonic, aspiring middle class—African American children; abused or handicapped children; children with developmental problems. But, in general, the social compact was fulfilled through the forms of adoption that prevailed, and in the 1950s and 1960s sometimes even these least wanted children found homes among parents who took very seriously their sense of being responsible for the welfare of society's children. Interracial adoptions, for example, were never intended to mimic natural families, but revealed the social contract in its most serious and effective form.

By the end of the 1970s, contraception and the accompanying sexual revolution, as well as other value changes associated with feminism, had altered premarital patterns and the views of what a family was and its role in society. Premarital sexual experimentation was the first arena of change. This change was probably earliest signaled by the publication in 1962 of *Sex and the Single Girl* by Helen Gurley Brown, but it was evident as well in the profusion of sex manuals (*The Joy of Sex* being the most aptly named), and the franker discussion of sexuality in magazines and public discourse. Young people, who had been restricted at home by parents and in college by parietal rules, were freer in their dating behavior and much more likely, once they left home, to live for a while with a boyfriend or girlfriend, or at least to spend nights at each other's places. In fact, these arrangements probably explain the large jump in the average age at marriage during this period and profoundly altered the usual transition to marriage pattern. Women's new independence also made a difference. Where the expectation in the past had been that girls would move from their parents' house to the home they created with their husbands, with college no more than a carefully guarded transit point, respectable women now lived apart from families. For the first time in the century, the number of people living "alone" in the census ballooned, inflated by young singles living on their own or in makeshift arrangements with other singles of either sex. "Between 1970 and 1975," historian John Modell discovered, "the proportion of young single men living by themselves more than doubled. Among young women, the gains in singles living alone were equally dramatic."[8]

Just as significantly, the number of children born plummeted. In 1978, the birthrate stood at 65.5, the lowest in the century and well below even the sharp depression-driven dip of the 1930s.[9] The baby boom had collapsed. While children were still being born and conventional households composed of parents and children continued to be formed, these were a shrinking proportion of census households. Side-by-side with the conventional families were a number of newly experimental patterns: a growing number of childless couples who long delayed childbearing (or decided against bearing children altogether); single people either living alone or with an "unrelated" individual; communal living patterns, some of which had developed out of the idealism of the 1960s; newly dyadic families composed of a mother and her child (or children). American households had always been more diverse than the ideal inscribed in the 1950s, but the proportion of these households now grew significantly. The last configuration of a mother alone with her children was overwhelmingly the result of the enormous growth of divorce. The challenge to conventions and to chastity and the emphasis on self-expression of the previous decades had very specific consequences for families which might have once remained intact in deference to community standards or for the children's sake. It also removed the terrible stigma that still attached to divorced women throughout the first half of the twentieth century despite its decades of familiarity with a growing divorce rate. The family paradigm of the 1950s and early 1960s had tended to enforce this stigma since divorced women were not only conspicuous in a culture of couples, but carried a whiff of sexual license. In the 1970s, with swinging couples in the news and premarital experimentation all around, the divorced woman became a much safer commonplace.

In this new mixture of family forms, a never-married woman with her children could also now find a place—no longer a scandal or a threat but an individual exercising her options. The stigma of illegitimacy, long removed from the law, was also withdrawn now in language as "out-of-wedlock" disappeared from the social work vocabulary. The result for formal adoptions was catastrophic. Children available for agency adoptions largely disappeared. The notable exception were those who came under the auspices of the Catholic Church, whose firm stand against contraception and abortion meant that "unwanted" children were still born. African American children without families to care for them often went unplaced; as did the handicapped and abused. In the case of African American children, the number of children unavailable for adoption actually increased, because black social workers began to oppose interracial adoptions, insisting that children needed to be kept within the racial community, rather than be viewed as a charge to the whole society.

In the 1980s, the desire for adoptions within a population many of whose older married couples could not easily conceive after their long delay, and marked by a merciless decline in the supply of babies, resulted in both panic and creativity. Not everyone wanted to be parents, but those who did and couldn't have their own children began to seek alternative routes to parenting. One of these was the development of largely unsupervised forms of adoption. These private adoptions were usually facilitated through a lawyer, rather than an agency. What had once been a form of underground black market in adoptions, used by those who had been rejected or passed over by agencies, became legal throughout the country. Open adoptions also came into favor. In those cases the birth mother remained involved with the child, who now had two mothers and possibly two sets of parents. So did other strategies. As Americans sought new sources for babies in an increasingly global economy, they turned to Asia (China and Korea), Latin America (Mexico and Peru), and, after the fall of communism, the orphanages of Eastern Europe and the former Soviet Union. Often the laws of these countries had not caught up with the new practice. Sometimes the would-be parents found that the children (abused or inadequately attended as infants) were not what they imagined. Infants were now not exactly sold or traded, but they had become part of a very private world where meeting the needs of the child was distinctly secondary to meeting the desires of the parents. While these children often found a home among good people, there was no one around to make sure that some larger social goal was established. Some of these adopted children were returned because they were not what the parents had expected, thus becoming twice rejected.[10] The delicate bargain of an earlier day, while it had left some disappointed, had at least assumed that the society had a stake in the transaction. The new world of adoptions had become a largely private concern. Whose children these were, which society they belonged to, who oversaw their welfare was a matter of chance and luck.

The change in adoption was emblematic of a much wider reality in the world into which children were now, less frequently than ever before, born. The refusal to judge family forms and relationships and the desire not to moralize led often to a failure to supervise children's welfare. This happened in many realms. In the area of television, the government increasingly withdrew from the stringent licensing and supervision of advertising that had once protected children's programming from the full force of commercialism. New educational programs on public television, such as the acclaimed *Sesame Street,* could hardly compensate for the decline of educational programming on the other networks. By the mid-1980s, most programs had been largely freed to float with the market. Children watched programs crammed with ads before, after, and during the show. Some shows were themselves nothing more than ads for toys. In 1990, the Children's Television Act seemed to restore restrictions on commerce, but the loopholes in the law, and the fact that its scheduling restrictions on violent or sexual programming were irrelevant in a new VCR and cable television age, rendered its controls largely meaningless.[11]

In the area of foster case, there was growing uncertainty and ambiguity about the state's role and what standards to apply in supervising families. Was it more important to keep families intact even if it was not clear that their nurture was quite "good enough" (and what, after all was a "good enough" family); was the child better off being adopted even if the parents still wanted her, or shunted among foster placements while the mother decided or cleaned up her act; could a filthy, rat-infested home be an effective place to raise children? The crisis in foster care grew throughout the

1980s and into the 1990s as more children found their way into "the system" and as the unstable families that had been long accumulating on their rosters were further devastated by drug addiction (increasingly common among pregnant women) and imprisonments. Gradually, the systems of supervision were cracking under the load they were forced to bear. Those cracks became more and more visible over time. By the 1990s they were exposed in public scandals when a New York City girl, who was supposed to be supervised by state and city welfare agencies, was abused and killed by her parents; or when a child in the Florida system disappeared altogether early in the new century. Almost all of these children were not white.

Child care, too, was largely unsupervised and overwhelmingly market driven. By the early 1980s child care had become an increasing necessity for the growing number of divorced mothers and households in which mother and father both worked full time, even when the children were young. From the 1970s to the 1990s, the age of children the majority of whose mothers worked declined step by step, from children under 6 years of age, to those under 2, and then under 1. In some ways, these households had fulfilled ideals of the feminist challenge to male power in the marketplace that was launched in the early 1970s. But in most other ways, it was the market that had triumphed, by incorporating the skills of millions of women while reducing the wages and salaries of most workers. The decline in real wages that was marked during the long recession of the 1970s and the shorter one of the 1980s was compensated by female work. Most households adapted to this economic reality, accepting women's work—no longer disreputable—as part of the modern bargain where goods rather than time and freedom had become the primary markers of class. The initial feminist agenda had rarely made any provision for children. But this left children at the mercy of private decisions and ad hoc arrangements—family care, young foreign nannies (still mostly illegal before the late 1980s), church child care, franchised day-care centers, nursery schools that accepted younger and younger children, or temporary baby sitters including extended kin. The state exercised some supervision over work conditions and health and safety provisions through licensing requirements in larger establishments, but none at all over quality. For many households where parents worked more than one shift, sometimes children were irregularly cared for by one or the other parent, making fathers now more responsible for the care of children, even if they had not quite adapted to the new reality. Above all, necessary child care, once assumed to be the work of mothers (who would remain home even if they were poor according to the legislation first established during the New Deal's Social Security package) had become a matter to be negotiated privately—each parent deciding who took care of the children and what he or she would settle for in terms of quality of care.

This new reality of mother's work ultimately destroyed the pact that had been made between the federal government and the poor, for whom Aid for Families with Dependent Children had provided some means for poor women to stay home and care for their children. In 1994, that pact came to an end when "welfare as we know it" disappeared during the Clinton administration, and with it the assumption that caring for children was itself a worthy form of social behavior, for which the state was willing to pay.

In the case of older children, the schools sometimes filled the breech in child care. As was so often the case in the past, the education of the "whole" child required that schools attend to more than academic concerns. This time they began to offer various after-school programs for children whose parents came home way past 3 o'clock. But the schools did this irregularly and unpredictably. Supervision, even after school, was still largely a parental choice and responsibility, and in a society where amusements had become cheap and plentiful, this often meant that children came home to fill their time with more and ever more fanciful toys. Some of these toys linked up with the world of television or movies; others were based on the rapidly evolving technologies relying on the silicon chip; still others were lodged in habits of serial acquisition as children collected sets of Ninja Turtles or Care Bears. Almost none of these were related to the toys of previous childhoods, once carefully selected by parents eager to pass on a tradition of play. Most came from television information, rapidly disseminated by school and child care chums. The supervision of toys, like the supervision of so much else concerning children, declined and gave way to commerce and guilt.

While parents were certain to want their children to benefit from the latest fad so as not to be left out from among their peers, they also increasingly provided their children with goods instead of time. In a new world of working mothers, where neither government policies nor social practices developed effectively as expressions of the society's interest in the child, parents found themselves in a time-bind. By the mid-1980s, time-strapped parents were more and more told that "quality" in time spent with children was far more important than the quantity that parents (still mostly mothers) devoted to the task. But, no matter how good the quality of their interactions, few mothers were completely reassured. Somehow the lack of time-intensive attention to children was taking its toll. Increasingly, this was experienced in parental stress and in exaggerated (but not altogether unfounded) fears about their children's safety.

Everywhere childhood itself seemed no longer what it once had been. The perfect childhood was always an illusion, something we want once to have existed, rather than something we really had. But since the middle of the nineteenth century, Americans had created more than an illusion in the commitment to a childhood protected from the market and given the chance to grow and develop through schooling, public health enforcements of clean water, and safe vaccines and drugs. In the 1950s, the invention of a vaccine against polio (previously a scourge of childhood) had made Jonas Salk into a folk hero. Laws also tried to protect girls from sexual exploitation and all children from abusive parents. The protections had always been firmly lodged in middle-class attitudes and were usually applied variously to the children of others. Still, they had raised childhood to a position of privilege for all, a kind of innocence from the worst kind of abuse that adults readily recognized was an all too human possibility. This protection, the middle classes thought they could certainly provide for their own children. By the 1980s, this belief was seriously challenged through the growing publicity about children's dangers. These dangers invaded deep into the homes of the middle class as parents worried about stranger abductions and discovered that their own spouses could steal their children and hide them away in what became a newly criminalized form of divorce-related behavior. (See Chapter 5 in this volume.) And schools, once the symbol of protected and extended childhood, had become less and less ideal.

In the 1970s, schools became first less community-centered as court-ordered desegregation took effect (an action grounded in a vision of public good), and then they became less and less safe as the growing drug problem (and the guns that often went with it) invaded high schools and junior highs, and then eventually even the lower schools. Similarly, the sexualizing of music, popular culture, and advertising was taking its toll on the outward behavior of younger and younger children, whose dress and tastes began to imitate their older siblings and models such as Cindy Crawford and media stars such as Britney Spears, as well as the Calvin Klein billboards that encouraged provocative looks and tight jeans. Many middle-class parents, hoping to protect their own children, fled to suburban enclaves and private schools (whose enrollments began to skyrocket in the 1980s) but found that the trends merely followed their children and their money.

What these parents were beginning to privatize more successfully was the good education that brought college admissions that had once been promised to all children through the public schools and which the race for excellence of the 1950s had delivered more effectively than in the past. By the 1980s, quality schooling tended to be more parceled out than ever since World War II, and more segregated since the end of the desegregation era, as the middle class began to protect its educational prerogatives. Public school districts in poorer communities found themselves strangled by lack of funds and forced to lesser programs at a time when going to college had become an imperative for economic success. By the 1980s, the great American system of education for all (great despite its many faults) became more privatized. Wealthy suburbanites raised property taxes or ran successful fund-raisers, sent their children to learning centers that taught basic skills like reading and advanced SAT preparation, while well-off city-dwellers sent them to selective and academically competitive private schools. Many others went to parochial schools. If these options were not possible, by the 1990s parents began to ask for a new choice, calling for "charter schools" where the public purse paid for a school that emphasized private goals and visions of superior education under parental control and supervision. This disassembling of the public schools into privatized components could not entirely save children from sex and violence, but it did reflect the growing eclipse of the vision of childhood as invested with common public goals.

Even money (maybe especially money) could not protect the children of prosperity from changes that technology and culture had deposited deep within the home. New devices such as microwave ovens and new expensive food purveyors made it possible to split up traditional meal times within families as working mothers had less time to shop, cook, and prepare what had once been a family's daily gathering. Parents' hours at work, children's hours at schools and sports meant fewer hours spent together. Often expensive vacations were intended to make up the difference. Too often, private family life became at once less private and more dependent on a variety of services performed by others while it also became less public-minded in its concerns and commitments. At the same time, these families could also not protect their children against the ultimate exposure that came with divorce, which revealed the family's painful emotional interdependence and its equally painful dependency on judicial intervention and public laws. No-fault divorce laws and new joint-custody decrees made women more autonomous but also less likely to be allowed to determine their children's lives. As parents remarried and blended their offspring into newer units, children often became members of several families—a new family form that joined the innovations of the 1970s. Psychologists debated the costs to children of their parents' divorces and subsequent blendings, but one cost was clearly an older sense of family autonomy.

Happiness seemed much more elusive than sexual satisfaction and freedom from the conventions of an earlier time. By the century's end, however, pharmaceutical innovations were beginning to compensate even for this. A whole range of drugs became available to treat depression in the 1950s and 1960s, with valium the best known, but these sedatives could never provide a sense of well-being. The sixties had begun a trend that normalized other kinds of drug taking, although these remained illegal and were taken surreptitiously and usually in groups. In the 1980s, a whole new category of drugs—serotonin re-uptake inhibitors—now provided a legitimate and increasingly widespread way for both sixties' youth and their children to feel good. At first given to the really depressed or dysfunctional in tandem with more conventional therapies, Prozac and the drugs that quickly followed in its wake provided relief from mood swings and psychological lows. In fairly short order, these drugs moved into the general society, widely prescribed and dispensed, and used by adults and more and more children and adolescents. In addition, children who were overactive in school were increasingly medicated (often as part of a school requirement) with a potent drug which calmed them down and allowed them to focus. In a brief time Ritalin became, in turn, a means to control overactive youngsters, a way for college students to concentrate during exams, and a drug sold on the black market for others to get high. Americans and their children had incorporated drugs into their daily lives.

Clone Age

By the late 1980s, physics as a source of technological wonder had been replaced by biology and electronics. Where once Americans guarded their nuclear secrets, now innovations in microchip technology and the new marketing attached to the Internet (initially a military sponsored technology) were providing American economic advantage. New fears about the theft of recent developments in this area were raising serious questions about the open nature of university research and its welcome to foreign students, and computers dominated not only the job prospects of America's ever larger college-bound population (now augmented through affirmative action programs) and grown to almost 60 percent, but their school tasks and desk equipment. Knowing how to use a computer became an essential part of growing up and increasingly necessary to the tasks the young were required to perform for homework. The new technologies were linking the children together over Internet-mediated games, while their common culture was being defined by movie characters and special effects in blockbuster movies.

The boldest new research on the frontier between social expectation and ethical dilemmas came in biology. The revolution that Darwin had initiated in the nineteenth century in the understanding of whole species now lodged in the genetic codes of the individual, and the technologies of cell division. Between them, these research fields had the potential to transform childhood in fundamental ways which had become genuinely frightening, but also highly desirable in areas of health and medicine. Research in this field promised new cures for cancers and ways to replace vital organs. It also predicted new ways to create babies.

That revolution was already glimpsed when the birth of a "Baby Conceived Outside the Body," was announced in the *New York Times*.[12] Born on July 25, 1978, and delivered by Caesarian section, Louise Brown weighed in at 5 lbs, 12 ounces. She was almost immediately labeled the first test-tube baby, but, in fact, Louise's first days were spent in a Petri dish where her parents' eggs and sperm had been mixed together, and thereafter she had developed inside her mother's womb like any other child. The original research that led to this potential "cure" for infertility was funded, among others, by the Ford Foundation, to aid in the development of contraception. The contraceptive revolution that had helped to transform sexual behavior and family dynamics had also created a new means to deal with the fertility collapse which had resulted, not all of it intended. Three decades later, Dolly the cloned sheep was born, also the product of Petri dishes and genetic research, but now much more completely through a different form of conception, since she was wholly the expression of her mother's genetic code. By 2004, copy cats, literally, were created (and later dogs) and sold at high prices to ease the grief of owners who had lost a pet. Despite widespread rhetoric, nobody really believed that the animal clones would not eventually be followed by a human version.

During those thirty years, fertility research and its associated medical specializations had created new hope for infertile couples, and new possibilities to tailor children to parental desires. What it had not created was an effective area of policy regulation or clear laws to govern a booming new field. Politicians vented their high ethical outrage, but could not control either the market for the innovations, nor the new global parameters of the scientific work being done.

By the mid-1990s, almost any undergraduate in America could pick up her college newspaper and respond to an offer to have her eggs harvested. If she was blond, tall, pretty, athletic, and had high SAT scores she might realize as much as $50,000 for this private transaction. Eggs were being bought on the Internet, accompanied by pictures and descriptions of personal features, which presumably were inheritable. The new techniques were making it possible to harvest eggs from a young, fertile girl (made more fertile through hormone treatments), combine them in a Petri dish with the sperm of a couple's male partner and implant them in the female partner. It was also making it possible for lesbian couples to conceive and for gay partners to father a child. The once imagined "natural" barriers to conception had been broken as sperm, eggs, and wombs became divisible components of a new birthing process. The division between sex and conception heralded by the contraceptive revolution of the 1960s had moved into a new world.

In that world, genetics was king. Genetic technologies that would eventually make the first breakthrough in laying bare the 20,000–25,000 elements of the human genome in 2001 were facilitating the identification of fathers in totally unprecedented ways. What had once been a social construct, became a testable biological fact. Where female chastity and marital fidelity had been the only way to lay claim to fatherhood, now a simple test made social practices irrelevant. This new fact was already transforming paternity suits, altering adoption contracts (as the Baby Jessica case made clear), and transforming the work of state welfare agencies as they pursued absent fathers for child support payments. "Out-of-wedlock" became truly meaningless in this context. As the genetic components of a child's DNA became the determinant of her social position, she increasingly belonged to or expressed her parents, rather than an identity established through agreed-upon community-established criteria.

Over the course of the second half of the twentieth century, the child's social position and her purchase on the community's commitments had steadily declined as the family, once an honorable social mediator, had been delegitimated. But the desire for children had not therefore declined. It now became a function of personal desire and the emotional need for self-expression. This is what baby-boom women discovered as their "biological clocks" began to tick down in the 1980s. Eager for the personal completion that having a child might offer, rather than the contribution they were making to a community good, or a family identity (historical or contemporary), women sought to become mothers, and the new reproductive technologies grew to meet that need. In this world of children as personal expression, why not tailor the genes to meet the desired image of the self just as the child could be made to wear the right "designer" labels. The desperation of some to create children with their own genetic materials (or at least that of their partner) at almost any cost, while thousands of children (not so well designed) were caught in the despondency of a deteriorating foster-care system, was perhaps as much a mark of ignorance as of selfishness, but it had become difficult to tell the difference.

At the core of the changes had been the eclipse of family as a meaningful social institution and the source of social identity. American families had never had the cultural meaning and weight associated with family in more traditional societies, but their private functions had been invested with social meaning since the middle of the nineteenth century. This was in some ways exaggerated by the social commitment to family life immediately after the World War and into the 1950s. By then, however, families had already shrunk in social terms, discarding resident grandparents who had still had a household place earlier in the century. Until the 1960s, this shrinkage of the connections between the intimate family and others that once created a sense of historical meaning had been hidden by the sheer size of baby-boom families. When the numbers of children declined sharply in the late sixties and seventies, divorce increased, and alternative residence arrangement blossomed, the family's weakness as a social link was exposed. With no obligation to an older generation whose care could not be paid for, and fewer children, the part that families had once borne in the social fabric began to seem weightless. Family relations still seemed to matter to individuals and the rhetoric of family values became ever louder in politics, but the family's real role in the society had shrunk. Despite the political noise around the subject, it found less real support in the political arena while actual families struggled more than ever to provide the resources of time, money, and knowledge on their own without much social support.

Technology had often been the source of change and a response to change during those fifty-five years, but rarely the sole explanation. By the turn of the new century, the many ethical issues that were being aired in relation to the changes in biological knowledge and changes in the family were too often attached to party labels, rather than understood as a measure of a broad social change that had led to a general disengagement from childhood. With some notable variation, liberal Democrats supported abortion, stem-cell research (which used embryonic cells), and contraceptives made available to young people; conservative Republicans supported middle-class school vouchers, adult sentencing for juveniles, and an end to welfare. Each side used the image of children to bolster its own position, and both vocally supported "quality schools." Indeed, schools became an important part of America's new competitive strategy in a new global market place, a necessary way to assure that Americans would stay ahead of the competition for highly skilled jobs. Neither side took children seriously as part of a fundamental social contract. Few politicians addressed the broad-range disengagement from children's welfare that had already taken place—the increasing privatization of adoptions; the substitution of genetic for family identity; the withdrawal of support from the families of poor children; the targeted marketing of goods to children; the loss of commitment to viewing everyone's child as a charge against the whole; the failure of nerve in making judgments about what was good for children and what was not, apart from the interests of their (voting) parents. Americans and increasingly the populations of Western Europe were haunted by the pedophile—the stranger come to prey on their children and to destroy their innocence. Few saw that their children had been made strangers to others, and that their innocence, once the potent source of protective legislation, had become little more than a politically convenient catch phrase. We had created a new childhood, but we were still using the images of the past. Understanding this changed childhood and protecting all our children would have to wait for another day.

NOTES

This essay was written for *The Columbia History of the United States: 1945–2000*, edited by Mark Carnes, and is reprinted here with permission.

1. The birthrate figures are from Thomas D. Snyder, "Education Characteristics of the Population," in *120 Years of American Education: A Statistical Portrait*, edited by Snyder, U.S. Department of Education, Office of Educational Research and Improvement, January 1993, Table 1, p. 12.

2. Michael Zuckerman, "Dr. Spock: Confidence Man," in *The Family in History*, edited by Charles Rosenberg (Philadelphia: University of Pennsylvania Press, 1975), 179–207.

3. Snyder, "Education Characteristics," Table 3, p. 16.

4. Erik H. Erikson, *Identity: Youth and Crisis* (New York: Norton, 1968), 128. The chapter in which this demand is made, "The Life Cycle: Epigenisis of Identity," was based on an earlier article that Erikson published in 1950.

5. *New York Times*, May 16, 1961, p. 39; *New York Times*, May 13, 1961, p. E13.

6. For new moves to incorporate blacks, see *New York Times*, April 15, 1966, p. 35. Malcolm X's experiences at school are remembered in *The Autobiography of Malcolm X* (New York: Grove Press, 1965).

7. Beth Bailey, *Sex in the Heartland* (Cambridge, MA: Harvard University Press, 1999), 200–202.

8. John Modell, *Into One's Own: From Youth to Adulthood in the United States, 1920–1975* (Berkeley: University of California Press, 1989), 275.

9. Snyder, "Education Characteristics," Table 1, p. 13.

10. Rachel Stryker, "Forging Families, Fixing Families: Adoption and the Cultural Politics of Reactive Attachment Disorder," Ph.D. dissertation (Anthropology), University of California at Berkeley, 2004.

11. Gary Cross, *The Cute and the Cool: Wondrous Innocence and Modern American Children's Culture* (New York: Oxford University Press, 2004), 182–184.

12. *New York Times*, July 26, 1978, p. 1.

BIBLIOGRAPHY

Excerpts from articles, newspaper clippings and other sources for many of the issues relating to children addressed in this essay can be found in *Childhood in America*, edited by Paula S. Fass and Mary Ann Mason (New York: New York University Press, 2000). The *locus classicus* for understanding the transformation of childhood in the late nineteenth century and how children were taken out of the calculations of the marketplace is Viviana Zelizer, *Pricing the Priceless Child* (New York: Basic Books, 1985).

On family life during the fifties and after, Elaine Tyler May, *Homeward Bound* (New York: Basic Books, 1988), and Arlene Skolnick, *Troubled Paradise* (New York: Basic Books, 1991) are good places to start. For Dr. Spock, see Nancy Pottishman Weiss, "Mother the Invention of Necessity: Benjamin Spock's *Baby and Child Care*," *American Quarterly*, 29 (1979), 519–546; and Michael Zuckerman who coined the confidence man term in "Dr. Spock: Confidence Man," in *The Family in History*, edited by Charles E. Rosenberg (Philadelphia: University of Pennsylvania Press, 1975). For a longer overview of the history of the American family, see Steven Mintz and Susan Kellogg, *Social History of American Family Life* (New York: Free Press, 1988). A good collection on contemporary family issues is *All Our Families*, revised edition, edited by Mary Ann Mason, Arlene Skolnick, and Steven Sugarman (New York: Oxford University Press, 2003).

For an excellent introduction to the history of childhood in America which also addresses many contemporary issues, see Steven Mintz, *Huck's Raft: A History of American Childhood* (New York: Oxford University Press, 2004). Child-rearing concerns and advice are ably discussed by Peter N. Stearns, *Anxious Parents: Trying to Measure Up in the Twentieth Century* (New York: New York University Press, 2003); Ann Hulbert, *Raising America: Experts, Parents and a Century of Advice about Children* (New York: Alfred A. Knopf, 2003); and Julia Grant, *Raising Baby by the Book: The Education of American Mothers* (New Haven: Yale University Press, 1998). A good measure of the growing contemporary revulsion against child-rearing advice and the illusion of parental control is Judith Rich Harris, *The Nurture Assumption: Why Children Turn Out the Way They Do* (New York: Free Press, 1998), which rejects the importance of parental influence altogether. Gary Cross, *The Cute and the Cool: Wondrous Innocence and Modern American Children's Culture* (New York: Oxford University Press, 2004) provides important insights into contemporary disengagement and the private dreams fulfilled by children. See also Cross, *Kids' Stuff: Toys and the Changing World of American Childhood* (Cambridge, MA: Harvard University Press, 1997), for the changing nature of toys and their growing dependence on children's taste. For media violence, see Sissela Bok, *Mayhem: Violence as Public Entertainment* (Reading, MA: Perseus Books, 1998). Adoption has not received the historical attention it deserves, but the place to start is E. Wayne Carp, *Family Matters: Secrecy and Disclosure in the History of Adoption* (Cambridge, MA: Harvard University Press, 1998); and Barbara Melosh, *Strangers and Kin: The American Way of Adoption* (Cambridge, MA: Harvard University Press, 2002). For the globalization of adoption matters, see Agnès Fine, *Adoptions: Ethnologie des Parentes Choisies* (Paris: Edition de la Maison des Sciences de L'Homme, 1998); Rachel Stryker, "Forging Families, Fixing Families: Adoption and the Cultural Politics of Reactive Attachment Disorder," Ph.D. dissertation (Anthropology), University of California at Berkeley, 2004.

Ricki Solinger, *Wake Up Little Suzy* (New York: Routledge, 2000), discusses how illegitimacy was treated in the fifties. A different perspective on modesty can be found in Rochelle Gerstein, *Repeal of Reticence: A History of America's Cultural and Legal Struggles over Free Speech, Obscenity, Sexual Liberation, and Modern Art* (New York: Hill and Wang, 1996). For changes in sexual behavior in the 1960s, see David Allyn, *Make Love Not War: The Sexual Revolution, an Unfettered History* (Boston: Little, Brown, 2000); and Beth Bailey, *Sex in the Heartland* (Cambridge, MA: Harvard University Press, 1999). For the sixties more generally, David Farber, *The Age of Great Dreams: America in the 1960s* (New York: Hill and Wang, 1994), and Farber, editor, *The Sixties: From Memory to History* (Chapel Hill: University of North Carolina Press, 1994). For college life in the twentieth century more generally, see Helen Lefkowitz Horowitz, *Campus Life: Undergraduate Cultures from the End of the Eighteenth Century to the Present* (New York: Knopf, 1988); Paula S. Fass, *The Damned and the Beautiful: American Youth in the 1920s* (New York: Oxford University Press, 1977); and David O. Levine, *The American College and the Culture of Aspiration, 1915–1940* (Ithaca, NY: Cornell University Press, 1986). For a statistical profile of the population and of the education of that population, Thomas D. Snyder, "Education Characteristics of the Population," in *120 Years of American Education: A Statistical Portrait*, edited by Snyder, U.S. Department of Education, Office of Educational Research and Improvement, January 1993. For schooling issues more generally, Diane Ravitch, *Troubled Crusade: American Education, 1945–1980* (New York: Basic Books, 1983); Paula S. Fass, *Outside In: Minorities and the Transformation of American Education* (New York: Oxford University Press, 1989). The federal government's sponsorship of university research is discussed in Ellen Herman, *The Romance of American Psychology: Political Culture in the Age of Experts* (Berkeley: University of California Press, 1995), and changes in the patterns of growing up in John Modell, *Into One's Own: From Youth to Adulthood in the United States, 1920–1975* (Berkeley: University of California Press, 1989). For life-course transitions and the changing composition of the American family, David A. Stevens, "New Evidence on the Timing of Early Life Course Transitions: The United States 1900 to 1980," *Journal of Family History* 15 (1990), 163–178; and Steven Ruggles, "The Transformation of American Family Structure," *American Historical Review,* 99 (February 1994), 103–128.

Matters relating to parenting and its relations to time and work and its consequences for children have developed a huge sociological literature, and growing attention among historians. Some of this can be glimpsed at the Web site of the Center for Working Families of the University of California at Berkeley, directed by Arlie Hochschild and Barrie Thorne (http://workingfamilies.berkeley.edu). In addition, Arlie Russell Hochschild, *The Time Bind: When Work Becomes Home and Home Becomes Work* (New York: Metropolitan Books, 1997); Anne Crittenden, *The Price of Motherhood: Why the Most Important Job in the World Is Still the Least Valued* (New York: Metropolitan Books, 2001). Among historians, Gary Cross has done some of the fundamental work; see *Time and Money: The Making of Consumer Culture* (London and New York: Routledge, 1993), and *An All-Consuming Century: Why Commercialism Won in Modern America* (New York: Columbia University Press, 2000). In addition, *Kids' Stuff: Toys and the Changing World of American Childhood* provides the necessary information on the development of children's toys and its relationship to consumer culture as well as insight into how this reflects on family relations. Also useful is Elizabeth Quinn-Lasch, "Mothers and Markets," *The New Republic,* March 6, 2000.

Issues of divorce and children are discussed in Mary Ann Mason, *The Custody Wars: Why Children Are Losing the Legal Battle, and What We Can Do about It* (New York: Basic Books, 1999), and some of the disagreement over the effects of divorce on children can be seen in Judith Wallerstein and Joan Berlin Kelly, *Surviving the Breakup: How Children and Parents Cope with Divorce* (New York: Basic Books, 1980), and E. Mavis Hetherington and John Kelly, *For Better or Worse: Divorce Reconsidered* (New York: W. W. Norton, 2002). The problems of the foster-care system and the conflict over policies has unfortunately developed a rich literature; see Nina Bernstein, *The Lost Children of Wilder: The Epic Struggle to Change Foster Care* (New York: Pantheon Books, 2001); Michael Shapiro, *Solomon's Sword: Two Families and the Children the State Took Away* (New York: Times Books, 1999); Elizabeth Bertolet, *Nobody's Children: Abuse and Neglect, Foster Drift, and the Adoption Alternative* (Boston: Beacon Press, 2000). Linda Gordon, *Heroes of Their Own Lives: The Politics and History of Family Violence* (New York: Viking, 1988), provides the historical context for the work of social agencies. For the politics and consequences of disengaging from welfare, see Jason De Perle, *American Dream: Three Women, Ten Kids, and a Nation's Drive to End Welfare* (New York: Viking, 2004). For the recent fears about child abduction, Paula S. Fass, *Kidnapped: Child Abduction in America* (New York: Oxford University Press, 1997); Philip Jenkins, *Moral Panic: Changing Conceptions of the Child Molester in Modern America* (New Haven: Yale University Press, 1998); and James Kincaid, *Erotic Innocence.: The Culture of Child Molesting* (Durham, N.C.: Duke University Press, 1998). *Clone Age: Adventures in the New World of Reproductive Technology* (New York: Henry Holt, 1999) provided me with the title for my section. The book by Lori B. Andrews will give readers a sense of the Wild West atmosphere surrounding reproductive technologies. Elaine Tyler May, *Barren in the Promised Land: Childless Americans and the Pursuit of Happiness* (New York: Basic Books, 1995), provides insights into the problem of childlessness and the search for answers.

PART III

Children of a New Global World

Introduction to Part III

A word with an impersonal and clumsy sound, "globalization," has often been invoked as a symbol of contemporary social change and a harbinger of a bleak future. As the following essays try to suggest, however, historians have been familiar with this phenomenon, if not with the word itself, for some time. The United States, one could argue, resulted from an earlier incarnation of the thrust beyond familiar boundaries as it occupied a new world and created an unfamiliar hybrid society with global resonances. But, globalization as it is understood today usually refers to changes that have taken place since World War II and have accelerated in the 1990s, as worldwide communications, free markets, and the massive migrations of peoples are remaking personal identities and cultural boundaries.

In this section, I try to use America's peculiar history as a means to better understand globalization today and specifically to evaluate the experiences of children in that world. This is especially the case in the first of these essays, Chapter 7, originally written for a conference on globalization in Łódź, Poland, in November 2001 and subsequently published in the *Journal of Social History*. In this, my first attempt to use the concept, I try to put what I knew about American experience to use in order to suggest what might be happening to children elsewhere when the conditions begin to approximate those in the United States in the past. I am proposing that American experience can even provide us with a way to anticipate changes elsewhere in the world today. To do this, I attempt to define the elements (such as work, consumption, schooling, and gender) that will likely be affected as the pressures of economic change, media saturation, and the exposure to diverse cultures spread. In this first foray in thinking about globalization and children, I assumed that the United States was both a force for globalization and a model of how it operated.

By the time I wrote the essay published here as Chapter 8, which looks at the effect of contemporary migrations on children, my sense of globalization had become far more dynamic. I now considered how the United

States as a participant in contemporary globalization was itself being redefined through the many pressures that the global world was creating. In this essay, I ask about the future of the United States and the different possibilities that the current new migration was creating. The United States is only one of the many societies in which migration is re-creating social life and social relations. The United States in this essay is no longer just a product of an earlier globalization and producer of the capital remaking the world today, but itself caught up in its strong currents. At the same time, this dynamic experience still needs to be understood within the historical context of previous American experience with many of these factors and issues. By looking at American society in this wider context, I began to reflect on the nature of childhood in a global future. This forced me to think about our commitments to a certain kind of childhood, how potentially fragile those commitments really are, and to assess their vulnerability to economic pressures generally.

The question of our commitments to children, how they came about, and their future in a new global world underlies the last of the essays in this section, Chapter 9. The paper published here is a revised version of an earlier essay written for a conference on children and youth in globalization organized at the School of American Research in Sante Fe, New Mexico, in April 2004. It was my goal to provide a framework for anthropologists and other social scientists working in this area. I am grateful to the SAR Press for allowing me to publish this essay here. It will be published in its original form in an SAR book, *Figuring the Future: Children, Youth, and Globalization* in 2007.

This final essay tries to grapple with two related matters: the historical circumstances and beliefs that permitted childhood to be imagined in noneconomic terms in a capitalist society, and what this offers us today in a very different world, where economic imperatives appear to drive a globalization that has the potential to threaten the kind of childhood that we have come to value. As will be clear to the reader, my views of globalization have become somewhat less sanguine and more complex. Nevertheless, in all three essays, I am trying to imagine childhood in a world context, not governed only by local conditions. I am also trying to understand how a worldwide set of ideals about children would function. By the end of this section, the cultural possibilities that were created in the West by the early twentieth century through a commitment to children's welfare and rights is one I find myself embracing and hoping to see further developed through a global commitment to children, despite my discomfort with the potentially hegemonic implications of such a view.

This last essay also suggests that the social experiences of children and the cultural definitions of childhood are closely related. In this sense, I am also bringing together the perspectives kept somewhat separated in the last two sections. Children's lives begin with adult definitions. And while they certainly do not end there, it is adults who must commit themselves to their welfare before children can thrive, and potentially move in their own directions. Thus the study of children in society and in culture must be seen as of a piece. This also brings us back to the question of how we study children historically. By studying children globally, historians are enabled to see in more complex ways, to compare different childhoods in different cultures across space and time, and to better make the connection between adult values and institutions and children's experiences.

7

Children and Globalization

Bringing Children into Globalization

Boy and girl prostitutes in Thailand hired by French tourists; child pornography on the Internet; five-year-old indentured textile workers in India making silk for American clothing; Eastern European adolescent girls assaulted and raped as they seek glamorous careers on Milan's runways: these are the startling images that confront us regularly now as the economy becomes a global network and as our means to communicate information penetrates into and out of every village and hamlet. We shudder at these assaults on the most vulnerable and ask ourselves if this is a portent of the future. As our planet shrinks in size, will we sacrifice children to the yawning and ever more visible gulf between the richest and poorest nations of the earth?

It is odd that children and childhood should be nowhere on the agenda of those who currently discuss globalization.[1] Children are most definitely part of the Western sensibility about globalization, and childhood is a particularly sensitive node for cultural contention in the politics of globalization. It is my hope that an understanding of children's history will help to make discussions of globalization both more realistic, since many children are and will be affected and more attuned to the peculiar Western sentiments that are evoked in the media's coverage of the conflicts over globalization. Children are everywhere present in this debate, but never heard from or addressed.[2]

Childhood is at once a universal experience, and one of the most culturally specific. Every society must have and raise children to survive, and each seeks to protect them in some fashion. Each culture defines and divides childhood as a stage of development differently, while devising unique means to express its views of what children are like, and practices relating to children through which it fulfills the culture's vision of its own future. So too, each of us has experienced a childhood, and we are therefore strongly attached emotionally to an image of what childhood is and should be like. Thus childhood is a critical point of social contention, a profound test of cultural autonomy, and a basic emotional reference point for all of us as we reflect upon the many meanings and consequences of globalization.

It is therefore not surprising that many of the starkest images of globalization's costs take children as their subjects.[3] And we can, I believe, expect that the continuing pressure toward global integration will expose the special differences invested in childhood practices. We can also expect that this tendency for change to affect this most intimate place, where culture as well as individual memories are created, to explode in very public reactions. There are two reasons for this. The first results from the strategic role of childhood as the point of socialization and therefore as the means by which each society tries to protect its own identity. The second results from the fact that in modern Western societies children have been invested with an especially heavy emotional load. Indeed, because it has become such an emotionally resonant site in the Euro-American West, childhood and its associations have most often provided the occasions in the recent past around which we have expressed larger cultural anxieties and our sense of anguish about a whole range of issues. In other words, in addition to being a sociological and anthropological site, childhood has been invested with enormous symbolic power. I will give you just one example, from many that I could choose. This one is very recent and very raw. First in the United States in the 1980s, and then in much of Europe in the 1990s, the issue of pedophilia and the sexual abuse and murder of children has often dominated headlines and resulted in widespread popular hysteria. Those reactions are almost always way out of proportion to the actual occurrence of outrages against children, but they express a much more general sense of vulnerability, and are often powerful ways to express a less clearly focused sense of grievance and fear about other matters—the police, the economy, changes in the family, new sexual practices, and gender roles.[4]

In order to understand both how globalization is likely to affect children and why we have come to focus so much power in childhood imagery, I would like to turn now to aspects of American social experience that can provide some insight into these matters. Such an examination of the old New World, so to speak, is an unusually good point of departure for this discussion. Not only does the United States today provide the most powerful engine driving globalization toward the creation of the new New World, but America provides a kind of microcosm of the early forms of globalization. After all, globalization today—the rapidly expanding domination of all forms of culture by market forces and the penetrating power of communications—continues patterns of development that began much earlier in the West, and most conspicuously in the United States. Here rapid economic expansion, the migration and mixing of populations, the breaking down of regionalism and localism, and the confrontation of disparate value systems took place first. The United States has experienced all of these within its own historical experience during the last 150 years. The United States was, after all, a nation whose dynamic capitalist economy and vast resources attracted tens of millions of immigrants to its shores, factories, workshops, and schools. I would like, therefore, to address three issues that are especially significant to this experience as it centered on children—the issue of children's work, the role of play in childhood development, and the problem of sexuality. Together these provide what I would like to call the contemporary "youth complex" with a powerful symbolic fuse.

Children's Work

When Alexander Hamilton, America's first Secretary of the Treasury, imagined and wrote about America's manufacturing future, he had no sentimental qualms about putting children into that picture.[5] Children, he assumed, together with their parents would work in the nation's mills and factories. And why not? At the end of the eighteen century when he issued his report, American children as young as five or six could be found working alongside their parents in farms, village shops, as well as throughout the homes of the nation. They also worked for others as apprentices, or as bound labor paying off a debt, or because they were put out to work by county officials as paupers or orphans. In the growing plantations of the American South as well as in places as far north as New York State, thousands of child slaves worked alone, and in groups, often in places that were quite distant from their parents or other relatives. Indeed, children worked everywhere. The lucky ones did so as part of a family economy where they could understand their contribution as part of a corporate effort. Those who were less lucky simply did so because of their master's orders. The sense of a childhood freed from labor and devoted to individual development and play (a protected period of innocence sheltered from the cares of adults) had not yet become a common point of cultural understanding, although Jean Jacques Rousseau had already proposed it half a century earlier as a theoretical possibility.

Today, we are shocked when young children are put to work for pennies a day in India, or China, in conditions of indenture that approximate slavery, or when they are kidnapped and enslaved in the Sudan. But it is important to remember that our contemporary response is the result not of our own historical superiority, but because in the nineteenth century the struggle over slavery, the development of humanistic sensibilities, and the sentimentalization of childhood in the United States and much of the Western world began to alter values as well as behaviors, among the middle classes especially, but increasingly among others as well. Those changes grew out of the rapidly developing market economy that was eclipsing slavery as a form of labor and swamping corporate identities of all kinds, while increasing the American commitment to the rights of the individual. It is that new sensibility which defines our reactions to issues of child exploitation today. But even in the nineteenth century, this perspective did not become universal at once in the United States, and it did not happen everywhere. It also took time for this view to envelop adolescent children, those 13 to 19 whom we regard as needing protection today but who were drawn into England's soot-filled "satanic mills" and those slightly more respectable versions of New England to work twelve-hour days. Single girls of fourteen, whom we would today call adolescents, stood for hours in Lawrence, Lowell, and Holyoke, Massachusetts, spinning yarn by the mile from sun up to sun down, while they lived away from parents and home under severe restriction. They were glad at first to get such good work, and even Charles Dickens and other visitors of conscience testified to their good health and high spirits. Not until the 1850s did they begin to see themselves not as exceptions to the degradation of industrial labor, but as hardly better off than slaves.[6]

One of the great turning points for the revisioning of childhood came when Americans began to weep over slavery, when Harriet Beecher Stowe made Americans visualize the family costs and inhumanity of an institution that affected white and black. In so doing, Stowe gave the Western world a picture of the pure innocence of childhood that helped to underwrite a new sentimentality. Together with other images of the time, but familiar to far more people, Little Eva and Uncle Tom and Topsy made childhood something to be treasured and carefully guarded. It was then, in the middle of the nineteenth century, that John Locke's *tabula rasa,* by then available for almost two centuries and well known to some, found a wide audience to instruct in the fundamentals of childhood. By the middle of the nineteenth century, the unquestioned assumptions that once did not shrink from employing children as young as six came to a stop. A combination of religion, of politics, and a new vision of what we owed, not just to our own children but to other people's children came to the forefront. That view, with some alterations, continues to organize our responses to news stories of children in India, Africa, and Thailand and adolescents in Slovenia today.

It is worth stopping for a moment to examine this vision and its consequences, since it not only alerts us to why the Western observer today is grieved by news stories of children's oppression elsewhere, but suggests what kinds of issues economic expansion may bring forward in the future. At the center of this vision stood what sociologist Viviana Zelizer has called "the priceless child," the child whose value stood apart from the economy, who literally had "no price" attached to his or her being.[7] This child's importance was measured in emotional terms which obligated parents and society as a whole to his well-being. In shifting the child from a ledger where he or she could participate in economic calculations and to which even his or her small contribution had weight, to a ledger in which the only legitimate calculation was how well he could be sheltered and provided for, the society experienced a paradigm shift. This shift was quite as significant, I believe, as the other, more commonly discussed change from seeing the child as primitive and unredeemed (the early American Calvinist child), to the child as innocent and cherubic expression of God's kingdom (the Victorian child). That innocent child had emerged earlier, in the eighteenth century, but had fewer immediate social and legislative consequences.[8] It was the change in the values to which children contributed—from the economic realm to the emotional realm, that made the great difference in the late nineteenth century. In salvaging children from the insatiable engine of market transformation and investing them with an alternative value, the West reserved in childhood an arena of innocence. It was only then that these two changes together transformed the way children were conceptualized and how they were treated among the white middle classes in the United States especially, but in other parts of the world as well.

It is through that now sometimes foggy lens that we continue to see the children of the world today. Let me repeat, in this new system of values and beliefs, the child was important not for what he or she could contribute economically, but for the emotional satisfactions his cultivation could provide to the family. This child could expect much since his value lay in his emotional well-being and effective preparation. Childhood was set apart as a period of innocence and vulnerability, which obligated adults to sheltering and protecting children. The child was also to be enjoyed now in and of himself for the special qualities he contributed to the family, and to the better future he promised to the society. In this context, the newly created discipline of psychology and other scientific explorations of emotional life began to develop, with their emphasis on the unfolding personality. The child was not only withdrawn from the calculations offered up by the market, but childhood was invested with the very origins of that individuality which Western values had enshrined as worthy of respect. With this view of childhood's essential role in molding the future also came the democratic extension of schooling.

To me this is an honorable view of childhood and one with a great deal to offer to civilized life. But it is a distinctly Western incarnation and it extends a whole network of Western values that carry other consequences in their wake. We might want to keep this in mind as we think about just what effects economic changes will have on the elaborate and complex cultures which are being challenged by globalization today. Americans withdrew children from the marketplace as a fulfillment and alongside of a range of beliefs and practices to which visions of childhood were attached.[9]

The United States population in the post–Civil War period was hardly composed strictly of the kind of urban middle class population devoted to science and nurture which most readily adopted these sentiments about childhood. In its own version of internal globalization, this largely northern middle class sensibility confronted a series of immigrant groups who were drawn to other features of the American promise—above all by an exploding economy and open borders. And within its own borders, the United States still contained layers of preindustrial rural populations whose visions of children's roles and obligations grew from an older set of values, as well as a large group of former slaves and their children. All these children often became the beneficiaries, and sometimes the victims, of the new vision of childhood and the various institutions constructed to fulfill it in the late nineteenth century. In this earlier version of globalization, what I have here called the Western view won out. But not without cost. Some of these costs are visible when we consider the institutions for children that spilled out from this vision and whose aim was to protect, instruct, and shelter them. The list is long, but among its most prominent components are the Children's Aid Society and a whole host of Societies for the Prevention of Cruelty to Children, orphanages, adoption and foster care, juvenile courts and detention centers, sports clubs and playgrounds, settlements and church social centers, and above all a refashioned and newly obligatory school and its counterpart, the reform school.

These institutions were developed to protect and to constrain, to assist and to evaluate people whose values and beliefs did not usually conform to its standards. And they began the construction of a picture of a normative childhood which conformed to the values of some, but not necessarily the habits of many. By the turn of the twentieth century, these institutions had affected more and more children, and for longer and longer periods of their lives. Many historians over the last generation have demonstrated that these high-minded institutions often had less than wholesome consequences. The protection of the children of the poor and foreign often served as a means to condemn their parents and their values and practices.[10] Over fifty years ago, Lionel Trilling explored how the liberal impulse to enlighten and uplift also resulted in the compulsion to control. This does not mean that this sensibility of protection was at fault, only that the extension outward from one's own children to the children of people unlike ourselves can harbor other emotions as well. In the process, those who are criticized and dispossessed in this way can experience confusion, insult, and outrage.[11]

This is only to say that many of the things we now take for granted in the United States did not take place without a struggle. As immigrants from Poland and Italy, Greece and Ireland brought their own visions of childhood, of upbringing, of religious training, of the proper road to full adulthood, and above all of generational relations and obligations, they confronted these new institutions, instructions, and definitions ready to take their children away from their past, their priests, and the church's order, and the work they were expected to do to relieve their parents' burden. They also took them from the respect that they owed to parents whose visions of the future increasingly differed from those taught to their children. This was a new world it seemed, in which economic possibilities beckoned in exchange for control over their children's future.

One example can be used to suggest how these changes could be experienced by those who came for their own purposes only to find that they were losing control over their children in the process. Italians throughout the northeastern United States resisted the institutions of schooling that were being imposed, and they resisted as well the extension of childhood into adolescence, into years, when from their point of view, children should be usefully employed, but remained instead idled by the regulations imposed by the state. In places like the state of Connecticut, officials complained that "Every year it has become apparent . . . that parents [of unschooled children] to a considerable extent are insensible to the wrong they are permitting to be inflicted upon their offspring." In these very same places, parents complained that American life was enforcing idleness among their children who did nothing but play. "When you pass by a school," one Italian mother complained, "all you hear is singing or the steps of dancing, or the noise of playing, playing, playing." One Italian father put it another way. "What good is it if a boy is bright and intelligent, and then does not know enough to respect his family. Such a boy would be worth nothing. That's the trouble with American kids . . . the schools don't teach them to respect their families."[12] As parents hoped to enforce an older discipline and an older understanding of the corporate welfare of the family as an economic unit, state officials increasingly insisted that the children needed to be protected; that they needed to be schooled away from their parents' habits and language; that they needed to play in order to express themselves as children.

This struggle over authority was often framed around issues of work, and as we confront globalization on a massive scale beyond American borders it is well to remember this earlier confrontation. After all, the work expected of children today, on shoes in China, or cloth in India, and which offends us deeply may just be the first stages of a process of change, which we who peer from the other side of that divide refuse adequately to understand, having forgotten our own experiences. It is by no means easy to predict whether children's work outside the home will lead to a pattern of development in which that work will finally be condemned from within the society. I have argued that in the United States the conjunction of many factors resulted in the special solicitude toward children that condemned child labor. But, it is hardly necessary to predict that this will work to stir opposition in international organizations who see through a Western lens.

In many ways, what we have seen so far is only the first glimpse of the change that globalization is sure to introduce as economic expansion makes the labor of children available in new and profitable ways. During this stage the same forces that bring more work to children also make their lives more open and known to those in the West who are observing this process. Thus, various international human rights organizations have already begun to expose the exploitation of children as the kinds of grueling work that horrifies our own sensibilities. That exposure leads others, often students on college campuses, to call for the boycotting of goods produced by children. And these boycotts may well lead to various new controls by international trade organizations. Our vision makes us want these children to be schooled, not to work. We assume that it is a child's right to play and to learn, not to work for a pittance. Here we are at a crossroads, not so unlike that of the Italian parents in the United States in the beginning of the twentieth century. From their point of view why should their children not produce these goods and help support their parents and give deference and respect to their elders in so doing? From ours, this is pure exploitation and our impulse is to control their parents' right to use their children in this way.

Add to this one other contention certain to peer out from the children's faces of the globalized economy—the conflict over gender. As we stare through the lenses fashioned in the late nineteenth century at those children's faces in the twenty first, we wear not one but two lenses. After all, in the United States, the extension of protections for children was offered to girls as well as to boys, and so were the opportunities for self-expression and the schooling aimed at their future development. But in most of the societies from which children came to the United States in the great immigration of the late nineteenth century, and the societies today being swept up in the forces of globalization, girls occupy a lesser place, protected in its own way, but hardly participating in the freedom of expression and growing equality that the United States was beginning to offer to its women. Italian parents in the United States were bewildered by the insistence that their daughters go to school, which merely reinforced their natural tendency to flirt with boys. As one parent put it: "When girls at 13 or 14 wasted good time in school, it simply made us regret our coming to America."[13] Today, globalization can be expected to create around issues of gender a serious point of conflict, both within the societies where the work of girls will likely raise serious challenges to patriarchal institutions, and from among those women's rights groups and organizations committed to improving the lives of women and girls around the world.

Consumption and Play

This questioning is only stage one. Stage two leads to other points of cultural and generational contention. The money that children are making, or are capable of making, however small and insignificant it appears to us, has its own powers of disruption. With the growing allurements of available cash and the growing exposure to Western habits and pastimes along television channels and over the Internet, the children caught in the new forces of globalization will begin themselves to ask why they should not participate in the pleasures that their earnings could provide—to visit McDonald's, buy tapes and CDs, and dress in the hippest Western clothing. Certainly, this happened to the sons and even to the daughters of the immigrants that came to America as early as the 1890s. At that point, the adolescent children of the old world began to go to the amusement parks and to the dance halls and eventually to the movies of the new world. With some cash at their disposal, it is difficult to halt the erosion of corporate family identity that first impels the child to labor outside the home. This does not happen at once or quickly, but it is sure to happen more quickly in a world of instant images of goods and enticements that are part of the entertainment society creating the realm of pleasure that beckons and surrounds youth everywhere. Even the early stages of this process are likely to create serious potentials for disruptions in parent-child relations, cultural continuity, and gender roles. From the point of view of the allurements offered to youth, all societies, whether they are ready or not to globalize, are likely to be affected just as immigrant groups in the

United States were, although some, like the Islamic societies, are likely to offer sturdy resistence.[14]

And here we begin to encroach on the second area I wish to bring to your attention—the problematics of play. Work and play for adults are, of course, opposite sides of the same coin since the energy invested in one can only be salvaged from time stolen from the other. But since the nineteenth century for young people in the West, play has been identified not as time stolen from work, but as the very structure of childhood. Historically this fundamental role of play for young people grew from two different sources. We have already caught glimpses of both here. In the nineteenth century, the emphasis on play grew from the new and different valuation of childhood that took root as scholars of childhood and of schooling, like Friedrich Froebel, Maria Montessori, G. Stanley Hall, and John Dewey began to view play as the terrain of development and learning, and of socialization itself. These designers of a science of childhood began increasingly to replace *homo faber* with *homo ludens* as the core of childhood preparation. Here the lessons of Rousseau began quickly to eclipse those of Locke, as play became not only a form of vitality, but central to education.

At first, play was restricted to certain times of day, or after school, or in playgrounds and gymnasia, as a form of respite from work. It is no doubt this early form of school activity that the Italian mother witnessed when she passed the public school, and which already made her uncomfortable and unhappy with what her children were learning in America. By the twentieth century, however, play began to infuse conceptions of curriculum as American schools adopted progressive approaches to instruction. Just as children were given years away from work for the sake of learning, as preparation for adulthood, so their schools began to define learning itself as linked to play. More play time and play space were introduced into classrooms that were loosened from earlier rigid plans and disciplines, and instruction was refashioned. Just as Americans worked hard in the nineteenth century, they learned to play hard in the twentieth. This emphasis on play has given modern American culture its aura of unruliness, and nowhere more so than in the upbringing of its children. While American schools produce some of the most creative children in the world, those who make new kinds of communications in their fathers' garages, they also produce some of the most out-of-control classrooms and unteachable children. Certainly, part of the fear associated with globalization in various parts of the globe has to do with the changes in education that are likely to follow the adoption of computers and Internet linkups, whose innovation were a product of America's unrestrained educational system.

But the specific forms of play for children in the United States also grew from the aggressive development of an untrammeled market economy, and that economy created spaces for play both as necessary outlets for the release of energy and in response to the new view of the specialness of childhood. Play and recreation became especially significant as outlets for adolescents, who worked at increasingly oppressive routines at sewing machines and lathes, in shops and factories, by clock time and not the more informal craft time of earlier apprenticeships. This kind of play as a complement to work, very unlike the play associated with community rituals and household routines, once integral to traditional modes of socialization, became segmented and commercialized. Jane Addams recognized its dangers vividly in her tract, the *Spirit of Youth in the City Streets*.[15] And just as commerce benefited from the work of children, commerce soon enough began to recognize the benefits that could be reaped from the play of children and adolescents. If children's work will, as I have suggested, increasingly become a subject of contention globally, we can expect that play will become probably an even greater flash point. Here the consequences of a cash-based economy that is defined by market mechanisms and new forms of work will produce ever more friction between traditional views of children's roles together with the parental limits imposed on their freedom of expression, and the appeal of new institutions to which the young turn after working hours and the profits that can be reaped from those same children in video shops and hamburger places.

As play and the objects associated with play become larger parts of our commercial world, its allurements become harder to resist. The toys and amusements that the West now offers to its children in abundance, and to which even Chinese city dwellers with their one-child restriction are in the process of adopting, have become a new realm of desire. The toys of childhood become increasingly irresistible as people around the world think about prosperity, and these toys will also become a stimulus to demands for higher wages and for the desire to approximate the possibilities of the West. Play and work together have the potential to disrupt profoundly traditional generational relations, cultural continuity, and the very definitions of childhood that go along with these.

Sexuality and the Limits of Childhood

And here we come to another issue certain to affect children in the new globalization. What, after all, is a child? In the United States in the early twentieth century, two especially significant and symbolic movements took place that would alter our understanding of childhood: the first was a significant extension upward of schooling into what we today call the teen years; the other was the creation of legislation in one state after another that raised the age of sexual consent for girls. Together these activities institutionally redefined the upper limits of childhood, so that 12–18-year-olds became both the objects of protection and the subjects of state regulation. There were other institutional changes, among them the rapid development of the juvenile court system which created a variety of means to express these expectations of a longer childhood. The court, designed to protect the young from full criminal responsibility for their actions, became a means to enforce strictures against behaviors that were considered inappropriate for children in their teen years. In all, by the second decade of the twentieth century, childhood had been vastly enlarged to include a period of life which pioneer psychologist and educator G. Stanley Hall had permanently enshrined with the name adolescence in his massive two-volume study of 1904. As a result, in the United States, adolescence became an extension of childhood rather than a preparation for adulthood, although its in-between status was meant to suggest how one could unfold into the other.

The creation of free, publicly supported high schools and requirements that enforced attendance by older youth, and the new laws making it a crime to have sexual relations with a female adolescent, variously capped by different states at from 14 to 18 years of age, were both symbolic and effective ways to create a much expanded childhood. It should not surprise us that immigrants, above all, became vulnerable to these new definitions, and that it was their children who were hauled into courts for sexual offenses and truancy.[16] The new sensibilities and the shift in paradigms around childhood in the second half of the nineteenth century had also created a new stage of life which those who came from the old world had a difficult time understanding. The Western view of childhood today often takes this view of adolescence, which Erik Erikson called a moratorium on adult responsibility, for granted. Not so, most of the rest of the world, for whom the transformational quality of adolescence may be recognized briefly or not at all, but which can hardly afford an extended moratorium.

By attaching adolescence to childhood we absorbed into childhood a period of life which is sexually potent and in which sexual energies are especially available. This sexual ripeness of adolescence is often recognized and carefully directed in traditional societies. In the United States in the twentieth century, in the context of an eager market economy and an emphasis on play and gender equality, it has been permitted to float freely in the culture as adolescents often serve as exemplars of beauty, of vitality, and of fashion. As a result, the image of adolescence has been absorbed into the special appeals of Western advertisements and popular culture in which, as we all know, sex sells.

In the long run, this meant that the ambiguous status of child sexuality was sure to become an unusually contentious and emotionally loaded issue since the boundaries within childhood between eight-year-olds and fourteen-year-olds had become more difficult to discern. Freud, after all, was just discovering the fundamental power of sexuality even among infants at a moment when Americans began to connect adolescence to an enlarged paradigm of protected childhood innocence. The volatile mix of age and sexuality sheltered under the umbrella of innocence was certain to create a powerful site for cultural politics and also for cultural anxiety. And so it has. Today, there is no more effective means to inflame our sense of a world gone awry than to point to the exploitation of children for sexual purposes. And we can expect a continuing parade of sexually exploited children to become one of the signs of the problematics of globalization.

The trend toward the consolidation of adolescence with childhood has also had other consequences, and their importance is best understood when we consider how disturbed we become when younger children imitate older children in their forms of expression. Young children in the developed world today are far more likely to imitate their peers than their parents (in speech, dress, language, and leisure habits) and this pattern is trickling down further and further among younger children. This tendency only fulfills the wider tendency of such children to be guided by signals that come not from parents and not from teachers, but from the popular media and popular culture. Here, I think we have finally come to the powerful mix that play and sexuality has deposited on our global horizons. Nothing is quite as fearsome today in our anxious representations of globalization and children—not child prostitution, not children in sweatshops, not even rape—as the problem of the vast, rapid, and unstoppable spread of youth-based American popular culture. At its core that concern is about the wildness, the sexuality, and the spontaneity of American forms of music, music videos, body styles, dress, and ornamentation most profoundly adopted into youth culture, whose potential reach seems to be all the children of the world. Thus do our children seem to rise up and threaten our very sense of a world under control, and nowhere more so than in those countries just on the cusp of the forces of globalization.

Before we succumb to this haunting vision, it might be well to remember what I said at the beginning of this chapter. Children have taken on immense symbolic weight in our culture and often they are the most potent means we use to frighten ourselves. It is this picture that is most often used by those opposed to the extension of Western values and invoked in the so-called clash of civilizations toward which our drive toward globalization is, these opponents claim, leading. It is surely the picture that will be used most vigorously to encourage all-out resistance to the West and its forces of self-indulgence and decay. It is in many ways a picture we have ourselves created, an inversion of innocent youth of the nineteenth century, a fearsome specter of the results of the West's special solicitude toward the young. At last, we have reached that point in our discussion. Before we trap ourselves in our own nightmares and projections, we need to pause to disentangle what we can expect to happen to children as a result of globalization from this looming image emotionally fed by the symbolic uses to which we have learned to put our children in the twentieth century.

This specter of youth, the rocking, highly sexualized teenager, created in late twentieth century America, is hardly a threat in most of the rest of the world. What happens to children there will be affected and moderated by the specific culture of each place, the speed of market developments, and each society's alacrity in adopting quite specifically Western values and beliefs. I have argued in this essay that American and Western beliefs and values emerged in a specific time and place, and while they were clearly fed by market developments that can help us to understand some of the changes likely to take place as a result of a new globalized market, they were not exclusively the results of market developments. We should not let ourselves become victim to the symbolic use to which we have put our children; nor should other parts of the world become victim to those visions. Nevertheless, some aspects of the development I have discussed with reference to American experience, are, if not inexorable, at least quite likely. And it is worth reexamining which of the changes in child life are most likely to occur as globalization proceeds.

First, work: Wherever global market forces penetrate, and development experts disagree about how widespread the process is likely to be, children, almost certainly, will become more conspicuously caught in the cash economy. While this may initially develop as an extension of their roles within the family and on behalf of their families (indeed, as we have seen in news stories, they may be sold for the good of the family), this work will itself lead in two directions: the Western sensibility is sure to be outraged by this work and this will be expressed in attempts to create various kinds of controls; the cash economy will erode some of the corporate links to family that first extends wage work to children.

It is difficult to tell how far these will proceed. It will depend on many factors internal to individual societies as well as the strength of growing international trade organizations that will likely regulate, to some degree, workplaces around the globe. It will depend too, on the pace and timing of worldwide prosperity as well as a host of political decisions and conditions. But, no matter the speed or the degree, there is almost certain to be some questioning of traditional gender divisions as this proceeds and this will create resistance and fear.

In the arena of play: It is impossible to believe that play will not change its character in most of the societies exposed to the new globalism, both as a result of the encroachments of Western definitions of childhood and because the commercial possibilities of play are built into the very nature of globalization. The developing world not only creates most of the West's toys, but it will increasingly want to consume them, and in so doing, it may want its children too to benefit from the positive views of play that underlie their creation. But play is so fundamental to the re-creation of childhood in the nineteenth century and so much a product of Western culture that it is not certain how thoroughly it will be adopted elsewhere as an essential of child life. To embrace it fully would be to engage Western culture at its core. Moreover, even in the United States today, play is being challenged by those who are concerned about overindulgent child rearing, as well as by those convinced that global competition requires that we impose stricter standards of disciplined accountability on our play-inclined children.

In terms of defining who and what a child is: Here I think most predictions are off. The extension of childhood into older periods of life is socially expensive and it is schooling above all that extends the upper limit of child life. Moreover, even in the United States we are witness to the beginning of a retreat from the full commitment to protection of innocence that adolescence once entailed. This is most clear in our increasing willingness to commit young people to adult jails. In other parts of the world, there will probably be a new sensitivity to how childhood can be protected and part of that will raise questions about traditional periods of transition from childhood to adulthood. Whether this will mean a full-blown extension of childhood into older ages in the American manner will depend on the prosperity of different societies, the degree to which they extend schooling and other quite culturally specific factors.

Finally, in the area of child sexuality: I think we can expect that the problematic tension involved in the combination of innocence and sexuality in our current view of childhood will repeatedly confront the specific and multitudinous differences in sexual views and practices in different societies around the world. In many of these places the investment of sexuality in children did not require a Freudian revolution, and in many of them innocence may not be congruent with the absence of sexual experience. Here we will face many arenas for potential misunderstanding, because the West has become so invested in viewing children in certain ways despite its own great differences and hypocrisies in the treatment of children (especially in the commercialization of adolescent sexuality). We will almost certainly continue to be outraged by the sexual exploitation of children in the world today, since this is one of the most sensitive fault lines through which we have learned to express indignation. But I doubt whether that will change the sexual abuse of children around the world with or without globalization.

Historians are notorious wimps when it comes to predicting the future, and I offer these thoughts with the usual historian's caveats. At the same time, I would like to suggest that historians should be fully included in current discussions of globalization. Their knowledge is essential to any complete analysis of the nature of the process taking place, whatever the accuracy of their predictions. Finally, it is simply foolhardy to discuss globalization, the cultural politics of globalization, and the social consequences of globalization without firmly situating children in that discussion. I say this not as an expression of mere sentimentality, but because so much of what will happen in the process of globalization and so many ways in which it will be resisted and criticized will have children at their center. If globalization is about the economies, the societies, and the cultures of the future, it is about the future of children and childhood and to that task we should be required to bring all the things we have learned over the course of the last fifty years about childhood in the past.

NOTES

This article was published in the *Journal of Social History,* 36 (Summer 2003), 963–977, and reprinted here with permission.

1. This has changed, of course, since this essay was written and children are more and more coming into the discussions regarding globalization and a substantial literature now exists on the subject. (See Introduction to this volume.)

2. For a number of these discussions, see *Culture Matters: How Values Shape Human Progress,* edited by Lawrence E. Harrison and Samuel P. Huntington (New York: Basic Books, 2000).

3. An especially effective version is Sebastiâo Salgado, *Migrations: Humanity in Transition* (New York: Aperture, 2000). Salgado's photographs have been traveling across the country as an extremely successful exhibition.

4. See Paula S. Fass, *Kidnapped: Child Abduction in America* (New York: Oxford University Press, 1997); Philip Jenkins, *Moral Panic: Changing Concepts of the Child Molester in Modern America* (New Haven: Yale University Press, 1998).

5. The relevant portions of Alexander Hamilton's s *Report on Manufacture* (1795) can be found in Paula S. Fass and Mary Ann Mason, eds., *Childhood in America* (New York: New York University Press, 2000), 248.

6. For the early industrial workers in New England, see Thomas Dublin, *Women at Work* (New York: Columbia University Press, 1983).

7. Viviana A. Zelizer, *Pricing the Priceless Child: The Changing Social Value of Children* (New York: Basic Books, 1985).

8. The innocent child has been extensively written about. See, among others, Anne Higonnet, *Pictures of Innocence: The History and Crisis of Ideal Childhood* (London: Thames and Hudson, 1998), and James R. Kincaid, *Child-Loving: The Erotic Child and Victorian Culture* (New York: Routledge, 1992).

9. See the discussions in Harrison and Huntington on how culture affects globalization issues. What I am arguing is not that culture will determine who will be globalized, but what consequences globalization may have for culture and for children specifically in those places that are drawn into the international market.

10. See, among others, Linda Gordon, *Heroes of Their Own Lives: The Politics and History of Family Violence* (New York: VikingPenguin, 1988); Mary Odem, *Delinquent Daughters: Protecting and Policing Female Sexuality in the United States, 1885–1920* (Chapel Hill: University of North Carolina Press, 1995).

11. Lionel Trilling, *The Liberal Imagination: Essays on Literature and Society* (New York: Viking, 1950). For a related perspective pertaining to children today, see Tobias Hecht, *At Home in the Street: Street Children in Northeast Brazil* (Cambridge, England: Cambridge University Press, 1998).

12. Quotes are from Stephen Lassonde, "Learning and Earning: Schooling, Juvenile Employment, and the Early Life Course in Late Nineteenth-Century New Haven," *Journal of Social History,* 29 (Summer 1996), 846; Stephen Lassonde, "Should I Go, or Should I Stay?: Adolescence, School Attainment, and Parent-Child Relations in Italian Immigrant Families of New Haven, 1900–1940," *History of Education Quarterly,* 38 (Spring 1998), 49.

13. Lassonde, "Should I Go, or Should I Stay?" 52.

14. On the matter of Islamic resistance to western influences, see Samuel Huntington, *The Clash of Civilizations* (New York: Simon and Schuster, 1996). Huntington, of course, believes that globalization will not take place in those parts of the world where strong, competing civilizations offer alternative norms and ways of life. I find myself generally at odds with Huntington's view that globalization will lead to a clash of civilizations, rather than a process of gradual interpenetration, although Islamic societies are certainly among those who have been more rigorous in their clear opposition to all the elements of pleasure and play with which Western societies beckon and repel.

15. Jane Addams, *The Spirit of Youth and the City Streets* (originally 1909; reprinted Urbana: University of Illinois Press, 1972). On the amusements of young people, see also Kathy Peiss, *Cheap Amusements: Working Women and Leisure in Turn-of-the-Century New York* (Philadelphia: Temple University Press, 1987); David Nasaw, *Children of the City: At Work and Play* (New York: Oxford University Press, 1985). For a very different view on this matter (much closer to Addams, in fact), see John Burnham, *Bad Habits: Drinking, Smoking, Taking Drugs, Gambling, Sexual Misbehavior, and Swearing in American History* (New York: New York University Press, 1993).

16. See Odem, *Delinquent Daughters,* and Eric C. Schneider, *In the Web of Class: Delinquents and Reformers in Boston, 1810s–1930s* (New York: New York University Press, 1992).

8

Children in Global Migrations

The growing reality of movement across borders has become a twenty-first-century theme and increasingly a focus for the anxieties and uncertainties about change in our time. When it is paired with children, its potential as a modern form of brutality becomes an almost irresistible excuse for sadness and poignant reflection. The Brazilian photo-journalist Sabastiâo Salgado is hardly alone in reaping the emotional and aesthetic harvest of this theme, but his moving exhibit "Migrations: Humanity in Transition—The Children," provides an exceptionally vivid perspective on this issue.

At the Berkeley Art Museum, one of the stops the exhibit made in 2002, it was seen by thousands of people. The normally empty exhibit spaces were jammed and extra galleries were opened to accommodate the huge range of his photographic record as he toured the world through the Americas, Europe, the Middle East, Africa, and the many parts of Asia to observe children, willingly and unwillingly on the move (mostly the latter). Here is a quote from the pamphlet that accompanied the exhibit: "In every crisis situation—whether war, poverty, or natural disaster—children are the greatest victims. The weakest physically, they are invariably the first to succumb to disease or starvation. Emotionally vulnerable, they are unable to understand why they are being forced from their homes, why their neighbors have turned against them, why they are now in a slum surrounded by filth or in a refugee camp and surrounded by sorrow. With no responsibility for their fates, they are by definition innocent."[1]

They are usually also the most attractive of their species and, however much they may be hostages to fate, their attractiveness is very effectively manipulated by the photographer toward his many purposes. I will argue later that children are hardly entirely victims or entirely innocent, but for now, I want to claim for them the aesthetic appeal of which Salgado and all those gathered to see his work were undoubtedly deeply aware. In today's PR world, where the image often becomes the reality, it is appropriate for us to begin with the images that Salgado, among others, has imprinted in the public imagination as the picture of child migration. As humanity in transit takes center stage in the twenty-first century, it is the children that are most memorable. Again, in the words of the exhibit pamphlet: "Migrations is the story of humanity on the move. It is a story of our times, with profound implications for the generations to come."[2]

It is important for us to consider those implications, and I take for this purpose Salgado's exhibition as my opening text since it helps to define the public mental space usually occupied by children's migration in the context of globalization. We need first to question the assumptions that lie behind this exhibit: that the normal state of child life is stability, and that children are naturally innocent and dependent. These assumptions have become deeply embedded in a Western ideal of childhood that is increasingly broadcast through Western media and international agencies to the rest of the world. In this sense, Salgado's exhibit is an expression of globalization as much as it records the migration that accompanies it. By situating Salgado's sensibility deep within the modern Western vision of childhood and understanding how that sensibility now takes global childhood as its subject, we can begin to appreciate some of the tensions and complexities of the subject we hope to understand.

Contemporary images of child migration usually assume that mass migration is both a new phenomenon and a threat to the stability necessary to child life and its proper development. In this chapter I will examine migration historically, as a subject long familiar to American historians, and as a contemporary phenomenon that has new features and significant new consequences "for generations to come." This is not an easy task, not least because the distance on their subjects that historians value is not realizable when examining a subject as protean as globalization, and one that is both now expressing itself and still changing. Historians are nevertheless quite well situated to make these evaluations because, unlike a photographer such as Salgado, historians are accustomed to recording change. Whatever Salgado's philosophical and ethical purposes, his is first of all an aesthetic project, one of whose goals is to transform the static photograph into something new and more commensurate with the movement it seeks to record. Salgado longs to expand what photographs can convey and do. For historians, however, fluidity and change define our imaginations and constitute the mental world of our discipline. And American historians, I believe, are especially well situated in this task. I have written elsewhere about why I believe that the history of the United States provides an unusually good point of departure for understanding globalization.[3] (See Chapter 7 in this volume.) Suffice it to say here that many of the ingredients of globalization—a large zone of free trade and largely unimpeded market development, the strategic role of rapid communications to that development, and mass immigration and cultural exchange among diverse groups—have been familiar features of American experience for the last two hundred years. I take these to be critical aspects of what we have come to call globalization in the modern world.

Migration and Children in the American Past and Present

The mass movement of populations, whether associated with war or with economic change (and since these are frequently related, to both), is hardly new. During the last several decades, colonial American historians have been hard at work demonstrating the fluidity of the seventeenth- and eighteenth-century world, a period when empires collided and brought large portions of the Americas, Africa, and Asia into the European force field. So expansive was that world that one historian, David Hancock, has described its innovative and wealthy beneficiaries as *Citizens of the World*.[4] These collisions created the strong currents that led to an immense migration within the Americas, in Africa, and across the Atlantic and Indian Oceans. Whatever else they are, today's migrations often follow the trade paths and social patterns established at that point in history. And whatever else these studies demonstrate, they make clear that many European, Amerindian, and African children could expect very little in the way of stability of hearth and home. The upheavals of the seventeenth and eighteenth centuries pulled children into their train, among them those as young as 9 or 10 who were kidnapped in London and elsewhere to become indentured servants in the New World.[5] When they were put to work in the "plantations" of North America, they displaced native children from stable villages and practices.[6] By the end of the seventeenth century, they were likely to meet on those plantations other young people who had been brought in shackles from Africa.

These strangers from three continents were hardly viewed in the terms of our time. Where in today's global perspective we see children, kidnapped or stolen, seventeenth-century ship captains and planters saw cargo and a source of much needed labor (and if the young were girls, also fair sexual game). They were no more or less precious than 20-year-olds. In this sense, the picture is entirely altered today, as journalists and others document the plight of 8- or 9-year-old girls working on cloth in India, or 11-year-old girls drawn into prostitution in Thailand and Cambodia.

That leap in our imagination of what children ought and ought not to do is the product of Western history and of the development of humanistic sentiments during the last two hundred years. Today, these victims are no longer, as they once were, merely a subset of poor people whose poverty makes them vulnerable or desperate. Instead, as children we respond to them in a special way and see their exploitation or abuse as unacceptable. This diffusion of Western sensibilities to embrace the children of the globe is a significant ingredient of globalization. The change from the eighteenth century to the nineteenth century that resulted first in outcries against slavery and finally in organizations against the abuse of children in factory labor required an alteration in Western sensibilities and a new humanitarianism that has been studied by Thomas Haskell and others.[7] By the end of the nineteenth century, this sensibility was prevalent among the middle classes in Britain, the United States, France, and in other places in the Western world.[8] Because we have inherited that sensibility, globalization today has a very different face than its antecedents did in the seventeenth century. In the seventeenth and eighteenth centuries, Western superiority was clothed in various guises of culture, color, and religion. Today, our Western commitment to child protection often incubates a similar sense of superiority which lays a claim to virtue in the vision of a proper childhood. As a result, at just the point when globalization is making knowledge of diverse childhood patterns widely available, age has become a sorting device by which we allocate sympathy and parcel out favor.

What is happening to children in other parts of the globe today is refracted through a Western lens. Some journalists, such as Nicholas Kristof in the *New York Times,* is conscious of the complex contradictions that these changes introduce, recognizing that for many of the children in third world countries factory work opportunities where they are made available by globalization are often far superior to the work which children have long done exploiting dung heaps for scraps, or in home manufacture. For his insights, he has been showered with outraged letters from readers.[9] But historians need to make the public aware that their current view of children (our view of children) is a product of a particular history. This will not resolve the ethical or intellectual dilemmas that globalization pose to the modern sensibility, but it can provide a much wider aperture from which pictures about the present can be viewed and evaluated. In this sense, the new history of children and childhood has come at a strategic moment as a necessary corrective to current popular fixations. Only as we begin to understand the degree to which children have a history in the Western world and one that, as many historians have demonstrated, includes large doses of child labor, will the readers of the *New York Times* begin to understand Kristof's point.[10]

While the history of child labor is useful for our understanding of how we "see" contemporary globalization, our knowledge of the history of race is another necessary part of our vision. As a consequence of earlier migrations, the United States became both a land of different races and a nation of immigrants, a product of the intersection of several worlds and of immigration from several continents. The migrations of the seventeenth and eighteenth centuries variously influenced subsequent generations. Sometimes they had treacherous consequences, as in the case of Africans caught in the Atlantic slave trade, and the disruptions and destruction of native peoples in the Americas. But the movement did not always proceed in these fearsome and humiliating ways that many of Salgado's photographs portend. Many immigrants to the United States came willingly and expectantly starting in the eighteenth century because they saw the change for which America became a byword as a promising outcome of migration.[11]

Historians of the United States have taken note of the fact that migration had very different consequences for children, with some becoming successful beneficiaries of the migration, while others became its victims, and that many of the differences were sharply etched along racial lines.[12] More recently, sociologists such as Alejandro Portes have sharply distinguished between voluntary and forced migrations and observed how these tend to be racially patterned.[13] Most, though not all immigrants who came willingly to the United States before the last half century were European, and even among these some were "racialized" in the late nineteenth and early twentieth centuries, that is to say that they were often described as if they were distinct races.[14] It is yet to be determined whether the current immigrants, almost all of them of non-European origin, will experience similar sharply drawn racial boundaries, or whether they will face a world where racial tendencies have subsided. The degree to which migrant groups continue to be racially defined will have huge consequences for their children because race, unlike ethnicity, has historically been viewed as an inheritable trait.

In the eighteenth and nineteenth centuries, the presence of large numbers of racial minorities (Africans and Amerindians) was a distinctly American variant of Western experience. Today, unlike the past, even countries like Denmark, Sweden, and the Netherlands have substantial numbers of racial minorities who have migrated as part of the globalizing process. Will their children remain ostracized outsiders, like the Jews of early twentieth century Europe or like the Chinese of the late nineteenth century United States (who were voluntary migrants but viewed as racial outsiders)? Or will the children of millions of non-European immigrants in today's Los Angeles be like European immigrants into early twentieth century New York, strangers with hopeful futures?[15]

Between 1955 and 1991, the numbers and proportion of Asians and Latin Americans who have migrated voluntarily to the United States has mushroomed. In the two years 1990–1991, a total of almost three and one-half million immigrants were admitted legally to the United States—a number larger than at any previous point in American history. Of that number, less than 10 percent were of European birth, while the rest were a combination of Mexican, South American and Asian immigrants. In the previous decade, between 1981 and 1990, a total of over one and one-half million came from Mexico alone, one-half million from the Philippines, over 400,000 from Vietnam, 388,000 from China, 338,000 from Korea, and 145,000 from Laos, and more than a quarter million from India. In addition, hundreds of thousands came from a variety of other Latin American countries, the Caribbean, and Asian societies.[16] Today, almost twenty-seven million people in the United States (legally) are foreign born, with a very large percentage of them children.[17]

The result is an enormous new American immigrant society, composed of groups whose presence is either entirely new to the American experience, or newly important because of sheer size. These migrants are re-creating the nature of American cities in all regions of the country where they and their children now often make up one-half or more of the population. Thus in Los Angeles (62 percent), New York (54.3 percent), Miami (71.5 percent), and Orange County (53.7 percent) immigrants and their children are becoming the dominant population.[18] In the United States, the reopening and massive increase of Asian migration and the unprecedented levels of Latin American immigration holds out the promise of a new nonracialized future. According to Richard Rodriguez, this future promises a hybridized "brown" society.[19] Is this something that all parts of the world, or even the United States with its fraught racial past, can truly hope to realize in the future? If the future of the United States is a brown one, it will be because children lose their consciousness of race in the process of their interactions to create a new hybridization (in both culture and bodies) that was once called assimilation when applied to European immigrants. If contemporary globalizations erase markers of race, as immigration over time and in the context of schooling and youth culture once effectively erased markers of ethnicity, then in the future the United States can expect to once again be at the forefront of a new kind of world identity just as it once created a trans-European identity. (For more about this process and its limits, see Chapter 3.) This would be a real expression of changes introduced by globalization. At the same time, it is well to remember that the evidence we have for children's interaction in school, on which so much of that future depends, indicates that over the last ten to fifteen years, American schools have become more, not less, segregated by race, hardly a good sign for the integration of children into a newly hybrid future. According to studies by Gary Orfield and his colleagues at the Harvard Project on School Desegregation, "For Latinos, an even more severe level of segregation [than for African Americans] is intensifying across the nation." This segregation is "particularly affecting our rapidly growing Latino communities in the West."[20] If this continues, American children will hardly be provided with the community and school context from which to create a new global society. Instead, globalization will mean a more complex world with more different kinds of people living side-by-side, and a culture with more diverse elements, but hardly a truly brown society.

Migration Is Often a Family Strategy That Affects Children Even If They Stay Put

Our vision of globalization will be very much enhanced if we understand that migration affects not only those who move but those who stay. This is usually left out of contemporary mental pictures of child life, but is quite an important and understudied product of contemporary migration especially since the character of those who leave has dramatically changed.

Family migration has never been a process in which all members of the family necessarily move together. Indeed, much of migration history concerns the disassembling of families in order to underwrite a family process of survival and/or success. Like those who migrate today, people in the past also maintained bonds across borders, with relatives in far distant places. Today, in the context of instant communication and rapid transportation, this is becoming an ever more normal way of life. Globalization has not only made migration more possible, but has affected the family decisions that frame migration. Many hundreds of thousands of Filipino women (some have estimated the total to be over six million) have traveled to Europe, the Middle East, and to the United States to clean other people's houses, take care of their elderly, their sick, and their children.[21] In most cases, these women leave their children behind with grandmothers, aunts, fathers, or other relatives as they send good parts of their wages back to improve the lives and prospects of their children and other family members. Most hope to return to better lives in the Philippines. Very often this lasts not for a few months, but for many years.

Historians are quite familiar with the pattern of transient migrations. During the height of immigration from eastern and southern Europe, in the late nineteenth and early twentieth centuries, hundreds of thousands of men left families, including children, behind as they went to the United

States, Argentina, or Brazil to find work. They sent back their wages on a regular basis, and then often themselves returned after several years' absence. Sometimes, they went back and forth repeatedly. The Chinese tried to do the same, but were cut off when the Chinese Exclusion Act of 1882 singled them out as the first group against whom a specific embargo was imposed, which thereby stopped most of this transitory process. But Italians and Poles did it regularly and Mexicans continue to do so into the twentieth-first century. In Mexico today, 41 percent of all household heads have had some migratory experience to the United States, and 73 percent of all households have a social connection to someone living in the United States.[22] Americans today are governed by ideals of family reunification because we have decided that the family's physical preservation is a desirable part of public policy, a policy enshrined in the Hart-Celler Act of 1965. (As I write, that policy is being rethought by the Bush administration in its proposals for temporary workers.) So we tend to find migration that disrupts a family's physical coherence troubling and even pathological. But international migrations, as they accompany international capital and information as part of globalization today, just as in the past, do not take issues of family preservation into account. And today, as in the past, families adapt and use the pressures and/or opportunities this presents. Family life, it is well to remember, is a process as much as a physical fact, and migration often accentuates one part of that process over others. In the seventeenth and eighteenth centuries, when travel was hard, expensive, and dangerous, the rupture of movement over the seas for the poor, such as indentured servants, was usually permanent. In the nineteenth and twentieth centuries, as the means of travel improved and became faster and cheaper, family ruptures were more often temporary. With travel ever cheaper and faster and when people everywhere can go almost anywhere by air, some families have become genuinely binational as children travel back and forth from the United States to the Caribbean or Latin America to visit with grandparents. Some stay during the difficult teen period to become truly bicultural in their orientation.

Perhaps the most potentially destabilizing part of the modern version of transitory migration which maintains family bonds is related to *gender*. Rarely in the past did women leave children behind as they sought to raise their family's prospects for survival or success, although single women could and did travel by themselves. Only in the context of the modern world in which female labor is often as valuable as, or more valuable than, male labor and where children no longer work in the countries to which their parents migrate has this become likely.[23] While journalists remind us that globalization often pulls children into new work contexts this is very unlikely to take place in Europe or the United States precisely because, after the late nineteenth century, Westerners began to view child labor as unnatural and abhorrent. We might want to recognize that by maintaining this posture toward children, a globalized twenty-first century makes it more likely that women will leave their children behind for long periods of their lives as they seek the work that is now available to them, but not to their children, work paid in valuable dollars and in euros. This means that women often have to depend on extended kin for child-care arrangements. This confirmation of dependence on intergenerational ties is utterly unlike the model of nuclear family mobility posited by Talcott Parsons in the 1950s when he argued that only integral nuclear families cut off from obligations to kin could allow for the movement essential for social mobility in the modern world.[24]

The female out-migration I am describing introduces genuinely new elements into the history of migration. In fact, there is no better demonstration of the potential for gender change that globalization offers (and threatens) than this new pattern.[25] Rhacel Salazar Parreñas shows that some Filipino women use migration as an alternative to seeking divorce for an abusive marriage in a deeply Catholic culture. So family maintenance may be less an issue than a new female boldness and the desire for self-determination that is using the possibilities offered by globalization. Thus, migration makes a kind of latent female empowerment thinkable and, in this case, a permanent rupture in family relations may well result from the contemporary phenomenon that Arlie Hochschild and Barbara Ehrenreich have called "global woman."

We know far less about the children left behind than about the women who move. But the increasing dependence of working women on child-care arrangements in the West is apparently affecting far-flung parts of the world. Parreñas and others have noted that the modern pattern of globalized female employment results in a progressive lowering of the status of child caretakers as European and American women employ lower-caste immigrant women, and these women, when they cannot turn to kin, employ much needier and lower class women to care for their own children. This process of "diverted mothering" is now an international phenomenon.[26] Gender patterns and maternal obligations lie deep within culture and contemporary trends affecting married women's migration in the context of globalization has as much, if not more, potential for cultural destabilization as child labor or child migration does. We need to understand this much more fully than we do as we think about the consequences of globalization for children today. Identity for women on the move and for the children they leave behind is deeply caught up in this process as traditional means of social reproduction are altered. So is identity changing for children who may shuttle between schools in the United

States or Europe while they are in the care of their working mothers, and vacation with grandparents in Latin America and other places.

Migration, Education, and Social Mobility

In order best to understand the affects of migration on education and authority, it is important to remember what social historians take for granted, that children's movement will have different consequences depending on where they move from, where they move to, why they move, and how old they are. Neither migration nor childhood is an undifferentiated experience. It is important to bring these differences to the fore as we examine globalization. While globalization is having effects worldwide, those effects are neither the same everywhere nor have uniform consequences.

Salgado includes in his exhibit (for the sake of symmetry, I think) Russian Jews who migrate to the United States. But the children of Russian Jews are markedly out of place in the implicit lamentation that defines the Salgado exhibit. They do extremely well in the United States, where they benefit from educational opportunities which they know how to utilize. In fact, however, effectively using educational opportunities is part of the phenomenon of contemporary migrations generally, and Russian Jews are not alone in doing well in school. We are all familiar with the extraordinary success of the children of Asian immigrants, including the Vietnamese boat people.[27] Many Caribbean and other Latin American children also benefit educationally from migrating to the United States. This is true despite the fact that Chicanos are perceived as lagging behind in high school graduation rates and college attendance as compared to other immigrants. As two of the most highly regarded researchers in this field, Carola Suárez-Orozco and Marcelo M. Suárez-Orozco observe, "research suggests that immigrant children are healthier, work harder in school, and have more positive social attitudes than their nonimmigrant peers. Every year, the children of immigrants are overrepresented in the rosters of high school valedictorians and receive more of their share of prestigious science awards. . . . Immigrant children in general arrive with high aspirations and extremely positive attitudes toward education."[28]

One of the strongest predictors of success is the reason that the migration took place and the *generation* to which the young belong. Of the 24 million Americans in the United States today who migrated since 1960, 40 percent came as children under the age of eighteen, that is to say of school age.[29] Scholars of migration and schooling, such as John Ogbu as well as Carola and Marcelo M. Suárez-Orozco, have taken note of the unusual school success of these children.[30] Thus, children born in the Caribbean and in Mexico are more academically successful, despite the apparent handicap of language, than their siblings born in the United States. The latter are more quickly and easily absorbed in local black and Latino peer cultures that often turn them against school. The "identities" of migrating children are often lodged in a self-conscious exploiting of opportunities, while the American-born long for acceptance in the anti-intellectual peer culture of inner city blacks or Latinos, something that is exacerbated by the increased segregation of these groups in the recent past. The very "marginality" of these migrating children makes them more ambitious and better students. As Ogbu has shown, young migrants who know how much better their opportunities are as a result of migration than in their countries of origin take advantage of the education they are offered, even if this is in poor neighborhoods with dilapidated schools. The experience of migration through its very dislocations and the contrasts this encourages, one might argue, has its privileges. Ogbu also differentiates the experience of minority groups who continue to view and define themselves as colonial dependents from voluntary immigrants who assume they are free to succeed. The latter arrive with purpose and a sense of potential opportunities, while the former expect to be discriminated against and do not expect much benefit from their migration. His data tend to bear out this distinction, though I think they are not conclusive. But Ogbu's work does encourage us to invest with significance the distinction between children who were born elsewhere from those who are born into resident ethnic groups.

The growing and complex literature on the schooling of immigrants is not alone in suggesting that the migration of children has important consequences for life-defining factors such as risky behaviors in delinquency and substance abuse. Indeed, some of the evidence suggests that length of residence in the United States as well as generation may influence these matters. The United States, as well as other countries to which migrants have gravitated (Denmark, the Netherlands, and Great Britain), provide excellent places in which the fact of migration can be distinguished from ethnicity, and historians would be well advised to take note of this new work on youth migrations. For a long time, American historians, like Joel Perlmann,[31] have documented differential school success along ethnic lines, and these distinctions have provided us with important information about immigration and schooling. Most of these studies have compared different ethnic groups at a particular time as well as the changing patterns of mobility of members of specific ethnic groups over time. Although ethnicity cannot be entirely separated from migration, one can begin to suggest that studying contemporary migrations requires that we examine the experience of young people according to migration status regardless of ethnicity. I do not know of any historians who have done this, because the dominant "assimilation" model that grew from European experience in the United States assumes that greater success comes with time and steady generational acculturation.

The assimilation model, which I have questioned elsewhere as inadequate to understanding the education of American high school students (see Chapter 3), may now be altogether inadequate, based as it was on the experience of European immigrants who came into a blue-collar work world. Where blue-collar parents could once produce white-collar children or grandchildren, such a gradual ascent may no longer be meaningful or likely in a globalized world. In today's white-collar-dominant West, where a combination of schooling and youth culture determine children's lives and their future, the simple assimilation model may be outdated and misleading. Thus, contemporary globalization may be effectively distinguishable from earlier migrations in its altered affects on patterns of social mobility.[32]

Today, many upper-status and highly mobile students from around the world migrate to take advantage of American higher education, especially its graduate and professional schools. Some of these students are privately funded, others are supported by their governments who save themselves the expense of investing in advanced laboratories and facilities. It is possible to imagine that a parallel migration is taking place, one in which poorer young people migrate for white-collar skills. For these aspirants even deprived and unsightly American elementary schools and high schools provide rich resources. We might also want to rethink some of the conclusions about educational deprivation that we have come to as historians. As Kathryn Anderson-Levitt has suggested in her studies of African schoolchildren, the desire to get beyond the school-yard gate, no matter how poor the school, may depend on where you stand.[33] Those migrating from poor countries may find the universal education offered in the United States a really golden opportunity. In the early twentieth century, many of these migrating young people were simply incorporated into work at an early age. In the United States today, high school attendance requirements means that migrating teens must attend school, and bilingual classrooms have become a necessary part of their integration into an age-defined curriculum. As a result, ambitious teenagers have far greater opportunities than in the past.

In the United States, it is also possible that we are seeing a situation in which the competitive educational success of migrants (from Russia and Asia, for example) may actually be displacing older ethnic groups from routes of mobility in a newly redefined and globalized economy. The effects of globalization for education in the United States are not hard to find. Over the past two decades, we have become familiar with recurrent educational "crises" as statistics on achievement at various school levels reveal deficiencies among American schoolchildren. The schooling speed-up that has resulted as we try to cram more information into students earlier in their lives and measure them against international norms, culminating most recently in the "No Child Left Behind Policy" of the Bush administration, is beginning to squeeze our definition of childhood and the role of play and a leisurely child-centered development in schooling. At a time when the social placement and success of their offspring has become ever more urgent and consequential to middle-class families eager to maintain their own and their children's status, the new globalized economy may be on the verge of redefining childhood expectations in the West as Asian children and children from elsewhere displace those who had assumed they were at the head of the line.[34] Thus, not only our definitions of assimilation, but our definitions of a proper childhood may be forced to change in the context of the global realignments of the present day.

Migration as a Move toward Cities

As we consider the specific nature of the migrations taking place, their motives and consequences, we also want to pay attention to matters such as the rural-urban trajectory of the migration. In the American South after the Civil War, quite a lot of migration (both white and black) took place, but much of it was rural to rural, a pattern that also defined much of the Okie exodus to California in the 1930s. Most historical studies I have seen suggest that rural-to-rural migration rarely helps the young or their parents to move out of poverty, although the migration may be necessary for individual and group survival. In fact, rural-to-rural migration may also have a greater tendency to cement intrafamily authority and encourage patterns of cultural continuity.[35]

Changes often attributed to migration generally are more likely a consequence of movement from countryside to city or from smaller urban places to larger urban places, than simply a result of movement alone.[36] Thus, unlike these earlier domestic migrations, the huge internal migration that took place in the United States during World War II was heavily toward city war industries that uprooted tens of millions of Americans. Despite the often described discomforts and difficult conditions to which these migrants were subjected, most believed that their lives and those of their children were greatly improved.[37] Today's migrations are overwhelmingly toward cities. The massive movement toward the cities that affected Europe and the United States in the nineteenth and twentieth centuries is now taking place throughout the world. It would be useful for us to remember that these movements were fraught historically just as they are today, and that the transition to city life often meant a confrontation between different mores, cultural disruption, squalor, and uneven economic development. Globalization is currently playing this out on an even grander scale, as large cities become huge, and smaller towns become substantial cities.

It is in this context that child prostitution becomes significant today. This is always one of the most disturbing issues in contemporary journalism and certain to incite reader revulsion. A recent feature in the *New York Times Magazine* has brought this home yet again.[38] In the late nineteenth and early twentieth centuries the issue of "white slavery" also evoked spasms of reformist rage as young country girls were supposedly abducted for the purposes of sexual exploitation, a widely feared phenomenon common to both Europe and the United States. According to many reports, girls (and boys) today are also being misled into believing that they are migrating for respectable employment and are then absorbed into prostitution rings, or they are quite literally abducted for that purpose. The campaign against the sexual slavery of children today reminds me of that earlier campaign.[39]

It is far from my intention to dismiss the current concern or to question its validity. Nevertheless, understanding how it repeats earlier historical experience is useful and necessary. First, we need to recognize the degree to which the journalism is addressed to the fears and sensibilities of the Western world. Most historians understand the nineteenth-century campaign against white slavery as, at least in part, a form of journalistic titillation feeding middle-class appetites about the experiences of the inhabitants of the city's lower depths.[40] The campaign came at a time when reformers were eager to redefine adolescence as an extension of childhood and to shelter girls from 13 to 18 under the protective umbrella being opened by upwardly revised age-of-consent laws.[41] In today's outrage at child sexual exploitation, are we at once repeating our fascination with the sexual irregularities of "other" people who may seem to be very distant but have become our unknown neighbors, and reconfirming our own commitment to child protection?

Child prostitution is not new either in the Western or non-Western context. In Thailand, as Kevin Bales has shown, a form of child prostitution where young country girls (from especially impoverished regions) were sold by their families to urban brothels has long provided a means for family survival, and a form of mobility for the girls.[42] Bales also makes clear that the contemporary globalized sex industry has vastly exacerbated this local pattern and that AIDS has made its need for young girls both insatiable and ever more dangerous. Nevertheless, it is worth understanding that prostitution has long been a rural-to-urban migration route for those we today define as children, but whom their families and communities may designate as merely young earners, providing supplementary income to family coffers. Like so many other features of globalization, modern Western beliefs about what is appropriate to childhood as well as *when childhood begins and ends* is deeply implicated in the discussion. It may well be the case that because of the differences in how childhood is defined in various parts of the globe, child prostitution may actually be growing in places where it exists, and it may also be encroaching on younger children. Today, globalization makes possible access to children for sexual purposes, including for Internet pornography, almost anywhere in the world. The problem is exacerbated by the fact that child prostitution is still available in other places while sex with children is now largely taboo in the Western world. The very construction of the innocent child in the West may even increase the exploitation of children elsewhere. This makes the subject especially vexed, since it at once titillates our imaginations and calls forth our most vociferous condemnations. It may also be an area where globalization is seriously increasing child endangerment.

Children Are Often an Active Driving Force in Migration

The *New York Times* recently featured the story of a Holocaust survivor who lived with his family in a hole in the ground of a Polish farm to which they had fled when the Germans arrived. All of them were kept alive through the insistence and tenacity of the children, who sustained their parents as they suffered from despair, hopelessness, and thoughts of suicide.[43] This is, in fact, not so unusual. Despite their so-called "innocence," children are remarkably insightful, resilient, and resourceful, and adolescents especially can sometimes initiate migration demands. It is important to recognize and acknowledge important differences between young children and older children. That children are a differentiated social group is important to our rethinking of the dominant images of childhood—as innocent, passive, and dependent. In fact, children today, especially older children, as well as such children in the past, have often acted with intent and purpose.

Contemporary American adolescents have become much more work oriented generally than those of a generation or so ago, mostly because they have been exposed to the costly allurements of a consumption-obsessed America. Many choose to work part time in order to buy the CDs, jeans, movie and concert tickets, and others necessities of teenage identity in our time.[44] So too, youths elsewhere in the world, whose identities as "children" hardly have the depth that one hundred years of history has provided to those in the United States, may nevertheless be eager to be *adolescents*—and to buy the identities that come with this designation in the world today. I believe that *adolescence* may have become a universal identity in the context of globalization as the accoutrements and culture of youth has spread everywhere through the very channels that has brought globalization. While modern adolescence was created in the West in the early twentieth century as an extension of childhood and especially schooling,[45] adolescence soon became a distinct product of Western capitalism.[46] Today, where childhoods can still remain somewhat culturally specific, adolescence is less and less so. As such, it may have become a globalized identity expressed through fashion, music, and other consumer habits. Adolescents may actively pursue this identity in many ways, by working, by consuming, by rejecting parental authority, by rebelling against their parents' ways, and by urging migration on their parents as they hope to improve their chances elsewhere. They may also leave their families to pursue it on their own, as many young migrants did historically when they came at an earlier time to the United States.[47] That loosening of youth from their moorings in the past is part and parcel of what globalization is all about.

Unlike their parents who cling to their homes and possessions, children cling to hope of the future. Migration may or may not offer them that, but it is not helpful to imagine that children, especially older children, are either helpless or passive in the process of change that defines today's world, and the migrations that are part of it. In that sense, we students of children's history need to detach ourselves from the connection made early in the twentieth century (often with good reason at the time) between children who were 5 or 6 and children who were 13 or 14. We can, I believe, do this without giving up entirely our desire to continue to shelter and protect older children. The role of children in the process of global migration is just now becoming a subject for careful examination and thoughtful appraisal. We should begin by looking to the past in an effort to understand both the active roles that older children especially can play, and to understand just what children introduce into the migration calculus. We tend to reduce authority in traditional societies to a one-way hierarchy, in which children are always at the bottom. But a more careful reflection will let us see that even in the most traditional and hierarchical societies and during periods of significant change, children may in fact be seen as the salvation of the family. We know that they are often the first to be put into new working situations—whether in factories or on the streets,[48] and we are increasingly coming to understand how they operate at battle frontiers in wars as lookouts and guerrilla fighters.[49] Here, they may gain knowledge and know-how that not only benefits their families in the immediate situation, but provides them with information about the change that would come with migration. Once they migrate, they become the translators at the margins between cultures, between generations, and between the past and the future. As informants and as people on the margins, children provide just the kind of outlook and knowledge that encourages migration choices and facilitates migration once it takes place.

It is exactly young people like these whom one could expect to do especially well in school, as John Ogbu found to be the case in many parts of the world. Urged toward the future and imaginative in finding ways to develop in a new setting, children can be the heroes as well as the victims of the migrations that are more and more part of what the modern globalized world is all about.

By examining migrations in the past and today, historians can begin to contribute to the current discussions about globalization, especially by bringing our growing knowledge about the history of children to bear on these discussions. Those discussions should include an understanding of education, of work and mobility, of family relationships, as well as subjects such as child prostitution and other survival strategies among children on the margins. We also need to understand how the images of children we carry around as citizens and scholars have been framed historically and how these frames organize our contemporary responses. An exhibit like that of Salgado makes us aware of how rapidly our world is changing, but that alone cannot be enough. As the world shifts before our eyes, we want to know exactly how it is changing, what we can anticipate from our historical knowledge and what kinds of changes, such as gender changes in migration patterns, are almost entirely unanticipated. For that, children's migration needs to be situated in a much larger field of historical knowledge than even the very best journalist can provide.

NOTES

This essay was written for a conference on Children and Globalization, gathered by Peter N. Stearns in March 2004 at the George Mason University. It has been published, together with several other conference papers, in the *Journal of Social History*, 38 (Summer 2005), pp. 979-991, and is reprinted with permission.

1. Sabastiâo Salgado, "Migrations: Humanities in Transition—The Children," University of California Berkeley Art Museum, January 16–March 24, 2002. Salgado has a book

which contains many of these images: *Migrations: Humanity in Transition* (New York, 2000).

2. Salgado, "Migrations: Humanities in Transition," exhibition pamphlet.

3. Paula S. Fass, "Children and Globalization," *Journal of Social History*, 36 (Summer 2003), 963–977 for an explanation of why I believe the United States provides a good basis for exploring issues of globalization in many parts of the world today.

4. David Hancock, *Citizens of the World: London Merchants and the Integration of the British Atlantic Community, 1735–1785* (Cambridge UK, 1995).

5. See Bernard Bailyn, *Voyagers to the West: A Passage of the Peopling of America on the Eve of the Revolution* (New York, 1986), 302–312.

6. See Evan Haefeli and Kevin Sweeney, *Captors and Captives: The 1704 French and Indian Raid on Deerfield* (Amherst, MA, 2003).

7. Thomas Haskell's articles on humanitarian sensibilities, which first appeared in the *American Historical Review,* are reprinted in Thomas Bender, ed., *The Anti-Slavery Debate: Capitalism and Abolition as a Problem in Historical Interpretation* (Berkeley, CA, 1992). See also Larry Wolff, "When I Imagine a Child: The Idea of Childhood and the Philosophy of Memory in the Enlightenment," *Eighteenth Century Studies,* 31 (1998), 377–401.

8. One of the earliest public examinations of child sexual exploitation which I have seen was in France in the mid-nineteenth century. See Ambrose Tardieu, "Etude Médico-Légale sur les Attentats Aux Moeurs," *Annales d'Hygiène Publique et de Médicine Légale,* ser. 2, vol. 9 (1858), 137–198. I would like to thank Katharine Norris for this reference.

9. Nicholas Kristof, "Inviting All Democrats," *New York Times,* January 14, 2004, p. A23. For the flood of condemnatory letters, see *New York Times,* January 16, 2004, p. 22.

10. For child labor, see Robert Bremner et al., *Children and Youth in America,* vol. II, part 5 (Cambridge, MA, 1971); Paula S. Fass and Mary Ann Mason, eds., *Childhood in America* (New York, 2000); Hugh Cunningham, *Children and Childhood in Western Society since 1500* (New York, 1995); David Levine, "Economics and Children in Western Societies: From Agriculture to Industry," in *The Encyclopedia of Children and Childhood in History and Society,* edited by Paula S. Fass, vol. I (New York, 2004), 295–299.

11. Thomas Archdeacon, *Becoming American* (New York, 1983); Thomas Kessner, *The Golden Door: Italian and Jewish Immigrant Mobility in New York City, 1880–1915* (New York, 1977); David M. Reimers, *Still the Golden Door: The Third World Comes to America* (New York, 1985).

12. Edmund Morgan, *American Slavery/American Freedom: The Ordeal of Colonial Virginia* (New York, 1975), has made the boldest statement concerning how white and black immigrants were played off against each other in the seventeenth century. This argument about the uses of "whiteness" has been pursued by a host of other historians, e.g., David Roediger, *The Wages of Whiteness* (New York, 1991).

13. Alejandro Portes and Dag MacLeod, "Educational Progress of Children of Immigrants: The Roles of Class, Ethnicity and School Context," in *Interdisciplinary Perspectives on the New Immigration: The New Immigrant and American Schools,* edited by Marcelo M. Suárez-Orozco et al. (New York, 2001), and the contributions by an array of historians in *Coerced and Free Migration: Global Perspectives,* edited by David Eltis (Stanford, CA, 2002).

14. John Higham, *Strangers in the Land* (Boston, 1948); Reed Ueda, *Postwar Immigrant America: A Social History* (Boston, 1994).

15. For the racialization of Mexican populations in the Southwest early in the twentieth century, see Linda Gordon, *The Great Arizona Orphan Abduction* (New York, 1999).

16. Ueda, *Postwar Immigrant America,* 58–80, Table A-7, p. 163.

17. Rubén G. Rumbaut, *The Immigrant Experience for Families and Children: Congressional Seminar, June 4, 1998,* edited by Richard D. Alba, et al., Spivak Program in Applied Social Research and Social Policy, American Sociological Association (Washington, DC, 1999), 9.

18. Douglas S. Massey, in *The Immigrant Experience for Families and Children,* 10.

19. Richard Rodriguez, *Brown: The Last Discovery of America* (New York, 2002).

20. Gary Orfield, Mark D. Bachmeier, David R. James, and Tamela Eitle, "Deepening Segregation in American Public Schools: A Special Report from the Harvard Project on School

Desegregation," in *Interdisciplinary Perspectives on the New Immigration: The New Immigrant and American Schools*, 121.

21. Rhacel Salazar Parreñas, *Servants of Globalization: Women, Migration and Domestic Work* (Stanford, CA, 2001); Barbara Ehrenreich and Arlie Russell Hochschild, eds., *Global Woman: Nannies, Maids, and Sex Workers in the New Economy* (New York, 2002).

22. Massey, in *The Immigrant Experience for Families and Children*, 5.

23. Saskia Sassen, *The Mobility of Labor and Capital: A Study of International Investment and Labor* (Cambridge UK, 1984); Sassen, "Notes on the Incorporation of Third World Women into Wage Labor through Immigration and Offshore Production," *International Migration Review*, 18 (1984), 1144–1167. For single migrating women early in the twentieth century, see Susan A. Glenn, *Daughters of the Shtetl: Life and Labor in the Immigrant Generation* (Ithaca, NY, 1990).

24. Talcott Parsons and Robert F. Bales, *Family, Socialization and Interaction Process* (Glencoe, Il., 1955), especially 3–131.

25. For related effects on gender, see Jennifer Cole, "The Jaombilo of Tamatave (Madagascar), 1992–2004: Reflections on Youth and Globalization," *Journal of Social History*, 38 (Summer 2005), 891–914.

26. Perrañas, *Servants of Globalization*, 69–79.

27. For Asian immigrants, see Ueda, *Postwar Immigrant America*; Reimers, *Still the Golden Door*. For Vietnamese boat people, see Nathan Caplan, John K. Whitmore, and Marcella H. Choy, *The Boat People and Achievement in America: A Study of Family Life, Hard Work, and Cultural Values* (Ann Arbor, MI, 1989).

28. Carola Suárez-Orozco and Marcelo M. Suárez-Orozco, *Children of Immigration* (Cambridge, MA, 2001), 2.

29. Rubén D. Rumbaut, in *Immigration Experience for Families and Children*, 10.

30. Margaret A. Gibson and John U. Ogbu, *Minority Status and Schooling: A Comparative Study of Immigrants and Involuntary Minorities* (Westport, CT, 1991), and the essays in Marcelo M. Suárez-Orozco et al., eds. *The New Immigrant and American Schools.*

31. Joel Perlmann, *Ethnic Differences: Schooling and Social Structure among the Irish, Italians, Jews, and Blacks in an American City, 1880–1935* (Cambridge UK, 1988). See also Paula S. Fass, *Outside In: Minorities and the Transformation of American Education* (New York, 1989), and above, chapter 3.

32. For a reassessment of the traditional model of assimilation, see Richard Alba and Victor Nee, *Remaking the American Mainstream: Assimilation and Contemporary Immigration* (Cambridge, MA, 2003); also Suárez-Orozco and Suárez-Orozco, *Children of Immigration*, 4–5, and passim.

33. Kathryn M. Anderson-Levitt, "The Schoolyard Gate: Schooling and Childhood in Global Perspective," *Journal of Social History*, 38 (Summer 2005), 987–1006.

34. For the squeeze on Japanese schoolchildren, see Norma Field, "The Child as Laborer and Consumer: The Disappearance of Childhood in Contemporary Japan," in *Children and the Politics of Culture*, edited by Sharon Stephens (Princeton, NJ, 1995), 51–78.

35. For southern rural migrations, see Jacqueline Jones, *The Dispossessed: America's Underclasses from the Civil War to the Present* (New York, 1992); for the Oakie migration, see James Gregory, *American Exodus: The Dust Bowl Migration and Okie Culture in California* (New York, 1989); for the rural to rural Norwegian migration, see Jon Gjerde, *From Peasants to Farmers: The Migration from Balestand, Norway, to the Upper Middle West* (Cambridge, UK, 1989).

36. Massey notes that most migration takes place from newly industrialized communities of Mexico rather than directly from the countryside to the United States, in *Immigration Experience for Families and Children*, 4.

37. For the effect on children, see William M. Tuttle, Jr., *"Daddy's Gone to War": The Second World War in the Lives of America's Children* (New York, 1993).

38. Peter Landesman, "The Girls Next Door," *New York Times Magazine*, January 25, 2004, p. 30.

39. See Ruth Rosen, *The Lost Sisterhood: Prostitution in America, 1900–1918* (Baltimore, 1982); Judith Walkowitz, *City of Dreadful Delight: Narratives of Sexual Danger in*

Late Victorian London (Chicago, 1992); Stephen Robertson, *Crimes against Children: Sexual Violence and Legal Culture in New York City, 1880–1960* (Chapel Hill, NC, 2005).

40. Walkowitz, *City of Dreadful Delight*, 15–39, 81–134.

41. Mary Odem, *Delinquent Daughters: Protecting and Policing Adolescent Female Sexuality in the United States, 1885–1920* (Chapel Hill, NC, 1995), 8–37.

42. Kevin Bales, "Because She Looks Like a Child," in *Global Woman*, edited by Ehrenreich and Hochschild, 207–229.

43. *New York Times*, January 14, 2004, p. A19.

44. For consumption and adolescents, see Gary Cross, *An All Consuming Century* (New York, 2000); for adolescence and work, Jeylan T. Mortimer and Michael D. Finch, eds., *Adolescents, Work, and Family: An Intergenerational Analysis* (San Francisco, 1996).

45. See Stephen Lassonde, "Learning and Earning: Schooling, Juvenile Employment, and the Early Life Course in Late Nineteenth Century New Haven," *Journal of Social History*, 29 (1996), 839–870; Stephen Lassonde, *Learning to Forget: Schooling and Family Life in New Haven's Working Class, 1870–1940* (New Haven, CT, 2005); Fass, *Outside In*, chapters 2–3.

46. See Thomas Hine, *The Rise and Fall of the American Teenager: A New History of the American Adolescent Experience* (New York, 1999), and Kelly Schrum, *Some Wore Bobby Sox: The Emergence of Teenage Girls' Culture, 1920–1945* (New York, 2004).

47. This was the case even for some young women, as shown in Glenn, *Daughters of the Shtetl*. As Richard Rumbaut notes, "Immigration," today "as always, is mostly the province of the young"; *Immigrant Experience for Families and Children*, 10.

48. David Nasaw, *Children of the City: At Work and at Play* (New York, 1985); Tobias Hecht, *Minor Omissions: Children in Latin American History and Society* (Madison, WI, 2002); Hecht, ed., *At Home in the Street: Street Children of Northeast Brazil* (Cambridge, UK, 1998).

49. See, for example, Anna Peterson, "Latin America: Wars in Central America," *The Encyclopedia of Children and Childhood*, vol. 2, 535–536, and Peterson and Kay Almere Read, "Victims, Heroes, Enemies: Children in Central American Wars," in Hecht, ed., *Minor Omissions*, 215–231.

9

Children of a New World

The United States invented neither the faith in the expanding market that underwrites what we usually mean by "globalization" today, nor the image of childhood which haunts it.[1] But it has made powerful contributions to the momentum of both and it practically invented modern adolescence and youth. It is therefore important for us to understand something of America's historical experience in these areas as we think about children, youth, and globalization. A clearer grasp of these matters can dispel mistaken notions that sometimes vex discussions of globalization, including the idea that globalization necessarily means the exploitation of children, or that globalization will lead inevitably to the re-creation of childhood in the rest of the world along the lines of the West. Indeed, while the valorization of childhood and an expanding market were both part of nineteenth-century American development, their parallel evolutions, though not completely fortuitous, were also not fatefully interdependent. And this history can alert us to the difficulties in the concept of globalization that describes it as unalterable, foreordained, and coherent. I will argue that in the United States, on the contrary, the modern idea of childhood came to represent a reprieve from the market and that its preservation today will require a renewed commitment to the hopes that it once enshrined. Childhood, as we know it, will not come with a world-encircling market. Youth as a modern Western experience, on the other hand, seems to have a life of its own in today's world and is deeply embedded in its commercial energy. It is necessary therefore that we understand the historical evolution of the several aspects of our concern as we wrestle with their implications in today's world.

The Early American Economy

Historians may still be uncertain whether the United States in the nineteenth century can be best described as a postcolonial or postimperial society as they contemplate our origins in the British Empire,[2] but few question that the United States after the Revolution was a special kind of European cultural outpost in which capitalism flourished in a large and rapidly expanding geographic terrain. Since it was born late in the eighteenth century, the United States was little hindered by earlier mercantilist beliefs as it looked toward its inland agricultural realm to the west while exploiting its Atlantic seacoast connections to Europe and the rest of the world. America's laissez-faire approach to economic development nevertheless provided a particular twist to early capitalism because its own vast continent was both labor poor and resource rich. While this unusual combination is not true today in most places experiencing capitalist development, many of the other elements we have come to associate with contemporary globalization are. These included a reliance on rapid transportation and communications as Americans built by far the largest railroad network in the world (with the aid of British capital) and invented and innovated in the uses of the telegraph and later the telephone. These inventions turned America's huge size into a massive market that encouraged American adventurers and investors to turn the hopeful possibilities established by the Constitution into the largest free-trade zone in the world.

Labor was trickier. The need for labor was an American problem well before capitalism took root. The British as well as other imperial powers had early brought slavery to the Western Hemisphere as part of the developing Atlantic trading system. In the case of British North America, there were already Africans present in Virginia by the early part of the seventeenth century, though the laws that differentiated these Africans from other kinds of servants did not appear until the 1640s.[3] Indeed, well after they had left their colonial dependency behind, Americans found it difficult to give up slavery as the continent expanded with the immense Louisiana Purchase lands that Jefferson acquired from Napoleon in 1803. These huge territories became an internal empire into which already established American habits of westward migration could find ample means for expression. These territories also provided the site for the continuing devotion to slavery and for the expansion of the agriculture of cotton on which it was based. The subsequent battle against slavery left an indelible mark on American culture and self-identity, and would eventually lead to its bloodiest and most traumatic conflict. Indeed, the growing antagonism to slavery in New England and the upper Midwest, the uses of negative images of Southern slaveholders to promote visions of humane and proper child rearing,[4] and the identification of American ideals of self-ownership in distinction to slave dependency would strongly mark attitudes toward childhood and children during the nineteenth century and beyond.[5]

By the early nineteenth century, however, the dominant economic commitment to free, not forced, labor encouraged unlimited European immigration for the rest of the century.[6] Indeed, the importation of slaves after 1808 was prohibited by the Constitution. Only the immigration of Asians, seen as truly threatening on the West Coast, was restricted in public policy, but even that limitation did not come until later in the century, and was often questioned.[7] Immigration came steadily and regularly as Americans set about cutting trees, digging mines, laying track, making steel, locomotives, electrical equipment and cloth, and processing the grain and carcasses of its always abundant harvests and pasturelands. Europeans came from everywhere, initially from the British Isles and Germany in the eighteenth and early nineteenth centuries, and then, first gradually and then rapidly and profusely from Ireland, the Scandinavian countries, Switzerland, Russia, the Austro-Hungarian Empire, the Balkans, Armenia, Poland, Italy, Greece, Portugal, Syria, and many other places. These immigrants included people of many religions, a matter of considerable disturbance to a Protestant-proud culture. But this extraordinary heterogeneity was also claimed as the substance of America's uniqueness. Thus Herman Melville observed, "We are the heirs of all time, and with all nations we divide our inheritance. On this Western Hemisphere all tribes and peoples are forming into one federated whole; and there is a future which shall see the estranged children of Adam restored as to the old hearthstone in Eden."[8] By the end of the nineteenth century there were few regions of Europe and the Middle East that had not contributed to the extraordinary dynamism of the American economy. In the twentieth century, the United States eclipsed its European parent to become the major driver of world economic growth, while it transcended European nationalisms to become the site of a newly hybridized white population whose multiple origins had created a genuinely new social and cultural phenomenon. None of this took place without social conflict and cultural tension, especially over the future of children, but all of it contributed to the substance of the American economy and the texture of American social life. It also anticipated (and some believe actually surpassed) the dependence on migratory labor that is today associated with globalization.

Thus America's development as a nation—its vast free market, economic differentiation, dependence on communications technology, and diverse migrating population—presaged in many ways the current developments as we observe a world opened up to investments, the recruitment of cheap labor, and a new global culture negotiated across national and ethnic boundaries.

Children in the History of American Development

The logic of economics, it is often said, knows no bounds and, in the American context, it recognized no children. Much of the labor in the seventeenth and eighteenth centuries, outside of New England (which was peopled in family groups), arrived in the form of unfree or semifree labor, as African slaves or indentured servants.[9] These men and women were only useful and worth their investment price if they were young and strong, and youth from the beginning was therefore an asset in America. As early as 1619 (a dozen years after its founding), the Virginia colony noted in a letter to the mayor of London that it "had been very grateful" for "those children to be apprentices" who had been sent that year and requested him to "furnish us again with one hundred more for our next spring."[10] The letter specified that they should start at around 12 years of age. Some thus came very young, but almost all came before what we would consider full maturity, to work in the fields, workshops, and homes of precapitalist colonial America. A century and one-half later, when Alexander Hamilton looked to the future of the newly formed republic, he saw beyond the still largely rural economy toward a producer population composed of the young and the available, children and women. "It is worthy of particular remark that, in general, women and children are rendered more useful, and the latter more early useful, by manufacturing establishments, than they would otherwise be." Noting that the English employed women and children in its "cotton manufactures," where they made up four-sevenths of the work force, he observed that "the greatest proportion are children, and many of them of a tender age."[11] Hamilton wanted to use, to the fullest extent possible, the resources of the American population. But, in drawing a picture of the country's future, he also thereby opened up new economic possibilities that would require more labor than was available. It was this impulse to future prospects that opened wide the gates of immigration.

The factory work that Hamilton intuited as he looked out at a not yet bustling countryside of the late eighteenth century grew into reality by the middle of the nineteenth, and with it everywhere one could find the child and youth workers of America. Useful for America's growing industries, these young workers were also valuable to their families' survival. Most child workers did not disappear until well into the twentieth century. One need only look at the textile workers of the American South in the 1930s and 1940s to observe the descendants of those earlier workers in the "lintheads," children literally raised in the work routine of factories in North Carolina and elsewhere. Southern families had replaced the Lowell girls of New England because labor was so much cheaper in the American South in the twentieth century.[12] Those textile plants are largely closed today, replaced by factories in Bangladesh, China, and Honduras, where children continue to work.

There was nothing particularly liberating about this work, but neither was it very much worse than the conditions these children had known before. The work of children, like the work of women, is one of the great unheralded features of our history.[13] It is remembered today largely because of the campaign against child factory labor that was mounted in the late nineteenth and early twentieth centuries. Before that time, it was not much commented upon because children were expected to work unless they were especially favored by birth to prominent or unusually wealthy parents. The majority of children, and certainly the overwhelming majority of those over the age of 12 or 13, worked in the United States as they did in Europe and elsewhere in the world.[14] In the nineteenth century, even school attendance did not significantly alter the routines of young rural workers, as school terms were established around the planting and harvest calendars.

In the late nineteenth century progressive reformers in the United States began to attack child labor, as part of the general attempt to save the children of the poor from degradation and exploitation. Thus, Felix Adler noted in the *Annals of the American Academy* in 1905:

At the beginning of 1903 it was estimated that there were in the factories of the South—chiefly cotton factories—about 20,000 children under the age of twelve. Twelve is a very early age at which to begin work; under the age of twelve, and 20,000? . . . Where are our instincts of mercy, where is the motherliness of the women of this country, whither is the chivalry of our men that should seek a glory in protecting the defenseless and the weak? . . .

The lack of adequate statistical inquiries makes it impossible to express in figures the extent of the evil of child labor. But wherever investigation is undertaken, wherever the surface is even scratched, we are shocked to find to what an extent the disease is eating its way underneath, even in those States in which legislation on the subject is almost ideal. . . . I find that in New Jersey, in one of the woolen mills, 200 children under the legal age are at work. In the glass industry of Ohio, Pennsylvania, and West Virginia, the evils of premature work and of night work are combined. . . . In one of the glass houses of Wheeling, W. Va., forty boys were seen by the agent, apparently from ten to twelve years of age; one child looked not over nine years old, "but too busy to be interviewed." In this place 3,000 children of the school age were found to be out of school.[15]

By the early twentieth century, such observations, and the sensibility behind it—that children needed to be protected by the "motherliness of women" and the "chivalry of men"—could be found endlessly repeated by those who worked hard to expose the "evil" of child labor. In so doing, child labor became an oxymoron, a self-negating idea. It was viewed as destructive of the child's health, morals, mental development, and future. As such it was destructive of the child.[16]

Finding Childhood in the History of Children

In this brief outline of American history we can find children, but very little childhood, at least not in the sense to which we have become accustomed to imagining it—a childhood of leisured, protected development, free from care and toil, nurtured through learning and play. Felix Adler was measuring the reality of the working children's lives in 1905 against this image of childhood. And by the early twentieth century, the image already had a long history of its own. After decades of familiarity with the argument of Philippe Ariès, most scholars and others have a pretty good sense that "childhood" as we usually understand the term is a product of modern Western development.[17] Ariès's now dated book is not sufficient, however, if we are to understand why and how these views came into being. No one today would argue that other societies do not have a conception of childhood and its specific intracultural requirements. The early Christians were eager to proscribe the exposure of children, common to the Romans, and thereby to distinguish their own "Christian" habits from earlier pagan civilizations; Shari'a law, in turn, has elaborate property protections and rules about appropriate treatment that defines Islamic childhood. No society leaves its progeny entirely to the hazards of nature and the whims of its parents, but more or less tightly swaddles young children in a set of social norms, which is called childhood. Many also have ceremonies that chart the child's progress into adulthood. For this miscue about childhood, Ariès is, at least in part, to blame, since he has often been read to imply that childhood, *tout court,* was a modern invention.

In fact, however, Ariès was pointing to a more specific phenomenon whose origins he sought by reading backward from current Western ideals. A careful reading suggests that he was looking to find the early European origins of a particular view of childhood as a wholly separate estate—a fortress-like idealization in which children are set apart and protected in an elaborated circle of institutions and cultural forms. It was this specific childhood (and its subsequent extension into adolescence in the twentieth century) that Ariès believed was invented in the late sixteenth century and developed over the last four hundred years. He emphasized especially the role of schools, created in the sixteenth and seventeenth centuries by church moralists, newly conscious of the potentials of the inner life as first realized in children, and devoted to protecting the physical virtue of the young. Children, according to Ariès, had once been raised promiscuously, catch-as-catch can, by participating in various rituals, games, and other expressions of the common life. By the seventeenth century, however, the family became more private and schools designated for instruction divested the community as a whole of its early, much more informal means of supervising and instructing the young. Along with these developments, Ariès also noticed a growing awareness of (even obsession with) age, so that the very boundaries of childhood were increasingly separated off and patrolled. In line with this new guarding of age and virtue, Europeans began to attach ideas of innocence as the very essence of childhood as a category.

While historians have cast aside many of Ariès specific arguments, especially his dismissal of childhood in the Middle Ages,[18] Ariès was correct to identify a newly refined, age consciousness with the evolution of modern Western childhood, and its emphasis on the innocence and preciousness of children. And although historians can see some of these elements emerging as early as the seventeenth century, most agree that the elaboration of childhood as a fully fledged social commitment in the Euro-American world did not take place until later and certainly quite a bit later as it concerned the child population as a whole. In art (a medium of the privileged few), it becomes visible in the early eighteenth century, in philosophy in the mid eighteenth century, and in literature by the late eighteenth and early nineteenth centuries with Rousseau, William Blake, and then the Romantic poets, Wordsworth especially. The heightened consciousness of age-appropriate behavior as something necessary to all children, and its subsequent extension to adolescence almost certainly did not appear until the mid to late nineteenth century.[19] And the extension of this vision of childhood to all children hardly appeared as a serious undertaking until the twentieth.[20]

Childhood was thus born as an idea well before it informed popular views of children. The most persuasive argument I have seen inscribes the growth of the consciousness of childhood deep in the Enlightenment sensibility, as Larry Wolff shows in a close reading of the abbé de Condillac's *Essay on the Origin of Human Knowledge*. Wolff shows how necessary childhood was to the elaboration of enlightenment views about the nature of human memory. Wolff and others have observed the centrality of childhood to Rousseau's philosophical texts and to his very popular novel, *Émile*.[21] Rousseau's vision of the child's natural vitality and innocence and

Locke's views about its malleability helped to define political discourse in advanced circles in Europe and America.

These ideas were especially attractive in literate circles in the American colonies by the mid-eighteenth century, where the revolutionary implications of an individuality and autonomy enshrined in a protected childhood and the possibilities of more democratic relations between the generations was played out in a revolution against the patriarchal authority of the king. Americans also very much identified their nation as the more innocent child to Europe's decadent parent and were naturally drawn to the ideals of the child as innately good, closer to nature, and charting an independent and better future. The equality enshrined in the famous American Declaration of Independence was far from a description of all members of the society, but became increasingly appropriate to a context in which sons could and did set out to find their own way in a nation of broad spaces and ample land, which they increasingly felt justified in doing with or without their parents' approval. Alexis de Tocqueville was much taken with this unusual generational relationship when he traveled in the United States in the early 1830s. Fathers and sons, he argued, were much more naturally comrades as the young were empowered to look to themselves and their own resources rather than submit obediently to the dictates of age, authority, and inheritance.[22]

While the Enlightenment possibilities rooted firmly in American soil and the Revolution established ideals of youth and autonomy, this did not automatically translate into a gentle path for children. The tenacious heritage of American Protestantism was at least as vigorous as the Enlightenment imports, and Protestant views of children could be harsh and unforgiving.[23] And, as we have seen, the American need for labor and the facts of immigration made the work of children a pragmatic fact of life for most. It was not simply Enlightenment ideas that stimulated the American commitment to childhood by the mid-nineteenth century. Rather, it was a confluence of factors native to the land. Indeed, it was often the very conflict between these ideals and facts on the ground that allowed childhood to flourish as a value to which a profound sentiment attached itself. For whatever the ideals of equal treatment for all and enlightened commitments to individual self-realization, the new United States was also still a society of brutal realities. Slavery provided the most profound challenge to those ideas, and its wretched presence became a sore on the Protestant conscience as well as a manifest denial of a rational Enlightenment ideology of free self-ownership. By the 1840s, these contradictions of the American belief system and American practices became a subject of widespread public awareness, and with it a new commitment to how the future could be made better through directed human action.

This heightened sensibility about the need for change as a fulfillment of an ideal created the context in which the special solicitude for children became a nineteenth-century American specialty, although certainly never exclusively American. Those who sought to mould the American future realized that it would require two parallel courses of action—the reform of adult habits (drink, crime, slavery) and the careful formation of child life. Having inherited both John Locke's *tabula rasa* and Jean-Jacques Rousseau's innocence, Americans understood the vital importance of a carefully formed child life, and they set about creating the institutional network to make it possible. Above all they created the school as a necessary component of American civic beliefs.[24] The American school was probably more widely available and commonly used than almost anywhere else in the Western world, and American literacy rates, for both boys and girls, were very high as a result.[25] Schooling became a necessary extension of child rearing. By the end of the century, reformers had also harnessed other institutions, such as orphanages and reformatories, to serve with the schools to project a vision of childhood as a necessary component of a more progressive future. In many ways, childhood itself became an altar to democratic possibilities—a childhood properly created and, where this was lacking, a childhood effectively reformed. Americans also developed a new set of institutions such as kindergartens, playgrounds, and juvenile courts. It is arguable that even that topmost invention of the American Victorian imagination, the ideal woman devoted to home, chastity, fidelity, and selflessness, was little more than a by-product of the need to create a perfected childhood. Since the child required just such a mother to care and nurture her.

Along the way, Americans inscribed such monuments to the child and to its special qualities as *Uncle Tom's Cabin, The Adventures of Huckleberry Finn,* and *Little Women.* The nineteenth century was the century during which the child's special qualities became a national obsession, although this child was by no means exclusively American. British literature of the nineteenth century (Dickens, especially) makes this clear. But, it was probably most fully effective in the United States, where it was used as a cudgel against slavery first, and then against the many immigrants who came starting in the mid-nineteenth century with childhood ideas of their own. (See Chapter 7 in this volume.) It brought these children into schools, social settlements, and kindergartens[26] to learn English and American ways, and it took these children from the homes that were perceived as inadequate and placed them on Western farms, in orphanages, reform schools, and foster care. The sentimental child was the single most important means by which assimilation took place in America. And while I think that the final product of that assimilation was a hybrid product, the oversight of its production was certainly under the terms created by the mid-Victorian ideology of childhood.

The Children of Immigrants and the Ideals of Childhood

The struggle to define a proper childhood and to create its conditions was thus central to the formation of American cultural identity. This was the context within which the campaign against child labor took place.[27] By the early twentieth century, various efforts aimed at the mistreatment and neglect of the children of the poor were the means by which the broader cultural definition of childhood was accomplished, and this brought all children, more or less, under the umbrella of a proper childhood. The sacralization of childhood and its separation from the taint of the market was the final implementation of a growing commitment to a particular social idealization in which Anglo-Americans invested their sense of themselves as a civilization.[28]

The struggles that took place around this idealization were most potent in schools. As Stephen Lassonde has shown, the very idea of what a child was and the governing American commitment to a finely graded metric of age were matters of contention between the schools and immigrant parents.[29] The child as understood by Italian immigrants was often significantly at variance with the consensus among educators and child savers who looked to extended childhood dependency as a force for the creation of citizenship. Where an Italian father might see a young person fully capable of making a significant contribution to the welfare of the family, school reformers saw a child of 12 who needed protection, advanced training in English, and close supervision. Whether this child was a girl or a boy mattered little to school officials accustomed to American coeducation. These issues mattered enormously to the many new immigrants who treated their girls differently from their boys, and understood protection in very different terms. For them, group ideals of social honor, community authority, and family obligation often carried a price tag in the work of children.[30] Americans had committed their schooling to an individualizing destiny, and the divergent nature of immigrant parent-child interdependence was viewed by American reformers as a form of exploitation. Thus Jane Addams, who was generally sympathetic and understanding of immigrants, often observed women puzzled when the settlements and kindergartens would not punish and discipline children severely. "One of them remarked to the writer . . . 'If you did not keep control over them from the time they were little, you would never get their wages when they are grown up.'"[31]

The American idealization of childhood was specifically embodied in a series of laws and regulations which gave American visions of childhood and its proper requirements precedence over foreign visions through child labor regulations, required school attendance and truancy laws. In addition, American child savers also supported mother's pensions, juvenile courts, and foster-care placements. Certainly, the implementation of these regulations were subject to negotiation among American enforcers and immigrants, as historians such as Linda Gordon and Mary Odem have demonstrated. David Nasaw has also suggested that children actively took part in this evolving story when they worked and played, often illegally, on the city streets that were increasingly patrolled in efforts to protect children from harm.[32] But that negotiation was always framed by a now taken-for-granted view of the preciousness of childhood, the ground laid by the native view of childhood.

In this historical process, the evolving laws of childhood trumped the laws of economics. For while economic laws may know no natural bounds, the evocation of childhood as a sentimental commitment was a potent cultural force for the creation of just such boundaries. As I have suggested, American sentiments about childhood also overwhelmed immigrant approaches to parent-child relations and immigrant economic calculations where these were most vulnerable, as immigrants turned to the state for assistance. And regulations for and about the child (and to a lesser degree the mother who was his caretaker) became the entering wedge of all kinds of legislation and regulations that began to hedge the market in the late nineteenth century and early twentieth century. In Germany and Britain, the worker and his need for security underwrote the growing power of the state and its regulations. In the United States, the mother and child she protected provided the critical opening.[33]

By the end of the nineteenth century, progressives envisaged childhood as a sacred trust that was to be protected from the market. This does not mean that the two were not related or that children had no market connections. By the late nineteenth century, middle-class parents sent children to school to improve their chances in the labor market; labor unions supported anti-child labor laws to increase the wages of adult workers and to encourage a commitment to a family wage; women developed institutions such as settlements and orphanages to expand their own place in the public arena and allow women to go to work; and Catholic immigrants built and marketed their own schools to compete for control over their children's future.[34] But these were responses to a cultural development whose impulses lay outside the market place and whose consequences were to put issues concerning children outside of market calculations as Viviana Zelizer has shown.[35] At a time in the late nineteenth century, when Americans could be found estimating the dollar value of each incoming immigrant, the child was removed from this form of calculation.[36] The creation of the "priceless" child was a brilliant invention, an extraordinary product of earlier intellectual developments and of the particular forces that created nineteenth-century American social life.

Enter the Adolescent

Together the perfected ideal of childhood and its growing power over children's lives, the potent American economy with its commitment to education, and the social expression of an ideal of womanly virtue would also lay the foundations for the creation of twentieth-century American adolescence. There was nothing natural about the extension of beliefs about childhood into later ages. By the late nineteenth century, only a very small proportion of American children (no more than 8 percent) went to high school. Thirty years later, 50 percent did. This veritable explosion of the attendance of young people past 14 years of age was the foundation for twentieth-century youth development. These young people went to school into their adolescent years in ways that did not identify them with or necessarily even prepare them for work and adult roles. Unlike European forms of schooling, the American comprehensive high school was dominated by academic and neo-academic curricula that had no necessary vocational connections, although industrial and commercial subjects did begin to develop in high schools during this time as well.[37] (See Chapters 1 and 2 in this volume.)

The specific development of the American youth phenomenon can be understood through a confluence of many of the same factors which we have been observing in regard to childhood, amplified by new issues which came to the fore in the twentieth century. Foremost was the extension of the age of school leaving in the context of the enormous size of the new immigration. By then schooling had become essential to the assimilation of the second generation, and keeping children in school longer became the primary means to curtail fears about disorder and crime. The continuing availability of immigrant labor at a time of a new labor union aggressiveness made labor spokesmen eager to find some controls over the tendency of the labor market to erode wage levels. They too looked to advanced schooling to stop competition from new and younger participants in the job market. Finally, the self-identification of women as caretakers of the nation (something which they emphasized in the push for the vote) made the protection of children, which women saw as their special domain, a pointed extension of their growing public presence. That urge toward protection was embodied in a variety of movements to which women made conspicuous contributions, including the anti-child labor campaign, campaigns to raise age of consent laws, and the social settlement movement. Many of these culminated in the successful establishment of the Children's Bureau.[38] Together these various elements resulted in the opening up of the high school to a much larger clientele, a reshaping of the curriculum, the creation of junior high schools, and the increasing pressure toward higher school-leaving age.

By the 1920s, public high schools became the symbol of American democracy and of community pride. Often the most imposing and modern structures in the city, the school building became the site of the massive elaboration of the high school curriculum and of the extracurriculum that was a uniquely American product. Athletics, student government, orchestras, dances, and dramatic productions almost overpowered the classroom offerings as schools aimed to keep their older and older "children" (now increasingly denominated adolescents) occupied in school and these "children" found ways to direct their own activities within the bounds of the high schools. (See Chapter 3 in this volume.) The high school was the most obvious means by which supervision could take place over young people, whatever the nature of their education. And just as innocence and play in the nineteenth century became defining characteristics of childhood, the schools helped to encourage them as values for adolescents as well. As a result, many of the beliefs about childhood were extended to those who would in earlier times have been seen as young adults or, at least, on the verge of adulthood and ready to be trained to adult economic roles.[39]

This supervision and the extension of the organizing ideals of childhood did not stop at the school door. The development of the school was accompanied by a set of other institutions that aimed to control and protect youth. Two of these, the juvenile court and age of consent laws, were particularly revealing and potent. Both drew their inspiration from the protective tendencies that were inscribed in schooling, child labor reform, and the powerful role of women in all of these arenas. In the very late nineteenth century and early twentieth century, female reformers came together to guard the virtue of adolescent women by protecting them from a too early sexual exposure and male deception. They changed the laws to raise the age of consent, once as young as 10, to anywhere from 16 to 18 throughout the United States.[40] In so doing, they absorbed into the sphere of innocence an age group whose sexuality was now problematized in wholly new ways. Similarly, by creating courts in which the young were protected from the full responsibility of their behaviors, and placing these behaviors into the hands of family-like judicial mediators rather than before a jury, Jane Addams and the others who helped to found the juvenile court beginning in 1899 protected those 14 to 18 years of age from full adult legal responsibility, but also made many of their marginal behaviors more open to adult scrutiny.

It was, finally, psychology that legitimated this extension and the psychologist who made the concept of adolescence a Western commonplace, G. Stanley Hall endowed youth with a spiritual, almost religious, quality, and looked to adolescence to provide a new hopefulness that earlier Americans had seen in childhood.[41] Similarly, in bemoaning the commercial abuse of youth in work and recreations, Jane Addams attributed to adolescents that natural vitality and insight with which Rousseau had endowed children, and she looked to youth's restless possibilities for the future in just the ways that romantic kindergarten proponents sought enlightenment in the spirit of children.[42]

There was always a danger in remaking these young people in the image of childhood. The danger was clear in the workings of the juvenile court, for example, when 15-year-old girls were forcibly subjected to intact-hymen examinations when they were caught experimenting with their boyfriends, and those boyfriends could be sent to jail. In supervising these youth as if they were children, the transgressing of childhood boundaries became a sign of social crisis, while its testing became a tempting target for youth.

By the mid-twentieth century, therefore, the American commitment to childhood had certain very specific qualities: It was universalizing and had, at least in theory and often through force of law, been applied to all children and indeed, after 1954, even to African American children in all parts of the country. It was age expansive, having spread upward into adolescence where it continued, against the odds, to view fifteen- and sixteen-year-olds as innocent and dependent. It had become a firmly enshrined part of American democratic self-identity, despite its quite separate evolution alongside but in contention with American market capitalism. And whether we noticed it or not, it was this experience that Americans brought into the new global world of the late twentieth century.

Children, Youth, and Globalization in the Twenty-First Century

The explosion of global capital in the late twentieth century together with the post-1980s telecommunications revolution may or may not be an altogether unprecedented phenomenon. Theorists differ widely on this subject, but historians are likely to notice a number of striking resemblances to earlier periods and events[43] and American historians in particular can connect it to factors in the nineteenth century when North America was developing a powerful capitalist economy. (See Chapter 7.) The United States, as I have tried to suggest, witnessed the confluence of several factors that are again today ingredients in contemporary world events, such as mass migration and new modes of communication. In the case of youth culture, globalization has taken over from previous American experiences, and the international dimensions of modern media have increased the tendency for youth to connect with each other across national borders in matters of music, clothes, and language.

So too, contemporary images of children abused and mistreated follow in a tradition familiar to Americans and other Westerners who, in the nineteenth century, were besieged by images of children (visual and literary) that forced themselves on their consciences. These included the poorhouses of Charles Dickens, the slave plantations of Harriet Beecher Stowe, the photos of working and slum children of Lewis Hines and Jacob Riis, and in Britain the ragged children of David Bernardo, and tales of child prostitution in Paris. In late nineteenth century Britain, conscience-stricken readers of the *Pall Mall Gazette* were invited to read about young girls "snared, trapped, and outraged, either when under the influence of drugs or after a prolonged struggle in a locked room,"[44] a description that is echoed today in similar stories we can read in the *New York Times*.[45] Just as she is today, the Western reader was upset by child slavery, child prostitution, child labor. Does this mean that what we call "globalization" will also bring with it calls for improvements in the lives of children as the appeal to reform did in the nineteenth century in the United States and Europe?

In part, of course, this has already happened as human rights organizations and the activities of nongovernmental organizations issue reports on the conditions of the world's children, in which the implied standard of comparison is always the well-nurtured, middle-class Western child. Most of these are funded by the West and appeal to the Western conscience. In that sense, Western ideals of childhood are already deeply implicated in global projects. Tobias Hecht has brought some of the complex and ironic results of their work to our attention in his discussions of how Brazil's street children have been used and misused by Western organizations and media.[46] And it is well for us to recognize the multiple uses to which images of child exploitation have been put historically.[47] Today Western outrage against child exploitation can provide us with a continuing sense of our superiority while it feeds an enjoyment of tales of children who are mistreated. That frisson of pleasure and sense of superiority was true of those who judged other cultures in the nineteenth century, usually people in their own midst, and it remains true today as we observe faraway people mistreat their children. The activities of organizations which help children can carry multiple messages home as well as to those whom they assist.

As this brief historical account of the United States suggests, solutions do not come automatically and they do not come free of cost. The source of the American commitment to child protection was located in intellectual and cultural commitments—in Enlightenment ideas and beliefs in the necessity for reform—which had specific European and New World sources. They made sense to some and were imposed on others. When we extended them to immigrants, they were often met with sturdy resistance from those with alternative visions. At the same time, we should not assume that there is no place for our ideals of childhood. As Americans conceived of childhood and visualized its operations, they saw it in universal terms, and whatever the weakness and limitations of those visions, they continue to provide us with a place to start.

Belief systems are both tenacious and ephemeral, they outlive the circumstances of their birth, but eventually die out. As we look around us today, we can observe the growing emphasis in the United States on adult sentences for young children from which the juvenile court was supposed to protect them; a new insistence on schooling as a form of competitive skills preparation rather than individual moral development and playful creativity; the hyper-sexualization of children in advertising; the inundation in the news of portrayals of young children as bloodthirsty murderers. All these do not bode particularly well for the continuation of our twentieth-century views of vulnerable childhood as a period of playfulness and of respite from the market whose payoff is a better future for the human race.

Americans have always spoken out of two parts of their mouths about children. Even in the nineteenth century, some children were seen as largely irredeemable and sent to institutions that were hardly better than prison breeding grounds. Much of today's discussion about the preciousness of children and its outrage at the exploitation of children has a similar tendency to separate out the valuable (middle class) child from the threatening (lower class or nonwhite) child. Nevertheless, reformers once employed the rhetoric of a universalized childhood and set themselves the goal of making it a real possibility. It is not necessary to trot out the old chestnut about the United States being the only country in the world (other than Somalia) not to sign the United Nations Charter of the Rights of the Child in order to make the point about the limits of our commitment. The issue is much more complicated.

In many parts of the globe today, the labor of children is seen as essential to the survival of families. This can be true in rural Thailand where girls have been sold into prostitution in Bangkok for centuries, or in the factories of China where nimble fingers work on Nikes. Where does our concern for children legitimately stop and our concern for the integrity of families and respect for their cultures begin? This question raises acutely the matter of the historicity of our learning and the universality of our ethics. What is our responsibility to children as children apart from their social context? In the early twentieth century, middle-class American reformers, many of them women, imposed schooling for longer and longer periods on the children of immigrants who believed it was an infringement on their authority as parents and on their rights to command their children's labor. In the end, American values which included the right of 16-year-old girls as well as boys to go to school won, but historians are not usually sympathetic to the reformers who are seen as imposing their own standards on the poor and less powerful. Today, this battle is being played out in the international arena. Are we still ready to defend the right of 16-year-old girls to go to school? If so, are we ready to insist that these schools be built? And are we ready to help pay for them? In the early twentieth century, because American values were underwritten by American pragmatism about the future of these immigrant girls as American citizens, we did both.

The question must be stated in the sharpest terms. Are we ready in this global age of the free market to continue to protect children from the competitive pressures of the market? Since the United States provides a major engine for global capitalism and world trade, we might be tempted to let the market set its own boundaries, overlooking the harms done to children as we once overlooked the harms done to slaves. I wonder also whether the particular, romantic, Western vision of the sentimental child may not have outgrown its usefulness, to become so cliché ridden that it can no longer cover the needs of children. Can we do this by at once valuing the special needs of children (and children do have special needs) while recognizing the exigencies of the many evolving economies and cultures in which child labor, and even child prostitution, are necessary?[48] This is not only complex, but urgent, and it may involve us in a variety of apparent contradictions as we become better aware of the particulars of our own historical experience and more sensitive to the many cultures on which global media and global capital is rapidly encroaching. But we should not automatically assume that because our values regarding children are the product of a certain time and place, that there is, as a result, no place for those values, or that children have to be left to the uncertain fates that are today often worsened by pressures of global economics. The very historical knowledge that we have gained about how our ideals developed does not exclude them from having a worth and a potential for the improvement of the conditions of children.

Too often today we hear that global economics is all powerful. But economics does not always rule. In the nineteenth century, Americans were also confronted by the ruthless laws of economics and the extraordinary developments of the marketplace that put children into factories and to work at very young ages. But reformers refused to accept that economics is the only way that children can be viewed. They created a real alternative to the exclusive sway of market calculation and one that, whatever its many faults, has provided American children with unusual opportunities for personal growth and development. And it also did so for adolescents. Today's brain science suggests that much growth and development continues to take place in children's minds even into their teen years and that children require certain conditions and opportunities to grow and prosper. These opportunities for our children we would not want to lose as we, too, become part of a new global marketplace where we compete for jobs, skills, and cheap labor. And a global perspective makes clear that no children are protected when there are others who are vulnerable. And if we are not to lose fundamentals of the childhood we value, we must be prepared to defend them in a twenty-first-century world and to defend them for all children, those who are ours and those who belong to other places.

NOTES

This paper was prepared for the conference "Global Comings of Age: Childhood, Youth and Social Re-Generation in a Time of Global Flows" organized in April 2003 at the School of American Research, Sante Fe, New Mexico, and will be published in *Figuring the Future: Children, Youth, and Globalization,* edited by Jennifer Cole and Deborah Durham (Sante Fe: SAR Press, 2007) and is published here with permission.

1. See Jeremy Seabrook, *Children of Other Worlds: Exploitation in the Global Market* (London: Pluto Press, 2001), for a direct comparison to the exploitation of child labor in the industrializing nineteenth century and in globalization today. Indeed, Seabrook sees child labor as a substitution for slavery.

2. Joyce E. Chaplin, "Expansion and Exceptionalism in Early American History," *Journal of American History,* 89 (March 2003), 1431–1455.

3. Edmund Morgan, *American Slavery/American Freedom: The Ordeal of Colonial Virginia* (New York: Norton, 1975), 296–297.

4. Rachel Hope Cleves, "The Problem of Violence in the Early American Republic," Ph.D. dissertation, University of California at Berkeley, 2005.

5. Erik H. Erikson understood this emphasis on self-ownership in an early and provocative essay on American childhood; see "Reflections on an American Identity," in *Childhood and Society* (New York: Norton, 1963), 185–325.

6. Eric Foner, *Free Soil, Free Labor, Free Men: The Ideology of the Republican Party before the Civil War* (New York: Oxford University Press, 1970); David Eltis, "Free and Coerced Migrations from the Old World to the New," in Eltis, ed., *Coerced and Free Migration: Global Perspectives* (Stanford: Stanford University Press, 2002), 33–74; John Higham, *Strangers in the Land: Patterns of American Nativism* (Boston: Athenaeum, 1955).

7. Reed Ueda, *Postwar Immigrant America: A Social History* (Boston: Bedford Books), 18–20. For challenges to anti-Chinese legislation, see Higham, *Strangers in the Land,* 107.

8. Herman Melville, *Redburn: His First Voyage,* quoted in Higham, *Strangers in the Land,* 21.

9. See Richard Hofstadter, *America at 1750: A Social Portrait* (New York: Knopf, 1971); Eltis, "Free and Coerced Migrations from the Old World to the New."

10. The text of this document can be found in Paula S. Fass and Mary Ann Mason, eds., *Childhood in America* (New York: New York University Press, 2000), 241.

11. The relevant portions of the text can be found in Fass and Mason, *Childhood in America,* 248.

12. Thomas Dublin, *Women and Work: The Transformation of Work and Community in Lowell, Massachusetts, 1826–1860* (New York: Columbia University Press, 1979); Jacqueline Dowd Hall et al., *Like A Family: The Making of a Southern Cotton Mill World* (Chapel Hill: University of North Carolina Press, 1987); Jacqueline Jones, *The Dispossessed: America's Underclass from the Civil War to the Present* (New York: Basic Books, 1992); Harry Hendrick, *Children, Childhood and English Society 1880–1990* (Cambridge, UK: Cambridge University Press, 1997). For a contrary view of the work of children, see Hugh Cunningham, "The Decline of Child Labour: Labour Markets and Family Economics in Europe and North America since 1830," *Economic History Review,* 53 (2000), 409–428, and "The Employment and Unemployment of Children in England c. 1680–1851," *Past and Present,* 126 (February 1990), 115–150.

13. David Levine, *Reproducing Families: The Political Economy of English Population History* (Cambridge, UK: Cambridge University Press, 1987). See also Levine's article, "Economics and Children in Western Societies: From Agriculture to Industry," *The Encyclopedia of Children and Childhood in History and Society,* edited by Paula S. Fass, (New York: Macmillan, 2004), vol. 1, 295–299.

14. See *Industrious Children: Work and Childhood in the Nordic Countries, 1850–1990,* edited by Ning deConinck-Smith, Bengt Sandin, and Ellen Schrumpt (Odense, Denmark: Odense University Press, 1997), for the Scandinavian countries. It should be noted, however, that much of what we know comes from the reformers who tried to eradicate the problem. See Seabrook, *Children of Other Worlds,* as an example of how some continue to use the reformers to define the problem of child labor and Cunningham, "The Decline of Child Labor."

15. "Child Labor in the United States and Its Great Attendant Evils," *Annals of the American Academy,* 25 (Mary 19, 1905), 417–418 (reprinted in Edna D. Bullock, compiler, *Selected Articles on Child Labor,* Debater's Handbook Series [H. W. Wilson Co., 1915]. It should be noted that this article had made its way into a debater's handbook in the late Progressive period, a sure sign of just how important the "issue" had become and how widespread knowledge about it was becoming.

16. Viviana A. Zelizer, *Pricing the Priceless Child: The Changing Value of Children* (New York: Basic Books, 1985).

17. Philippe Ariès, *Centuries of Childhood: A Social History of Family Life,* trans. Robert Baldick (New York: Random House, 1962).

18. See, especially, Barbara A. Hanawalt, *Growing Up in Medieval London: The Experience of Childhood in History* (New York: Oxford University Press, 1993), and Linda A. Pollack, *Forgotten Children: Parent-Child Relations from 1500 to 1900* (Cambridge, UK: Cambridge University Press, 1983).

19. For art, see Marilyn Brown, "Images of Childhood," in *The Encyclopedia of Children and Childhood,* vol. 2, 449–462; for philosophy, Larry Wolff, "When I Imagine a Child: The Idea of Childhood and the Philosophy of Memory in the Enlightenment," *Eighteenth Century Studies,* 31 (1998), 377–401; and in literature, Jay Fliegelman, *Prodigals and Pilgrims: The American Revolution against Patriarchal Authority, 1750–1800* (Cambridge, UK: Cambridge University Press, 1982). For adolescence, see Joseph Kett, *Rites of Passage: Adolescence in America, 1790 to the Present* (New York: Basic Books, 1977); John Gillis, *A World of Their Own Making: Myth, Ritual, and the Quest for Family Values* (New York: Basic Books, 1996). For a contrary view of the development of views on children, see Philip Greven, *The Protestant Temperament: Patterns of Child-*

Rearing, Religious Experience, and the Self in Early America. (New York: Alfred A. Knopf, 1977).

20. Steven Mintz, *Huck's Raft: A History of American Childhood* (Cambridge, MA: Harvard University Press, 2004).

21. Wolff, "When I Imagine A Child"; Fliegelman, *Prodigals and Pilgrims.*

22. Alexis de Tocqueville, *Democracy in America.* Originally published in 1835 and 1840 I have used the two-volume Henry Reeve text, edited by Phillips Bradley (New York: Vintage, 1990) vol.2, 192–197.

23. See especially Greven, *The Protestant Temperament.*

24. For the development of American schools in this context, see especially Carl F. Kaestle, *Pillars of the Republic: Common Schools and American Society, 1780–1860* (New York: Hill and Wang, 1983). Also, Michael B. Katz, *Reconstructing American Education* (Cambridge, MA: Harvard University Press, 1987).

25. For Sweden's very high rates, see Bengt Sandin, "In the Large Factory Town: Child Labor Legislation, Child Labour, and School Compulsion," in *Industrious Children.*

26. For American kindergartens, see Barbara Beatty, *Preschool Education in America: The Culture of Young Children from the Colonial Era to the Present* (New Haven: Yale University Press, 1995); Ellen Berg, "Citizens in the Republic of Childhood: Immigrants and the Free Kindergarten, 1880–1920," Ph.D. dissertation, University of California, Berkeley, 2004.

27. For excellent documents on the anti-child labor campaign, see especially Robert Bremner et al., *Children and Youth in America: A Documentary History,* vol. II, part V, (Cambridge, MA: Harvard University Press, 1970), 601–755.

28. See my discussion of kidnapping as a means by which we enforce our commitments to children, in Paula S. Fass, *Kidnapped: Child Abduction in America* (New York: Oxford University Press, 1997).

29. Stephen Lassonde, "Should I Go, Or Should I Stay? Adolescence, School Attainment, and Parent-Child Relations in Italian Families of New Haven," *History of Education Quarterly,* 38 (Spring 1998), and *Learning to Forget: Schooling and Family Life in New Haven's Working Class, 1870–1940* (New Haven: Yale University Press, 2005).

30. For an insightful discussion of how intimacy and market calculations can, in fact, be part of the same calculus, see Viviana A. Zelizer, "The Purchase of Intimacy," *Law and Social Inquiry,* 25 (Summer 2000), 817–848.

31. Quoted in Jane Addams, *Democracy and Social Ethics* (New York: Macmillan, 1907), 45.

32. Linda Gordon, *Heroes of Their Own Lives: The Politics and History of Family Violence, Boston, 1880–1960* (New York: Penguin, 1988); Mary E. Odem, *Delinquent Daughters: Protecting and Policing Adolescent Female Sexuality in the United States, 1885–1920* (Chapel Hill: University of North Carolina Press, 1995); David Nasaw, *Children of the City: At Work and at Play* (New York: Oxford University Press, 1985).

33. Theda Skocpol, *Protecting Soldiers and Mothers: The Political Origins of Social Policy in the United States* (Cambridge, MA: Harvard University Press, 1992).

34. Lawrence B. Glickman, *A Living Wage: American Workers and the Making of Consumer Society* (Ithaca, NY: Cornell University Press, 1997); Sheila Rothman, *Woman's Proper Place: A History of Changing Ideals and Practices, 1870 to the Present* (New York: Basic Books, 1978); Kriste Lindenmeyer, *"A Right to Childhood": The U.S. Children's Bureau and Child Welfare, 1912–46* (Champagne-Urbana: University of Illinois Press, 1997). For parochial schools, see Paula S. Fass, *Outside In: Minorities and the Transformation of American Education* (New York: Oxford University Press, 1989), chapter 6.

35. Zelizer, *Pricing the Priceless Child.*

36. See Higham, *Strangers in the Land,* 17.

37. Hal E. Hanson, "Caps and Gowns: Historical Reflections on the Institutions That Shaped Learning for and at Work in Germany and the United States, 1800–1945," Ph.D. dissertation, University of Wisconsin, Madison, 1997.

38. Lindenmeyer, *"A Right to Childhood."*

39. European schools for older children were much more vocationally oriented and did not encourage this to nearly the same degree. See Hanson, "Caps and Gowns."

40. See Odem, *Delinquent Daughters,* for a discussion of age of consent campaigns and the resulting legislation.

41. For Hall, see Dorothy Ross, *G. Stanley Hall: The Psychologist as Prophet* (Chicago: University of Chicago Press, 1972); Anne Hulbert, *Raising America: Experts, Parents, and a Century of Advice about Children* (New York: Alfred A. Knopf, 2003).

42. G. Stanley Hall, *Adolescence* (New York: D. Appleton and Company, 1904); Jane Addams, *The Spirit of Youth in the City's Streets* (1909; reprinted, Champaign-Urbana: University of Illinois Press, 1972); Berg, "Citizens in the Republic of Childhood."

43. See, for example, Frederick Cooper, "What Is the Concept of Globalization Good For? An African Historian's Perspective," *African Affairs* 100 (2001), 189–213.

44. Quoted in Judith Walkowitz, *City of Dreadful Delight: Narratives of Sexual Danger in Late Victorian London* (Chicago: University of Chicago Press, 1992), 81.

45. Peter Landesman, "The Girls Next Door," *New York Times Magazine,* January 25, 2004, 30 ff.

46. Tobias Hecht, *At Home in the Streets: Street Children of Northeast Brazil* (Cambridge, UK: Cambridge University Press, 1998).

47. Anne Higonnet, *Pictures of Innocence: The History and Crisis of Ideal Childhood* (London: Thames and Hudson, 1998); James Kincaid, *Erotic Innocence: The Culture of Child Molesting* (Durham, NC: Duke University Press, 1998).

48. See the articles in *Minor Omissions: Children in Latin American History and Society,* edited by Tobias Hecht (Madison: University of Wisconsin Press, 2002); and *Global Woman: Nannies, Maids, and Sex Workers in the New Economy,* edited by Barbara Ehrenreich and Arlie Russell Hochschild (New York: Metropolitan Books, 2003), for a sense of the many issues involved.

Index

About the Author

Paula S. Fass is the Margaret Byrne Professor of History at the University of California at Berkeley, where she has taught for thirty-two years. Before moving to California in 1974, she was raised in New York City and received her degrees from Barnard College and Columbia University. She is the author of *Kidnapped: Child Abduction in America,* *Outside In: Minorities and the Transformation of American Education,* and *The Damned and the Beautiful: American Youth in the 1920s.* She is the editor of the three volume *The Encyclopedia of Children and Childhood in History and Society,* and (with Mary Ann Mason) *Childhood in America.*

Paula Fass has also been frequently interviewed about matters relating to the history of children in the press, on television, and on the radio.